are not universal, but are also so similar to that of all teenagers: filled with navigating regular problems like falling in love for the first time, getting ready for college, or finding a prom date. What pervades all of their stories however is the simple reality that these young people are growing up amid a terrifying rise of anti-trans bigotry—where new laws and policies create real barriers to their abilities to thrive. *American Teenager* provides an intimate window into the stories that the anti-trans hate machine doesn't want you to hear: the real experiences of trans kids and their families." **—IMARA JONES, CEO of TransLash Media**

"As a transgender woman who transitioned during childhood, *American Teenager* resonates deeply with me. With heartfelt empathy, Nico Lang uncovers the human stories overshadowed by political rhetoric, showcasing the struggles and resilience of transgender youth amid adversity while simultaneously amplifying their voices, which are all too often silenced. In a society where ignorance and bigotry seek to vilify the most vulnerable among us, Lang's sincere portrayal pulls back the curtain to unveil remarkable youth who simply want to be kids. As a child, I would often say, 'Get to know us, you'll love us.' *American Teenager* allows readers to meet these extraordinary kids along with their families and fall in love with their hearts, minds, strength, and, most of all, the courage to embrace their authentic identities and face the world as their true, beautiful selves."

—JAZZ JENNINGS, author of *Being Jazz:*
My Life as a (Transgender) Teen* and *I Am Jazz

"The transgender children and their families who are finally given the megaphone in Nico Lang's *American Teenager* love this country. Unfortunately, it so rarely loves them back. Lang weaves this broad bleak terrain with warm insights and a clear immediacy of message. In Lang's pages, these families aren't talking points bandied about on Capitol Hill or coastal elites out of touch with 'real America.' They are real America—and in Lang's expansive and compassionate writing, they'd rather be stretching a dollar and going to soccer games than being forced onto an unnecessary political battlefield."

—GABE DUNN, *New York Times* bestselling
author of *I Hate Everyone but You*

"Nico Lang's *American Teenager* is an urgently necessary book, bringing the voices of trans teens (and their families) to the forefront of a conversation that has been about them and around them, but which has all too often ignored their actual words and experiences. By allowing trans teens to tell their stories themselves, with all the messiness and complications that come with being teenagers, Lang has given them—and by extension, all of us—a great gift."

—HUGH RYAN, award-winning author of
When Brooklyn Was Queer

"*American Teenager* provides a beautiful—often uplifting, occasionally heart-wrenching—window into the lives of contemporary trans kids and their families as they navigate their teen years amid ever-increasing anti-trans legislation and prejudice. Tune out the politicians and pundits and pick up this book if you actually want to learn more about trans kids."

—JULIA SERANO, author of *Whipping Girl: A Transsexual
Woman on Sexism and the Scapegoating of Femininity*

"*American Teenager* is an incredibly important, humane account of the joys and struggles of so many youth currently under attack in our country. I pray this book will one day be seen as a historical work that sheds light in a dark world and that Lang's message of love and acceptance becomes the story we carry forward into the future."

—GARRARD CONLEY, *New York Times* bestselling
author of *Boy Erased: A Memoir*

"*American Teenager* speaks profound truths about the modern experiences of trans youth and their journeys toward becoming their true selves. Nico has crafted a vivid portrait of the environments and challenges that trans teenagers navigate daily. Helping readers understand that these kids just want to be kids. They long for the simple pleasures of youth—friendship, acceptance, and the freedom to explore their identities without fear or judgment. I hope everyone picks up *American Teenager* to gain a better understanding of these young lives, beyond the hate and prejudice that too often cloud public perception. This book is not just a collection of stories; it is a call to recognize and celebrate the humanity in all of us."

—MAXWELL POTH, photographer and author of *Young Queer America*

"In their powerful new book, *American Teenager*, Nico Lang shares the very raw, very real experiences of trans youth and their families at a moment in time when so much and so many things are conspiring against them. In doing so, Lang reminds us all of our shared humanity—and most especially, our capacity to find joy even in the hardest of times. I am grateful for this excellent reporting, which will absolutely help soften hearts, change minds, and create a lasting difference."

—BRIAN K. BOND, CEO of PFLAG National

"An evocative and authentic story of the love and resilience of transgender teens and their families. Lang's storytelling is intimate and illuminating, walking a tightrope between the complex narratives of trauma and joy, without ever leaning too heavily into one and discounting the importance of the other. Simultaneously heart-wrenching and heartwarming, *American Teenager* is an absolute must-read."

—RODRIGO HENG-LEHTINEN, executive director of the National Center for Transgender Equality

AMERICAN TEENAGER

AMERICAN TEENAGER

HOW **TRANS KIDS** ARE **SURVIVING HATE** AND **FINDING JOY** IN A **TURBULENT ERA**

NICO LANG

ABRAMS PRESS, NEW YORK

ABRAMS The Art of Books
195 Broadway, New York, NY 10007
abramsbooks.com

To Terri Bruce and Henry Berg-Brousseau,
who gave their lives for us.

To Nex Benedict and Acey Morrison,
who deserved better.

"Real isn't how you are made," said the Skin Horse. "It's a thing that happens to you. When a child loves you for a long, long time, not just to play with, but REALLY loves you, then you become Real."

"Does it hurt?" asked the Rabbit.

"Sometimes," said the Skin Horse, for he was always truthful. "When you are Real you don't mind being hurt."

"Does it happen all at once, like being wound up," he asked, "or bit by bit?"

"It doesn't happen all at once," said the Skin Horse. "You become. It takes a long time. That's why it doesn't happen often to people who break easily, or have sharp edges, or who have to be carefully kept. Generally, by the time you are Real, most of your hair has been loved off, and your eyes drop out and you get loose in the joints and very shabby. But these things don't matter at all, because once you are Real you can't be ugly, except to people who don't understand."

—Margery Williams Bianco,
The Velveteen Rabbit

CONTENTS

FOREWORD

Behind every headline about some new law—several hundred of which have been proposed and dozens passed in recent years—that makes being transgender in America more difficult, especially for young people, are untold thousands of individual lives upended by this legislative onslaught. According to one recent study,[1] somewhere between 130,000 and 260,000 trans Americans and their family members have already become internal refugees, relocating from hostile states to more supportive ones to escape this recent tsunami of repressive laws and policies. Depending on how the presidential election goes in November 2024, that wave could well inundate the entire county.

Award-winning journalist Nico Lang puts names and faces to eight individuals who make up a tiny fraction of those troubling statistics, all of whom are teenagers sprinkled from coast to coast and border to border. Lang offers space for them to tell their own stories while providing helpful context for the audience. The stories Lang's subjects tell are heartbreaking, sweet, infuriating, and inspiring in equal measure. They are stories of ordinary kids fumbling toward adulthood in all the usual ways while burdened by extraordinary historical circumstances that demand of them unusual levels of grit and clarity. Their stories can inform and enlighten; they should also be wake-up calls for anybody who hasn't fully tuned in to what's happening to trans folks in this country these days, and galvanizing calls to further action for everybody who already has.

I had a chance not long ago to speak with the parents of trans youth at a meeting of my local chapter of PFLAG, a national advocacy organization for families with LGBTQ+ members. They wanted me, as both a historian of trans life and a sixty-something-year-old Boomer-generation trans woman who transitioned decades ago, to put our present difficulties in perspective. I told them it was unlike anything I'd ever directly experienced myself or studied in our longer past.

So much of the rhetoric one hears these days is about how trans youth are part of a fad, caught up in a social contagion, victims of made-up maladies like "rapid onset gender dysphoria," innocent dupes of agenda-driven medical providers out to make a few unscrupulous bucks, even the hapless prey of predatory groomers and pedophiles. Trans people are represented as harming women and girls by our mere existence, threatening sexual violence simply by using sex-segregated public facilities, destroying fair competition in sports every time we lace up our athletic shoes. One powerful way to upend those false and misleading narratives is simply to listen to trans young people themselves, like the eight in this book, and to take what they have to say about themselves seriously.

I was once one of those trans kids. I know there's nothing new, nothing chosen, nothing malicious about being trans. I know my life would have been really different if I'd been able to transition at five when I realized this about myself, or twelve when I freaked out about puberty, or nineteen when I first came out privately to a romantic partner, instead of having to wait another decade before it felt possible to become publicly who I privately always knew myself to be. I also know that my life has been worth living, even though I had to wait. There's hope and solace in that knowledge, as we face a future when gender transition undoubtedly will be more difficult than it has been in recent decades. But I also know it would be a better life for the eight young people profiled in this book, and for the thousands of others in similar circumstances, if they didn't have to wait, and we had their backs far better than we do today.

—Susan Stryker, PhD
Transgender History: The Roots of Today's Revolution
OCTOBER 2024

INTRODUCTION

"I don't know what to do," Kimberly Shappley repeated over and over, the shock emptying her of emotion. "I don't know where to go."

In April 2021, Kimberly paced her lawn in her bathrobe, clutching a cold glass of white wine in her hand as she attempted to grasp her new reality: that she could soon be imprisoned for simply supporting her child, a spirited and stubborn ten-year-old transgender girl named Kai. A recently introduced bill sought to update the Texas Family Code to target families of transgender children by amending the definition of "child abuse" under the decades-old statute.[1] Republican lawmakers in her state were fighting to update that law to include allowing a transgender minor to access a "puberty suppression prescription drug or cross-sex hormone" or undergo surgery for the "purpose of gender transitioning or gender reassignment," per the legislation's text.[2] If the proposal were to be signed into law, Kimberly would have faced a potential first-degree felony should she be found guilty of "abusing" Kai—a charge punishable by a maximum sentence of up to ninety-nine years in prison and a fine of ten thousand dollars.[3]

Even if Kimberly weren't jailed for letting Kai access puberty suppressors or other gender-affirming medication, her daughter could still have been taken away from her. The courts could have then placed Kai into the home of a foster family who would deny her the right to be herself, by detransitioning her and forcing her to live as a boy.

Through the years I've spent reporting on the political struggles facing transgender youth and their parents for outlets like *Rolling Stone*, *Vice*, and *The Daily Beast*, I've gotten to know the Shappleys extremely well, but I had never witnessed Kimberly like this. Kimberly is one of America's loudest and most visible activists fighting discrimination aimed at families like hers, but that day, she seemed lost and distraught, almost fragile. I could feel her disorientation like a heartbeat, and I listened silently, unsure of what to say or whether I should try and comfort her. That hesitance led to the idea for this book: In the absence of a response, I decided to chronicle what Kimberly's family and the families of so many other transgender youth were feeling and experiencing as they tried to make sense of the world they suddenly found themselves living in.

The Shappleys had already been fighting this war for years, and they were exhausted. The first time I interviewed Kimberly was for *LOGO News* in April 2019,[4] back when Texas was considering a proposal to allow discrimination against LGBTQIA+ people on the basis of faith. Kimberly and Kai were spending every second of their free time trying to stop the bill's passage, making regular visits to speak to lawmakers at the Texas capitol who would shake their hands and then vote against them. That legislation didn't pass and neither did the child abuse bill, but those experiences reinforced a lesson that Kai had already learned long before: that others' limited worldviews could be weaponized against her. In 2017, Kai's family moved away from Pearland, a conservative Houston suburb, after her school refused to let her use the bathroom with the other girls. While Kai was permitted to use the single-stall restroom in the nurse's office, the door was locked anytime the nurse was out, leaving Kai to wet herself.

Kimberly had relocated her children to the outskirts of Austin, hoping that there Kai could be seen and loved for the girl she is. Despite their new house's extremely diminutive size—five people sharing four hundred square feet, including a twenty-foot loft that fit four twin beds—it seemed like maybe, for a time, things might be OK. The Shappleys had pet chickens and roosters roaming the yard, and of course, they still had each other.

But Kimberly sensed that their tentative utopia wouldn't last, and the day she called me, feeling crushed under a wave of helplessness, she correctly predicted the fate that would eventually befall her family. She knew deep down that Texas would win its battle to make her daughter a second-class citizen and that the Shappleys would have to leave the only home they had ever known. Kimberly, a former evangelical minister, and her children had already given up their religious community and most of their extended family, including Kai's biological father. Kimberly wondered how much more they could sacrifice and whether getting out of Texas was even possible.

"We have limited options," she said during our call. "All the places that are safe for my daughter are too expensive, and I don't know if we can afford it or whether I'll find a job there. We've been looking at a map trying to figure out what's next, and I don't have any answers. We shouldn't have to do this. We shouldn't have to keep leaving everything behind, again and again and again, just so my daughter can live."

The Shappleys' story is sadly familiar as America grapples with the emotional and psychological violence being inflicted upon transgender youth and their loved ones. One year after our conversation, they would join countless families in fleeing discriminatory legislation. They moved to Connecticut in August 2022 so Kai could live in a safer state where she would no longer have to look over her shoulder. But for many transgender kids and their parents, the worst was still to come. By some counts, around seven hundred and twenty-five bills were introduced in state legislatures in 2023 seeking to infringe upon LGBTQIA+ Americans' rights—whether by limiting medical care for transgender youth, preventing transgender people from correcting their birth certificates, or banning transgender students from fully participating in school sports, to name just a few.[5]

Most of these proposals did not pass, but their very introduction was a warning ringing out in the night. Among the worst were versions of the same fights that the Shappleys and other Texas families had been embroiled in for years. Legislation introduced in seven states—including Indiana, Michigan, and yes, Texas—sought to classify the provision of gender-affirming medical treatments like puberty suppressors or hormone replacement therapy (HRT) as "child abuse."[6] Meanwhile, Florida pushed a bill that would allow courts to assume "temporary emergency jurisdiction" of a transgender child if a parent allowed them to receive gender-affirming surgery or take medications to help them transition.[7]

At least seventy-five of 2023's unprecedented slate of bills were ultimately signed into law—the largest number of anti-LGBTQIA+ bills ever enacted in a single year.[8] That includes the Florida custody bill, even after critics warned that its passage could result in transgender children being "legally kidnapped" from their homes.[9]

It's impossible to measure the human cost of the war being waged on transgender youth, the homes and communities destroyed and the dreams indefinitely delayed. For a transgender child taking their first steps into the person they were meant to be, few blows are more devastating than losing access to the medical treatments that help them become themselves. Although critics of transgender medicine allege that the field is experimental and its benefits unproven,[10] study[11] after study[12] has shown that the impacts of gender-affirming care for transgender youth[13] can be profound.[14] When administered safely and in the hands of medical professionals, treatments like HRT and puberty suppressors have been linked to drastically lower rates of suicidal ideation, depression, and anxiety.[15] Virtually every mainstream US medical association supports the use of gender-affirming medicine, including the American

Medical Association, American Psychological Association, and American Psychiatric Association.[16]

This book is an attempt to understand the ongoing toll of a battle for basic equality and to survey the damage being done to innocent kids who never asked to be public enemy number one. It also aims to tell a more authentic, nuanced story about the lives transgender youth are leading during historically challenging times. For so long, mainstream narratives defined queer and transgender existence as inherently tragic, our lives fated to end in sorrow as punishment for defying the paths others expected us to take, the norms assigned to us without our consent. While the LGBTQIA+ community has in recent years reacted to these weary tropes by demanding space for joy and celebration in our storytelling, life as so many of us live it is a series of peaks and valleys, both a tragedy and a comedy unfolding on the same stage: a play informed by our bliss, sorrow, and all the in-between. We are never just one thing, and neither should the stories about us be.

Although media representation often treats transgender kids as if they were a hitherto undiscovered species found lurking at the bottom of the ocean, they participate in the world just as the rest of us do, with the same preoccupations that have bedeviled the minds of teenagers for generations. They want to be able to hang out with their friends at the beach, go to parties, and drive around on a Saturday night on their way to nowhere. They want to get asked to homecoming by that special person they've had their eye on all semester and slow dance under dollar-store gymnasium streamers. They want love, belonging, and acceptance, to feel like they're making the most of their youth while also preparing for an adulthood looming on the horizon. Many—but not all—cisgender kids get the chance to be young and free, to make mistakes and learn from them, and to take time figuring out what they want for themselves and their lives; transgender youth are yearning for that same liberty, to be permitted the experience of being fully alive.

It's hard for transgender kids to feel that they are part of society when so many are refused the acknowledgement of the names and pronouns that best tell the world who they are, the right to make decisions about their health care, and the ability to use the restroom that feels most comfortable for them. And yet, they are not only living but thriving even still. Transgender youth are carving out lives of fulfillment and splendor while navigating immense challenges that now include the full force of political might brought to bear on them, the banal evil of others' prejudice. They are creating safe spaces at their schools, trying out for the senior play, going on first dates, falling in love, getting their hearts broken, patching them up again, and realizing what it means to be a person with all the resplendent complications that humanity entails.

To tell these stories—of transgender youth surviving despite every attempt to eradicate them—I traveled the country to document the daily lives of transgender teens and their families. I spent nine months with seven families in seven states, beginning in September 2022 with a visit to South Dakota, where a sensitive high school student struggled with his unrequited love for his home state. After a brief moratorium in light of the busy winter holidays, my journeys took me to Alabama, where a popular senior worried he wouldn't be ready for prom; West Virginia, where a lonely theater kid yearned for community; and Texas, where a community college student met her dream guy at the worst possible time. They continued in Illinois, where a Muslim teenager claimed space for himself in his faith; Florida, where two siblings were helping each other live to see their adulthood; and California, where a spoiled seventeen-year-old tried to enjoy the perks of her liberal bubble, even as it appeared ready to burst.

The conversations with transgender kids and their families recorded in this book—which spanned hundreds of hours—strive to be as myriad and wide-ranging as the community they represent. Estimates suggest that, on the very low end, around 1.6 million American adults are transgender,[17] representing a population whose members often have little in common with one another aside from their desire to express their fullest selves, without apology. Transgender narratives span geographies urban and rural, conservative and liberal, religious and secular, and everywhere in between; they traverse divides of race, class, and national origin, and so do these dense volumes. No single work can represent the illimitable richness of transgender experience, and as a nonbinary person navigating my personal privilege in my nonprofessional life, I do not pretend this one does. This book is merely a beginning, a gesture toward the stories that remain, a prayer that many more projects like it come to fruition.

My aim was to find the universal in the anecdotal and the anecdotal in the universal. Rather than putting forward a grand unified theory of transgender teendom or exploiting these stories to advance a polemical argument, I attempt to avoid flattening the complexity of their experiences. This book eschews sweeping statements in favor of the small moments that illuminate a life, sidesteps overgeneralizations in favor of the rich detail of human experience, and attempts to allow transgender kids to express everything they've never been given the chance to say. Anti-LGBTQIA+ lawmakers have been able to dehumanize transgender people and their communities through the power of omission. By excluding transgender kids from the story of their own lives and denying them agency, that silencing permits politicians to fill the void with misinformation, fear, and lies, thereby making it easier for them to scare the public into discriminating against children. I strive, in some small way, to return their voices to them, to restore a stolen power.

Any person truly curious about whether transgender kids are being abused or mistreated by parents who affirm their identities need not wonder. They would tell you, except that they aren't used to being asked.

They are instead accustomed to people who don't know them and have never met them speaking on their behalf. This is, in part, because most Americans still say they do not have transgender people in their lives—not as coworkers or casual acquaintances, let alone friends or family members—and thus, even fewer are likely acquainted with a transgender child.[18] Research shows that when a cisgender person knows someone who is transgender, whether they be a young person or an adult, they are more likely to support their right to exist, to believe that they should have the same legal protections they do, and to vote for their ability to lead full, abundant lives.[19]

For those who do not know a transgender young person, I hope that in reading *American Teenager* you feel as if you do, that you feel as if you are part of the fabric of these kids' extraordinary, ordinary lives. I hope that you laugh with them, you cry with them; that you share in their hopes and desires; that you can learn something about yourself and the world by seeing life through their eyes. I hope that you see them as profoundly human, that you recognize parts of yourself in their thoughts and their words. For those who do know and love a transgender child, may this book be a small comfort during hard times, a document of survival and resilience. And for transgender children themselves, know that you are not alone, that you deserve to be loved just as you are, that you are a blessed gift to a country that desperately needs you. The title of this book is not an accident; it is your continued presence that makes America great, not the genocidal erasure that demagogues and charlatans so eagerly seek.

The Shappleys were unable to participate in *American Teenager* because they're still getting settled in their New England home after being forced out of Texas last year. Their journey, however, is not only emblematic of those you will meet in this book, but also of the stories of parents and children as yet untold, the countless voices that still haven't been heard.

In August 2022, Kimberly, Kai, and Kai's older brother, Kaleb, left Texas with just a suitcase for each of them, a plastic container filled with sentimental keepsakes, a fifty-pound dog in the front seat, and three cats crammed inside a crate in the rear hatch. Kai's eldest siblings were unable to relocate with them, but Kimberly was desperate to leave, in order to ensure her daughter could have the life that Texas wanted to take away from her. She drove twenty-seven hours nearly straight through, stopping every three hundred miles to nap, walk the dog, and breathe as deeply as she could. She was perhaps too exacting in her haste: They arrived so early that their apartment wasn't ready, forcing them to sleep in a hotel for two days.

While the adjustment has been difficult, the Shappleys' timing was fortuitous. They were able to get out before Texas fulfilled its fervent wish of discriminating against transgender kids: In February 2022, Governor Greg Abbott (R) issued an executive order targeting families of transgender children,[20] and the following year, the state's legislature passed a youth medical care ban.[21] (Both of these policies will be discussed in depth later in this book.)

Now that she's far, far away from a state that was so intent upon making her life harder, Kai is soaring. After celebrating her twelfth birthday, she recently won the role of insecure nail technician Paulette in her middle school's forthcoming production of *Legally Blonde,* a musical adaptation of the early aughts girl-power comedy. Her new friends all know that she's transgender. Her friend group is so supportive that all of them have even bought her book, *Joy to the World*, a semi-autobiographical illustrated novel in which Kai writes for herself the happy ending that Texas denied her.

Although her family is now in a better place, Kimberly is often exasperated with the political obliviousness of the other adults in her blue bubble, with how little they know about what transgender children and their parents go through. That's why Kai, who speaks over the phone as she prepares to celebrate her brother's birthday, believes that it's important for transgender children to have the ability to express themselves. They deserve to be truly heard and appreciated for what they have to say, Kai says, rather than being silenced and exploited by people who have their worst interests at heart.

"When you listen to stories and hear them, it can move people to action," she says. "We know ourselves better than anyone else. We have stories that we want to tell. We should tell them."

WYATT

SIOUX FALLS, SOUTH DAKOTA

SEPTEMBER 2022

I. MR. WYATT

As South Dakota's end-of-summer heat cools for an evening-long respite, a teenage boy with silver braces looks on while a circle of young ballerinas practices becoming animals. As the girls assemble in the "purple studio," an unassuming room of corkboard walls lined with plum trim and lavender accents, three aides instruct the tittering gaggle to refashion their tiny bodies as birds; the class, obediently following the edict, transforms into butterflies and toads and fish. Each of the young students is around five years old, and so while the finer points of form and technique may be lost on them, fauna they understand well. The most senior instructor says that the tiny tutees must now morph into baby kangaroos, gesturing to red, orange, yellow, and green potholders spread out in a straight line across the floor. "Do kangaroos jump with one or two feet?" she asks as the girls leap from one mark to another, attempting to avoid stepping into a fuming lava floor. "Two!" the group answers in shrieky unison.

Grinning parents watch through gossamer glass, intently following each evolution as their children transcend their bodily selves, but some of their adult compatriots face away as they tend to grown-up needs; they huddle over unbalanced checkbooks as unanswered emails light up their phones. One ballerina stands apart in the waiting area, besieged with the shapeless concerns that sometimes overtake five-year-olds. "I don't want to be a ballerina!" she cries, a tantrum that has, thus far, stretched on for the entire duration of today's class. Her mother attempts to console her by waving to a girl with wispy hair and a teardrop face who proves to be the purple studio's most animated dancer. But the sobbing child is unmoved by the promise of company, resuming her wail as her friend practices in a droopy tutu.

The glittering braced boy, whose name tag reads "Mr. Wyatt" in sharp handwritten letters, steps away from his charges and into the waiting area to intervene. Brushing his straw-colored bowl cut out of his eyes, he offers to chaperone the girl in exchange for participating in class. "Do you want to be my dance partner today?" he asks, his voice rising an octave in hopes of seeming less threatening and sounding less like the imposition of authority. When she rejects the offer, he asks her favorite color. "Pink," she offers with a truncated sniffle, her emotions beginning to wear down. "I bet you I could get you some pink ribbons," he says to an approving *oooh* from the student's mother.

Some additional coaxing is necessary before the girl is ready to join the animal kingdom, and she offers one remaining condition: She will only partake in the menagerie if she is seated in her mother's lap. "But you won't be able to dance!" her mother protests.

Wyatt Williams, who has been performing with the youth company for two years, is used to the occasional outburst by now. Wyatt teaches at the studio twice a week and attends dance classes most weeknights after school, where he is currently in the tenth grade. His company is the best in Sioux Falls and among the most prestigious in the state: The lobby includes three shelves lined with glowing trophies, and according to Wyatt, there's a fourth case stashed away somewhere in the back. Framed posters neatly arranged along the studio's walls chronicle the company's most acclaimed recitals, including performances of the stage musicals *Seussical Jr.* and *Annie*, as well as at least nine iterations of *The Nutcracker*, a Yuletide perennial. Some of the company's students have gone on to study at top dance schools and to perform on Broadway, but for now, most of them are still teenagers or on the cusp—not merely of adulthood but of a greatness promised to them.

Despite the shadow of prestige that envelops him, Wyatt has much less lofty goals. Just a few weeks shy of turning sixteen, he is proudly one of the least distinguished dancers in his company, immeasurably behind his peers. Many have been performing for most of their lives—birthed right into ballet flats, pirouetting before they could walk—while Wyatt only started dancing three years ago. But Wyatt, a lifelong overachiever with a 4.0 grade point average at school, finds peace in not being as good as everyone else, not being able to spin as fast or leap quite as high, as if he were a kite held down by invisible strings. Later that day, while we drink mandarin sodas at his favorite restaurant, Wyatt tells me he feels a sense of abandon in the imperfections of a rigid art form, in playing with the timing of a move even if it means he is scolded for it. "I know there's a definition of 'right' and 'wrong' in ballet, but for me, it's what feels right, what looks right, and what makes me feel good," he says. "That's been a challenge with ballet, being OK with teachers saying, 'Hey, that's not how you do it.' It's about being OK with doing something that doesn't make everyone else happy."

His own personal beliefs about what ballet should be—a space for liberty—frequently put him at odds with the company's directors and other instructors, one of whom he says recently told him: "You have to be a masochist, Wyatt. You have to search for the pain and hold on to it." A sensitive boy whose pink face is perpetually twisted in a contemplative squint, he cried in class one day after a teacher screamed at him; the watery paroxysm was a considerable faux pas for a ballet student. "You're never supposed to cry," Wyatt explains as he slurps his neon drink through a straw, sitting at a picnic table with an empty dog bowl at its wooden feet that falsely promises Jack Daniels whiskey.

Wyatt is unwilling to surrender the purity of his artistic ideals, in which ballet operates not as a repository for suffering but a way to rise above it. Embracing the limitations of his own body is what helps him withstand the unimaginable burdens he has been tasked with carrying as a transgender teen in South Dakota who is simply trying to survive his own childhood. After his breakdown in class, Wyatt came out as transgender to his ballet company's commandeering director on the steps of a nearby United

Church of Christ congregation, hoping that the added information would better contextualize his aversion to perfectionism. The twilight conversation, which took place under the loom of a massive rainbow Pride flag hanging from the church's clock tower, ended with both of them in tears, holding one another for comfort as blubbery apologies were exchanged.

If ballet is a coping mechanism, his studio is even more than that. It's where Wyatt gets to be what he is so often denied: a child, no different from the other bouncing frog moppets. Because he's been forced to grow up so fast—by a political apparatus that stripped him of the luxuries of innocence—he has a difficult time comprehending the banal preoccupations of most adolescents, feeling as if no one can really fathom all he's gone through at such a young age. He spends many days at the base of a bottomless well of loneliness, staring at his own reflection in its solitary waters. Adults tell him that he's "very mature" or that he's an "old soul," but Wyatt insists that he never had a choice in the matter. "I feel like my teen years have been stolen," he says. "Even if I have good memories, it's always like, *Oh, this is the year the bathroom bill was introduced*, not *This is the year I went to Disney with my family*. I wish being trans wasn't my whole life—because it's really not—but it does affect a lot of my life."

For as much as Wyatt resents the confines of ballet, the shame of being corrected by a teacher every time he dares to express his individuality as an artist, partaking in his Monday night men's class is among the few times he can remember feeling true joy in South Dakota; there, dancers are allowed to bend the rules with lessened reproach. Prior to starting ballet, he used to get terrible migraines every year before the gruesome commencement of the state's legislative session, when elected lawmakers converge on the barren capitol building in January for three grueling months of debate. When Wyatt was only nine years old, South Dakota became the first state in US history to pass a bill forcing transgender students to use restrooms and locker rooms that coincide with the sex they were assigned at birth, rather than their gender identity.[1]

The legislation was eventually vetoed by former governor Dennis Daugaard (R) in March 2016, but multiple anti-trans bills have been filed every single year since: from proposals to ban transgender people from correcting their birth certificates to attempts to prevent transgender youth from receiving gender-affirming medical treatments like HRT and puberty suppressors.[2] Not one of these efforts found success for another six years, when conservatives' patience paid off. In February 2022, South Dakota governor Kristi Noem (R), signed SB 46, a law barring transgender girls from participating in K–12 sports,[3] a year after vetoing a nearly identical bill.[4] Then eyeing an ultimately scuttled 2024 presidential run, Noem authored the bill herself, announcing its pending introduction just days before Christmas.

As the sports bill inched toward passage, Wyatt deleted social media and deinstalled all the news apps from his phone, attempting to block out the rapidly proliferating evils of the world. He couldn't read headlines about the legislation without that old familiar ache in his head; hearing lawmakers argue over his rights and the simple fact of his existence used to make Wyatt so physically ill that he began exceeding the maximum allowable days away from school. "I was making myself sick from being so worried," he tells me back at home, resting the back of his head on the arm of a sofa in his parents' basement as he stares up at the ceiling. "I don't think anybody that isn't trans understands how genuinely painful it is. I could have been doing kids' stuff—like going to parties—but instead I was staying home feeling sick about what my future might be."

With nothing standing in their way, Wyatt knows South Dakota lawmakers will just keep turning up the boil, pushing even more bills intended to make it progressively harder and harder to live in the only home he has ever known. My plane lands in South Dakota during homecoming week, but the scheduled assemblage of dress-up days—Hawaiian shirts and board shorts for Teen Beach Tuesday, pink for Mean Girls Wednesday, fanny packs and mom jeans for Grown-Up Thursday—is impossible for Wyatt to enjoy as the days lumber toward January, ever closer to three months of watching helplessly as his personhood is stripped away from him.

But as the 2023 legislative session too rapidly approaches, Wyatt is attempting to claim every spare moment of ecstasy while he still can. Homecoming week ends with a 41–22 victory in which his school's football team mounts a major comeback against its crosstown rivals, and before the game, Wyatt performs "The Star-Spangled Banner" with other students from his American Sign Language (ASL) class. Wearing black t-shirts that read "Homecoming 2022" in the style of the Hollywood sign, his classmates stand in parallel lines facing the crowded bleachers; the stands are so full that parents have been forced to park in the field and on the shoulders of the school's well-past-capacity parking lot to catch the evening's entertainment.

ASL is Wyatt's favorite subject in school, in part because he got a major head start. Although this is his first year of formal instruction, he has been studying the language privately since he was eleven due to auditory processing issues that make it difficult to understand others' speech, especially if multiple people are talking all at once. Aside from the utilitarian benefits of learning ASL, he was drawn to it for similar reasons as ballet—the exuberance in tinkering with its foundations, of making up his own rules. But the difference between ballet and ASL is that the latter encourages discovery and play as students develop their own style of signing. While the vernacular is built on basic syntactic principles, just as spoken languages are, ASL users can add their own flair to a sentence, exaggerating certain words through their wrist motions or facial expressions.

Wyatt is particularly fascinated by the fact that ASL contains its own regional dialects and variations, such as that the word for "Sunday" in South Dakota is nearly identical to "hallelujah." In other places, the first day of the week is signed with palms out in circles—similar to the washing of a car—but here, the motion is more akin to two hook hands reaching for the sky. Despite those linguistic quirks, Wyatt says that he admires ASL because it's very direct; he appreciates a language that leaves little room for misinterpretation. "Some people make things overly complicated in English, even if they don't realize it," he tells me as his classmates stand waiting for their cue to begin. "In ASL, you have to be literal because otherwise nobody's going to understand you. If I were to tell you I'm going to the store, I would just say, 'Go store.' It saves time and it's more efficient."

As the golden hour steadily grays, the homecoming signers appear to be asynchronous and out of step with one another, their hands each finding their own beat in the music, as if dozens of different national anthems were all being performed at once. The symphony of carefree limbs looks a little like something that Wyatt is searching for: freedom, whether to express himself without reprisal or to exist without political scrutiny.

While we drive home from the game, I ask Wyatt who he is at his innermost core, to name the things that define him. The most age-appropriate aspect of him, the one way in which he is not wise beyond his years, is that he doesn't know how to answer, as if he had never thought to sketch his own outline. Like the flouncy tots that he hopes to someday make into prima ballerinas, Wyatt is himself still in transit, not yet arrived; with his ultimate destination not yet in sight, he is trying to just be. His interim hours are spent laughing at bumper stickers that say "Gay As Hell" at the quirky variety store in downtown Sioux Falls, driving around town with the windows down while his hair blows in the wind, or taking photos of things he thinks are beautiful, like the sunlight bouncing off a windowsill or the shadows cast by tree leaves. His free time also includes drinking homemade smoothies and eating oatmeal chocolate chip bars—specialties of his adoring parents, Jeremy and Susan—and crowding around the TV with his younger sister, Elli, and the family dog, a mini goldendoodle named Rocky.

While Wyatt doesn't know yet who he is, he knows that he is loved and that he has so much love to give, a depth of feeling that is even more expansive because he has learned not to take it for granted. He is so many things all at once—a mess of disparate likes and passions that both do and don't define him—and just like every other fifteen-year-old, all he wants is the space to figure himself out. "There's this weird balance that I want to achieve, where on one hand I really just want to be a teenage boy and just live my life and on the other hand, I want my story to be out there," he says. "I have a lot to say. I'm just scared it's going to be taken the wrong way."

II. PAPA-TIERRI

As we sit under the low lights of the family basement, Wyatt peruses the airbrushed artifacts of last year's freshman yearbook, which he believes explains everything anyone would ever need to know about his high school. A sand-colored husk wrapped in cornfields that sits just outside the Sioux Falls city limits, the school's population is an eclectic mix. Wyatt's peers include rich kids whose parents work in health care and banking, the prevailing industries of Sioux Falls; the children of farmers, some of whom drive up to an hour to attend school; and a disproportionately large contingent of Deaf students, a byproduct of the closure of the South Dakota School for the Deaf in 2011[5] after years of alleged mismanagement by the state.[6] The pictures in his yearbook reflect this hodgepodge: A senior poses with a private plane and red sports car rented by his father, while another in camouflage military dress slings a hunting rifle over his shoulders. The yearbook's most Dadaist—and potentially criminal—entry is a student who rides a zebra while wearing a sweatshirt advertising Cheetos corn puffs. "I stole a zebra for this," the caption deadpans.

High school, for Wyatt, is a mirthless pursuit—a place where he feels that no one really understands him, where others get to be dumb kids while he has to deal with adult problems. He isn't fully out as transgender to his classmates, although some who went to elementary school with him are aware of his gender history. He came out in 2018 during the fourth grade, and the other kids around him were supportive, he says, because they hadn't yet been conditioned otherwise. On the day that he first told his classmates, Wyatt had a joyous celebration with a friend after school, throwing stuffed animals down the stairs and then jumping into the downy mess they had made. That friend, who lives in a blue house down the street, is now a fervid supporter of former President Donald Trump.

"He welcomed me with open arms," Wyatt says. "That's what kids do before they're taught. These kids all around me were just so happy to see another person be happy, and we were having fun. I was just one of the boys."

The students who have known Wyatt for a long time, since the days when his long hair tangled itself into a maelstrom of knots due to lack of attention, are aware that he is transgender. Those he met in middle and high school usually aren't because he rarely raises the subject, having watched people's opinions of his identity harden over the years. His favorite teacher began misgendering him after learning of his identity, and all Wyatt could think was: *What are you doing to me? What did I do to deserve this?* The uncertainty of who is aware—or might have been told by a friend—creates a paranoia and unease that strangles Wyatt's school days. In the hallways between class, he feels the creep of unseen eyes following him like paintings in a haunted house, and when other students throw back at him a knowing glance as they whisper to each other at their desks, his loneliness begins to feel like a permanent condition.

"I'm really scared to become friends with new people," he says with a tremble in his chin. "I don't really get the choice of when to come out to people."

There are out LGBTQIA+ students at Wyatt's school, but surviving the passive bigotry of teenagers takes an unyielding confidence that his poet's soul has not yet developed. A gregarious transgender classmate, Kris, found himself at the center of South Dakota's debate over inclusion in athletics after making the boys' football team—a first for the state—and the media attention only made him more popular and well-liked on campus. After all, he was in the *news,* the subject of a February 2022 photo spread in *GQ* magazine, in which Kris's blurry feet lift off the ground as he races across the field in his football helmet. Wyatt wishes he could emulate the defiant spirit of the queer senior who wore a full face of pastel makeup on picture day, but gesturing to the boy's yearbook quote, Wyatt knows he's just not that kind of person. "Being gay isn't a choice," the photo's caption reads, paired with a recalcitrant smirk demonstrating that its maker knows he's way too good for this. "It's a game. I won."

As thoughtful as he is shy, Wyatt just wants to be in a place where he doesn't have to develop an entirely new personality to survive, where the person that he already is can thrive. He and his parents have discussed sending him to school out of state if South Dakota—which was one of the earliest states to propose regulating transgender youth health treatments—ever passes its long-gestating medical care ban.[7] Even if that bill is never enacted, Wyatt still wants to graduate a year early so he can leave South Dakota as soon as possible, believing that this place cannot nourish him in the way he needs. In addition to the abundance of legislation targeting his right to exist, South Dakota lacks a comprehensive statewide law banning anti-LGBTQIA+ discrimination in education, housing, or health care.[8] The only city with its own anti-bias ordinance is Brookings, a college town that's nearly an hour from Sioux Falls in good weather, and good weather is a luxury in the upper Midwest.[9]

Although Wyatt's city is often described as a blue dot in a red sea, even Sioux Falls is only progressive to a point. When Wyatt came out as transgender, about half of his family's innermost circle cut off contact, along with most worshippers at the conservative Baptist church the Williamses no longer attend. The one-story structure isn't much to look at—it sits across from the budget delicatessen Jimmy John's and resembles a pointy office building—but for eighteen years, its movable pews of plush green chairs were where Jeremy, Susan, and then their children spent Christmases and Easters, a place for making memories and saving souls.

The handful of family friends who have stuck with them say that Susan and Jeremy were "icons" in their church before the fallout: the couple that everyone wanted to be, held up as an example of the exaltation made possible by embracing God's plan for humanity. Jeremy balanced the church's budgets and Susan oversaw the children's ministry until her part-time work selling Mary Kay cosmetics blossomed into a successful career. The daughter of evangelical missionaries, Susan was almost literally born into the faith; her parents met in 1971 while stationed in Brasilia, just fifteen years after construction began on the Brazilian capital. The small clinic in which Susan was brought into the world had no screens on the windows, just mosquito nets.

"For a long time, I've tried not to think about the church because how it all ended was so painful," Susan tells me over the kitchen table as we share jagged bricks of her signature coffee cake, a gooey cinnamon confection that dissolves the moment it hits the tongue. "I used to play the keyboard or the piano for worship during church. Now it's hard for me to listen to worship music. If I hear a song somewhere, it might hit me as a song that we used to sing. I have to turn it off, or I have to leave."

These untended wounds remain so raw that Susan finds it too agonizing to drive by the church, even though it sits alongside the most convenient route to downtown. After Susan and Jeremy sent an email informing church leadership that Wyatt would be socially transitioning and using new pronouns, word quickly spread. The church received so many calls that the week's Bible study had to be canceled, an unprecedented occasion. In a series of closed-door meetings held to debate *what should be done about this*, some parishioners claimed that people who are transgender are confused and said that allowing Wyatt to express his identity was "child abuse." The fallout continued as news of Wyatt's transition spread in a tight-knit community: Susan lost Mary Kay clients and her coworkers stopped associating with her. She had to find a new chiropractor and new childcare when a babysitter insisted that to use Wyatt's name would be to reject God. "In the beginning, He created them male and female," she told Susan in a text message, believing that the clarification would be helpful.

Ultimately, Susan and Jeremy opted to leave the church in support of their son, a choice they say they would have made a million times over. That doesn't mean that the decision wasn't agonizing or that they don't still feel its punishing weight. Before they stopped driving past the church, Elli's eyes would fill with tears each time she saw its somber façade slip through the tinted blue glass of her car window. "Oh, I miss it," she would say, plaintively, her face pressed against her mirrored self. For weeks, Susan cried almost every single day and night, feeling as if the life she had known were suddenly taken from her and she hadn't even had the chance to say goodbye.

The operatic emotion of those early days was a hard lesson for Wyatt in what it would mean to be transgender: that his transition would be a matter of balancing his needs and desires with others' reactions to those very yearnings. Neighbors spent years shunning the family—over time, they've upgraded to a passive head nod—and it seems to Wyatt as if other people are mourning a person he never was. Some of his family members still hang in their homes pre-transition photos of Wyatt that have his deadname printed on them, even though he has requested to have them taken down. When he looks at the pictures, Wyatt sees not what they see—a memorial to the past—but the acute agony of unwanted memories.

"It's like watching a funeral from the third person," he says, describing an out-of-body sensation that felt very literal during a summer trip to see extended family, when a seven-year-old cousin asked who the "girl" was in an old photo. "He doesn't know I'm trans. He was one year old when I came out. He couldn't grasp the alphabet, let alone me being trans, but he walked around asking, 'Who is this? Did someone die?'"

Despite the pain his family still lives with, Wyatt insists that theirs isn't a trauma narrative, of misery and brokenness as manifest destiny, the kind of suffering that ballet told him to worship. Their story is about finding each other, about the ways in which they are messy and imperfect and unfailingly generous toward one another as a balm for the world's cruelty. Conversations with Wyatt are often interrupted by texts from his parents announcing the arrival of Rice Krispies Treats cooling on the stove; reminding him not to stay up too late, even though Susan and Jeremy know his thoughts will invariably keep him awake until 2:00 a.m; or saying "I love you" for the fifth time that day. Their hurt has taught them to be generous: with affection, with words of affirmation, and even with the assigning of nicknames. After several days of standing in the backyard together in hopes of catching the faint glimpse of constellations in South Dakota's big skies, they gift me the endearment "Uncle Nico," a sign that family means so much that they are always willing to expand theirs.

Wyatt frequently describes his household's singular warmth as "wholesome," echoing a manufactured nostalgia for an America that never really existed. And yet, as a guest in their home, it's easy to believe that the television dream promised by family sitcoms like *Leave It to Beaver* was real, not just a flimsy cardboard set. Among the Williamses' myriad winsome qualities is their sometimes laborious dedication to family tradition, with no occasion too small to merit its own generations-spanning ritual. Every family dinner ends with Rocky, who was adopted as an emotional support animal for Wyatt, cheerfully licking away the leftovers, a mutually understood sign that the meal has finished. "He's the best dishwasher in the house," Jeremy says, an oft-deployed line that would be accompanied by a laugh track on the silver screen. When children in Wyatt's extended family reach their teen years, the aunts, uncles, and grandparents celebrate the imminence of adulthood with a group vacation, although the destinations tend to be humble in their ambition. Wyatt's trip was to Omaha.

Tradition was a major part of Jeremy's upbringing in a rural area of south-central Nebraska, where he grew up the child of corn farmers. His family never went on vacations and only dined out once a year, at the all-you-can-eat buffet at Bonanza Steakhouse, a once-ubiquitous restaurant chain with just a handful locations left in the US; the treat was unveiled as part of an annual advent calendar counting down to Christmas. "In each little envelope was a slip of paper," Jeremy says over the dining room table. "We did something special every day in December. One day it would be, 'Let's put up the Christmas tree!' One day would be like, 'Hey, open up a gift early!' One of them was almost always: 'Let's go to Bonanza.'"

That love of custom carried over into how Jeremy raised his children. Each year, they plan a family Halloween costume, although the 2021 attempt at paying homage to the teen truancy fantasy *Ferris Bueller's Day Off* was thwarted when Elli—ever the iconoclast—dressed up as a plague doctor instead. Christmas can be an all-day affair; family tradition holds that each gift giver hands out presents one by one, along with an explanation as to why the item was selected. Jeremy swears the unwrapping ceremony gets shorter every year, but Wyatt disputes that characterization. "It took eight hours last year," he interjects, "with three breaks!"

As a temporary constituent of the family, I am invited to partake in celebrating the seventy-third birthday of Susan's father, a retired pastor and mechanical engineer who everyone calls "Papa Terry." The family's sing-songy pronunciation makes the appellation sound almost Italian to my ears, somewhere in the range of *Papa-tierri*, a mondegreen that elicits no shortage of laughter among guests. Before Papa Terry blows out the candles on a green-and-white-frosted cake bearing the logo of John Deere, an agricultural manufacturing company that has achieved God-like stature in South Dakota, the mutually understood rules dictate that each family member says one thing they appreciate about the celebrant.

Going around in a circle, Wyatt offers the first tribute, thanking Papa Terry for teaching him how to drive and how to collect wood for the fireplace, although presumably not at the same time. Jeremy adds, in the same vein, that he admires Papa Terry's willingness to be an extra hand around the house whenever it's needed. "You're always willing to find a way to make something work," he says. I was warned ahead of time that someone always cries during gift-giving, and today is Susan's turn. "I didn't know how much like you I was," she says, holding back a sniffle. She praises her father for continuing to volunteer at the church following a very short-lived retirement, while also driving a bus twenty to thirty hours a week. "One of the things I learned from you was work ethic. I always put everything into my work, and I got that from you."

There's an unofficial motto that has carried their family through both good times and bad, one passed down from Papa Terry himself: "We don't quit." The saying was inspired by his father, a stoic farmer who worked long hours in the field and had a pragmatic approach to injuries. One time when Susan was a child, she broke her arm after she fell off a horse, but the wound wasn't bleeding and didn't look swollen; after her grandmother fashioned a sling using a homemade dish towel, her grandfather sent her back out to finish mowing the grass. "We used to tease your dad that he would still be farming and die out in the field because he couldn't get it out of his blood," Susan tells Papa Terry. "That's ingrained in me, and you as well."

Susan pauses for a moment to consider the implications of her latter remark, and twisting her neck to face Wyatt, she offers a curt warning. "*Don't* let that happen," she says, her eyes uncharacteristically intense. Every pulsing bruise they have endured to get to this moment—the doleful phone calls with the church, the melancholy holidays of that first year, the harsh gaze of Wyatt's classmates—flashes across the boy's face, and he smiles. "It's a bit too late for that," he says.

III. HAHA COUNTY

The words "Haha County Jail" hover in the distance as Susan speaks, giving a speech she's delivered many times before. Dressed in a pinstripe sweater with her hair spun into perfect curls, she is presenting a Trans 101 workshop to the Sioux Falls Police Department, using a PowerPoint to explain to officers the difference between concepts like sex, gender, gender identity, and gender expression. Susan initially studied elementary and special education at the University of Sioux Falls before switching her major at the end of her junior year, finding the monotony of classroom life too constricting, but those years of training are evident in her demeanor. Susan is unfailingly bouncy, as if she's several cups of coffee and a stick of dynamite ahead of everyone else.

The presentation is held at police headquarters in downtown Sioux Falls, a glass and brick building directly adjacent to the Minnehaha County Jail, whose name is accidentally truncated by the only window in our conference room. Susan warms up the small crowd by asking the officers where they are from—most have lived in South Dakota their entire lives, although a stone-faced woman with a slick ponytail recently moved from Mississippi after growing up in Honduras—before launching into a series of personal examples intended to bring to life the colorful PowerPoint she has prepared.

"Someone who may dress a certain way or present a certain way, it doesn't necessarily mean that they're transgender," she says, gesturing like an air-traffic controller to land her points. "My sister dresses in camo all the time—wears a baseball cap, does the whole hunting, fishing thing. That's her gender expression, but she is a girl. She identifies as a girl. Her pronouns are she/her. She's cisgender, somebody like me."

The workshop is designed to help police officers better understand the needs of South Dakota's transgender population, and Susan attempts to humanize an often-misunderstood group by telling them about her son's journey, which in some ways is also her own. Wyatt's coming out is the story of how his family came out with him—in which his honesty gave those around him permission to be more authentically themselves, more courageous because of his example. Wyatt has always known who he is; the people who loved him just needed time to catch up. The version that Susan tells as part of her workshop is abridged, and I will get the longer one over the course of the next few days, first over iced teas in a Sioux Falls bistro that used to be an auto garage, then on a road trip across the state.

Susan would have never guessed this was what life had in store; she had never even met a transgender person before Wyatt came out to her at ten years old. Those who have known Susan for a long time say that she is perhaps the last person they would have expected to become one of the state's leading advocates for LGBTQIA+ youth. A few days earlier, Jessica Meyers—a bubbly blonde with a pert nose who describes Susan as her "ride or die"—had told me that she used to call her friend "Kimmy Schmidt" in the days before Wyatt transitioned, a reference to the Netflix dark comedy about an ingenuous young woman who moves to New York City after being rescued from a doomsday cult. "If you would have offered Susan candy to get in the van, she would've said yes," said Jessica, who today serves as the president of the Transformation Project, a statewide nonprofit that Susan founded in 2019.

When presented with this anecdote, Susan agrees with the characterization wholeheartedly. "I would," she says with a vigorous shake of her head. "I would have gotten in the van."

The day that Susan saw an envelope addressed to her sitting on her dresser, she didn't realize that the lid to her own bunker was about to be ripped open. Inside was an eight-page, single-spaced letter from Wyatt in which he came out to her as transgender and begged her to accept him for who he is. "I love you so much," stated its brief cover page, which implored Susan to wait until she was alone to keep reading. "The following note expresses my feelings. They are all true. And I need your help. Please."

In the letter, Wyatt explained what he had been trying to tell his parents for years: that he was not their daughter and had never been their daughter. He had been male since as long as he could remember, spending his early childhood days playing in the mud and climbing trees with the other boys in his neighborhood. Growing up, Halloween was always his favorite day of the year because it meant he was allowed to perform masculinity without scrutiny, his deepest longings expressed through the plausible deniability of pretend. His favorite costume was a hand-me-down Captain America superhero outfit that had been donated to a friend's mother, the first person he told he was transgender; this was years before he was ready to share the information with the people he loved the most. He would have told Susan right away, except that he was so scared of what she would say, that she would reject him the same way that his church later would.

But as he explained in the letter, Wyatt didn't want to have to hide anymore, and he wasn't sure he could keep going if he was forced to live this way. "I want to be myself for once," he wrote. "Every day, I think about being a girl and making my family happy. Or, being a boy and being happy and accepting of myself. I have to be a boy fully."

Susan says that she wept as she read Wyatt's account of the trauma that he had experienced from posing as someone he wasn't for so long: a girl with long hair who wore velvet dresses with big bows to Sunday church. The letter ended with Wyatt signing his name for the very first time, and opening the door to his room, Susan saw him sitting on the floor, waiting for her to see him for who he always had been. She scooped him up, hugged him, and told him that nothing could ever make her break her promise to always love him, no matter what. "We're going to make it through this," she said as they held one another close, joined soon after by a sobbing Jeremy. "We're going to do everything we can to help you."

That promised aid was immediate, its quickness intended to remedy years of Wyatt trying, in vain, to find the words to proclaim his maleness, only to find he was speaking in a language those around him didn't yet understand. Four days after Susan opened the letter, they went to get Wyatt the haircut he had always wanted: combed back and shaved on the sides, just like the deific jocks to whom he served water as the pee-wee football team's student manager. The hairstylist, not understanding the task at hand, gave Wyatt the feminine equivalent of the reference photo he had shown her: a pixie cut favored by many of the girls in his fourth-grade class. The unwanted angular bob only reinforced Wyatt's dysphoria, and after he spent two days pleading with Susan to fix the error, a barber at the discount salon Great Clips chopped it all off.

Susan knew that she and Jeremy had made the right decision in allowing Wyatt to be himself when they saw how happy he was during the family's annual pilgrimage to Disney World, which happened to have been scheduled for the following week. Wyatt was no longer the sullen child prone to cryptic tantrums but rather a beaming boy whose newfound glow charged the air. He burned the most bright any time the amusement park's costumed workers called him a "little prince," a one-time park tradition that has since been discontinued. "He was so full of joy," Susan will tell me later during our car trip, as the prairie wind slams its persistent fists against our vehicle. "We had never even met this child before—somebody who was completely full of energy and couldn't get enough of life."

During their Disney vacation, a woman whose daughters had been incessantly squabbling approached Susan while the Williamses sat and watched fireworks pop in the night sky. "Oh, you're so lucky to have a boy and a girl," the stranger said. Susan had spent so much of her time grieving since Wyatt came out—lamenting the prom dresses and wedding

32

veils that would never be bought, the abrupt cessation of a lifetime's worth of plans—but suddenly, she realized that the other mother could see what she had been so blind to.

Wyatt's parents took time to adjust to their new reality, and Susan claims that she barely spoke for weeks because she was reading every book she could find on transgender youth. Ever the type-A parent, she sent packets to close friends and family members that contained a letter asking them to call Wyatt by his new name and pronouns, along with printouts of research studies explaining the importance of affirming a child's gender identity. The quickest family member to adapt was Elli, who was more troubled about being pulled away from her video game than she was by Wyatt's transness. "Duh!" she said when her mother attempted to sit her down for a conversation. "Just call him 'he' already!" Although her exasperated reply has since become a treasured part of family lore, Elli did actually have one grievance with her brother's transition: He began taking dozens of selfies a day, clogging the family's iCloud account with Live Photos that show him happy, smiling, and ever so faintly wiggling.

Susan's mission in retelling her family's story so often is wanting others to know that no matter where they come from, they have the capacity to love and support the transgender people in their lives. Her message varies in its reception: That Wednesday in a conference room set fifteen degrees too cold, not a single officer with the Sioux Falls Police Department asked a question following Susan's forty-minute presentation. Arms folded, they looked right past her, staring into a frigid nothing. The female law enforcement agent who had relocated from Central America hung back when Susan approached her, making cordial small talk with a cautious half grin, but her colleagues filed out of the room as the hum of lunch orders filled what was left of the silence. On that particular day, they decided to order burgers from the fast-food chain Five Guys.

While being upstaged by takeout might embitter some, Susan's optimism remained unshaken; that resilience is a testament to how long she's been fighting for her family and how many days like this she's had. After Wyatt came out, a fellow mother verbally berated her while she was waiting in line at a Starbucks café, accusing her of being a bad parent for allowing her son to transition. "I can't believe what you are doing," said the woman as Susan stood there in her morning workout gear. "When I was a kid, we lived out on a farm. All my friends were boys. I wanted to be a boy more than anything else. I think of what would have happened if my parents would have let me do that." Instead of dismissing her, Susan asked this person—whom she had at one time considered a friend—out to lunch to tell her about what her family had been through. By the end of the meal, both women were crying, in mutual recognition of the other's humanity.

"My goal is to plant seeds across South Dakota, and if I can open hearts with the stories I share, then maybe I can change some minds," Susan tells me in the car, pausing to consider the chilly reception from the police. "I don't think I changed minds, but I hope I planted a seed."

These kinds of conversations cemented the foundation for what has since blossomed into the Transformation Project, the state's largest organization advocating for the rights of transgender youth. It began three years ago as a support group in the Williamses' basement, which was then populated by Mary Kay boxes and fold-up tables, and families would travel from halfway across a sneakily long state just so their kids could spend a few hours with other children like them. Sometimes parents came alone and shared their own struggles, such as the complications of finding resources in rural areas and the shame of being rejected by people they had known their entire lives. Many who sought out the group were alone, cut off from their community and closest loved ones, and had nowhere else to go.

One day, while parked in the drive-through at the B&G Milkyway ice cream parlor, Susan asked Wyatt what he thought of her making the support group into a nonprofit and devoting her energy to it full time; she wanted other parents to know that they had someone to call if they needed help or even just a hug. The idea initially shocked Wyatt because Mary Kay had been such a major part of Susan's life for so long that he never considered who his mother might be without it. Susan had spent seventeen years as a sales director for the cosmetics brand, earning enough in annual revenue to qualify for eleven free cars. She operated a unit in Brazil and spent much of her time traveling back and forth, but Wyatt knew that other people needed what he was so fortunate to have had. He had parents who greet him with a hug as soon as he comes home from school every day, along with a sister he is so much like that they can open each other's iPhones with their faces, and he realized that it was time to share that good fortune with everyone. "I believe in you," Wyatt told Susan. "I think you'd do great things."

Wyatt was correct in his prediction: Since Susan first created the Transformation Project, over 90 percent of the anti-trans bills put forward in their state legislature have failed to become law. That outcome is due, in no small part, to joint lobbying efforts mounted alongside the advocacy organizations Equality South Dakota and the American Civil Liberties Union (ACLU) of South Dakota. Together they organize groups of parents and supporters of LGBTQIA+ equality to testify before lawmakers and share with them the stories of transgender youth—stories like Wyatt's.

It was Susan who insisted that I join her road trip to see that, despite the occasional cold shoulder, she has experienced so much beauty and resplendence in South Dakota. Our varied excursion carries us to the Corn Palace, a multipurpose arena adorned with seasonal murals of woven corn; a gas station that has tanning beds for winter depression and prom season; and a coffee shop connected to a thrift store, the latter of which has an unexpectedly stellar selection of used DVDs. Over yet another iced tea at the nineties-throwback café, with its prodigious library of used books and backroom stage home to a full roster of local bands, a friend of Susan's explains that her city had a transgender prom king and a bisexual prom queen for two straight years. Stopping at a conference for mental health practitioners, Susan is treated like a rock star: So many people ask thoughtful questions after her brief speech, a version of what she presented to the Sioux Falls Police, that the discussion spills out into the lobby, making it difficult for the next presentation to begin. For all the resistance she faces and the people who don't care to listen, Susan is making a difference, slowly making the state a better place for kids like hers.

After hands have been shaken and warm laughs exchanged, we sip our final teas at an Applebee's with trucks as big as houses in the parking lot. Susan isn't hungry—she filled up on gas station snacks—but the enthusiastic welcome has put her in a reflective mood. Although some might think of her as South Dakota's unlikeliest transgender advocate, Susan's life today is just another version of what she's been doing for years: ministering to people. Working in the church showed her the importance of building fellowship, and Mary Kay taught her how to help others see the elegance within themselves, the shine that had always been there. Now she does both. "I saw this quite often when I was doing Mary Kay: If you're sitting down with a woman and she starts taking her makeup off, she also starts to open up and share her heart with you," she says as I cautiously fork my strawberry salad. "I definitely see that in my work. People bare their souls."

What Susan does not admit, though, is that her soul has also been bared. Just a few years ago, she was so afraid that her perfect life was over, never to return, but she traded for something even better: She got to finally meet her son, and he showed her who she truly was—more than a pastor's daughter, more than anything she'd ever imagined. She was a survivor; she had survived.

IV. PREDATORY WASPS

Watertown's annual homecoming parade grinds to a halt as a convertible stalls, a taupe Chevrolet Styleline Deluxe resembling a porcelain stick of butter. Discontinued in 1952, the doomed vehicle holds two of the remaining members of Watertown High School's Class of 1947, who look down in horror as plumes of smoke rise from the dashboard. A group of volunteers springs to action, pushing the automobile down the boulevard as children in purple headbands read the sign taped to its passenger door: "You Said You Graduated When?!"

The octogenarian alumni, although a longtime fixture of the homecoming festivities, were not intended to be the main event. Wyatt drove one hundred miles from Sioux Falls today to take in the parade's most revered attraction: a fleet of vans with sawed-off roofs that are painted each year by members of the senior class. The most boisterous students bounce up and down as their creations bob across downtown, powered by human hydraulics. The vans are typically painted in homage to a grab bag of youth-oriented films and television shows, and this year's fleet includes tributes to pop culture mainstays like the retro musical *Grease* and the Disney animated film *Lilo & Stitch*. The most unintentionally unsettling float is the one Wyatt, who arrived just in time for the festivities, dubs "the Joker van" in a low whisper. The ominous jalopy features a portrait of the late Heath Ledger's gleefully depraved antagonist from the Batman neo-noir *The Dark Knight*, paired with the Joker's "Why so serious?" catchphrase scrawled in muddy green.

Susan's friend and fellow LGBTQIA+ advocate Amy Rambow has been waiting all week for the parade, and her anticipation is generously remunerated. The standout entry also happens to be one that her son, Alex, helped design: Depicting characters from the 3D video game Minecraft, Alex's vehicle mirrors the blocky aesthetic of its choose-your-own-adventure gameplay. The team is awarded the annual Most Artistic prize, a welcome result following a prior fracas in which another group deemed their vehicle the "Fag Wagon," which had allegedly not resulted in disciplinary action from Alex's school.

Dressed in a "Be a Good Human" t-shirt that is a staple of her wardrobe, Alex's beaming mother is the founder of Watertown Love, a surprisingly well-attended LGBTQIA+ support group numbering around eight hundred members. As part of her vision of a kinder, gentler state, she created the organization to send an important message to kids like Wyatt: that no matter how lonely they might feel, they are never alone. And like Susan's own Transformation Project, Watertown Love also arose from abrupt necessity. Two years after Alex came out as transgender, a bisexual classmate took her own life, and Amy worried that her son could be next. "I very easily saw that I could have been the parent planning a funeral for our kid because they didn't feel loved or wanted, like they had a community here," she tells me as soldiers in military garb march by hoisting American flags.

Watertown Love's kickoff meeting was held in April 2019 at an abandoned elementary school, and Amy arrived that first day carrying fifty dollars' worth of pizzas. Gathered in a circle of folding chairs, the thirty or so attendees talked about being excommunicated from their families and other traumas—surviving physical, mental, and sexual abuse—but they also spoke of healing. Those present expressed a desire to move past the pain that had defined much of their lives. "People were completely free," Amy recalls. "It started with sharing names, and people just started sharing their stories. It wasn't even prompted. There were good stories, there were bad stories, and then there were hugs."

Amy knew that Watertown Love would grow into something more when she saw how much that space meant to people, and she didn't have to wait long to be proven right. Watertown's first Pride festival was held just five weeks later, on a punishing one-hundred-degree day that Amy describes as so hot that you would "melt standing still." Although rumors circulated that teenagers planned to target the event by spraying attendees with urine-filled squirt guns, the section marked off for counter-protesters was empty that day. More than three hundred and fifty people came to the event, including an elderly couple who attended in support of their gay grandson and a man in cowboy boots who cried on Amy's shoulder as he told her how much that day would have meant to him growing up.

As she watched kids run around the park wearing Pride flags around their necks like superhero capes, Amy hadn't realized yet that she was also creating space for herself. She came out as bisexual in June of this year, a revelation that was as much a surprise to her as it was to others. For all the Watertown Love gatherings that have taken place in her home after that very first meeting, the youth who have sat around her dining room table eating Lay's potato chips and mini-muffins procured from the local Hy-Vee grocery store, she had never stopped to consider that the gesture wasn't motivated by allyship but membership. "I've thought a lot about this," Amy tells me with furrowed concentration. "I've always said that all of this is for Alex. Now, looking back on it, this was just as much for me. I didn't realize that I needed this, too."

Genuine community can be elusive in South Dakota, owing in part to its size and the intensity of its winters. Everything in South Dakota, the country's fifth-least densely populated state, is intimidatingly far, and that distance can be dangerous after the first October snow, when the roads freeze and never really thaw for more than a few days until spring. Having an emergency kit stashed in the back seat is helpful in case of breakdowns—to prevent the possibility of being stuck in the middle of nowhere with no heat—and South Dakotans rush to get their Christmas lights up as early in the year as possible, to avoid having to go outside again until it's safe. In addition to its equally miserable politics, Wyatt tells me on our drive back to Sioux Falls after the parade that the winters are why so many people eventually move away. He remembers a blizzard whose bluster was so ruthless that it knocked the power out, forcing him to huddle in the living room for warmth in a play tent his father had set up. They listened together as the wind screamed from outside their home; that awful sound was the only thing they could hear.

Wyatt had driven all the way to Watertown because he couldn't bear to go to school, looking for an excuse to avoid the kids who laugh about his painted black fingernails and who—even on a good day—he feels as if he is babysitting without pay. He is at the age where everything hurts and where that hurt feels like it might last forever, and all he wants is what Amy has found for herself and for her son: to feel at home among his people. He has felt that so rarely in his life, and the places where he has experienced that kind of radical acceptance weren't in South Dakota, this state that he loves so much but that he doesn't think will ever love him back. He met his best friend, Ben, over the summer when they went to the same transgender youth camp in New Hampshire, passing a shared journal back and forth in which they professed how nice it was to have someone who gets it, who doesn't require explanation.

"It was like having an extension of yourself," Wyatt remembers of the time they spent together. "It's very clear when somebody's actually listening to me or when they're thinking about something on their own. He would tell me stories of how he was when he was younger and the passion that he has now. We clicked on a level that I hadn't yet experienced."

Alternating in blue and purple ink, the letters left in that black Moleskine are a lot like Wyatt: emotionally direct and achingly vulnerable, a heart beating outside the safety of a body. Wyatt confesses his homesickness, missing the comfort of his parents, and Ben thanks his new friend for his unconditional support. Although their bond wasn't a romantic one, they were inseparable during the week they spent together, swapping sweaters to make sure the other stayed dry during rainy days and wading in the lake as they listened to music. "I hope we stay friends for life," Ben writes in his gaunt script, a record of which Wyatt has saved on his phone to keep his friend's words close. "The bracelet you made me will always remind me of the connection we made. I've learned so much from you in such a short time."

Even before the two part, Wyatt's entries take on a melancholic tone, grieving a loss of their closeness that he knows is coming soon. "I'm really proud of you, and I do genuinely mean that," he writes in perfect bubbles, later adding, "I'm gonna miss holding your hand."

Wyatt takes his time driving back from Watertown, stopping at an Indian grocery store, a café across from a grain silo, and a Bosnian restaurant that sells the biggest dolma—grape leaves stuffed with rice and minced meat—that I've ever seen. Although Wyatt resents that he had to leave South Dakota to find what he's been looking for his whole life, meeting Ben showed him that, contrary to his worst fears, he is worthy of love. He deserves the same human connections that seem so easy for other people. Maybe he'll never find that in South Dakota, but he has begun looking into attending college at Gallaudet University, a school for Deaf and hard of hearing students located in Washington, DC. He finds so much inspiration, he says, in Deaf Power, a movement originating among Gallaudet students in the late eighties that pushed to reframe the narrative around deafness. Often doctors and physicians would use the term "hearing loss" to describe the unique way in which they experienced the world, but as these activists saw it, being deaf was no one's loss; their existence was not a deficit.

Although Wyatt doesn't identify specifically as Deaf, that act of reclamation resonates as someone who has heard so often that his transition was a little death, that his parents had *lost a daughter but gained a son.*

That sentiment is meant to be a positive one, but Wyatt insists that his transness is not something that others must suffer: If he's the happiest that he's ever been, shouldn't others be, too? "I don't think anybody's losing anything," he says, his voice rising with a touch of anger as he clutches both hands more firmly to the steering wheel. "You're gaining somebody who's happy and you're gaining somebody who feels safe enough in their identity to share it with you. That is a privilege."

Knowing that his community is out there somewhere, waiting to meet someone just like him, has inspired Wyatt to start writing poetry, which he has come to feel is a natural progression of his sly, rebellious streak. His grandmother gave him a collection of Walt Whitman poems last Christmas, and he was struck by the free verse progenitor's willingness to break the rules, to throw out meter and rhyme in favor of idiosyncratic rhythms that are always changing and turning over on themselves. The epic poem "Song of Myself," which celebrates the multitudes within each of us, reminded him of what it was to be alive. It also helped him reconnect with what he had been searching for in his ballet practice: Dancing, like poetry, gave him permission to evolve, permission to ache for more.

Wyatt's first poem, fittingly, was written in appreciation of Ben, of the moment in which its author realized that he would no longer have to be alone, that he had found someone to show him the world could be different. "My eyes met yours as our hands parted, not wanting to let go," he writes of the end of their fleeting summer. "Soft smiles were spoken, our hands hovering apart/Daring to break the darkness/Just to live it again." As I read his words alone later that same day, it feels predestined that Wyatt—a Sufjan Stevens fanatic who draws "predatory wasps" in his journals in ode to the alt-folk musician's own ballad of summer camp longing—would eventually find himself in literature. He has always been a poet; he just needed to wait for a moment worth writing about.

On my last day in Sioux Falls, Jeremy prepares for us one final "porch meal"—Elli's name for the HelloFresh meal-kit dinners that her father whips up on evenings when it's his turn to cook—and we will pass the time playing board games, laughing, and taking photos for Susan, who has left for a week-long retreat in Montana to unplug. I am due to leave in the morning but not before stopping at the airport souvenir shop, with its barnyard-print ashtrays and unexpectedly risqué t-shirts advertising South Dakota as "Big Cock Country." Before I depart, I will discover a letter in my carry-on bag from Wyatt telling me how much these conversations meant to him; spending two weeks talking about his feelings and working through long-buried emotions has helped him think about what he wants from life and made him feel more prepared to claim it. He is considering that maybe he doesn't want to wait for college to get out of South Dakota, having begun researching ballet schools in other states where he can feel a little freer. If he ends up with no choice but to stay in Sioux Falls through graduation, he hopes to transfer to another high school or to finish up his studies at home, where he can find some serenity.

During the last of our many car rides in Sioux Falls, Wyatt confesses that "being a trans kid in the US is very lonely," and he is just now beginning to reckon with that. "We're all suffering because of this legislation, and you're in a state where not a lot of people are like you and you're being directly targeted," he says. "It's hard to come to terms with. There are days that I wish I could just stay home and lay on the floor. For trans kids, it's this neverending loop where we're dealing with hard things, and we don't necessarily get the grace that somebody else would. This is just our lives. We have to learn how to deal with that loneliness because it's never necessarily going to go away."

As we discuss what the future has in store for him, we swap control of the car's stereo, trading music recommendations. While the dreamy distortion of "When You Sleep" by the dream pop act My Bloody Valentine warbles in the background, Wyatt says that his plans include visiting as many countries as possible and trying to express himself however he can, any way that makes him feel like he's being heard. While we are stopped in traffic, Wyatt sees an unusual pillar of clouds jutting out from the sky, which flows against the grain of the other formations around it. As we take photograph after photograph of the clouds, trying to distill what makes them so striking, he selects "Let Down," a heart-wrenching ballad from the art-rock band Radiohead about overcoming life's myriad disappointments. In the wake of our failure to do justice to the casual wonders of nature, Wyatt tells me that he'd once had one of the most profound moments of his life listening to this song in the car on his way home from the doctor. I ask him what about the music resonates so deeply, and he finds it difficult to put into words. We agree that beauty is hard to capture.

RHYDIAN

BIRMINGHAM, ALABAMA

JANUARY 2023

I. EMBRACE THE SUCK

Rhydian Gonzalez-Herrero has been waiting years to take the next step toward becoming the boy he wants to be, and he just found out that he'll have to wait even longer. His family is all gathered in the finely kept living room of Rhydian's elderly grandmother, Mima, as his mother delivers the news. Mara practiced the message earlier in the day, as she sat in the car between routine errands. "You will not be getting top surgery this month," Mara said, locking eyes with herself in the rearview mirror, telling her reflection that they might, unfortunately, have to wait until his birthday in September. "Until you're nineteen," she tells him now, the emotion drained from her voice, "they can't do it."

Dressed in a black t-shirt with his curly hair pulled back in a top knot, Rhydian leans forward to rest his elbows against his crossed legs as he makes sense of the situation. Mara tells him that the surgeon—who specializes in double mastectomies for breast cancer patients, not transgender medicine—had been unfamiliar with the specifics of SB 184, an Alabama law that bans minor patients under the age of nineteen from receiving gender-affirming medical treatments like puberty suppressors, hormone replacement therapy, and breast augmentations.[1] Although Rhydian turned eighteen last year, he does not cross the age of majority under the state's definition for another eight months.

Typically stoic, Rhydian's face is flushed all the way to his impressive sideburns. He's frustrated but also immensely confused: *Wasn't the surgery already scheduled? Didn't they already have a date?* "I asked off work!" he protests, running a hand across the creases in his forehead. Although he is still in his last semester of high school, Rhydian works at a nearby AMC theater that is screening the latest *Avatar* sequel and

M3GAN, a campy horror comedy about a dancing, homicidal robot doll. He comes home five days a week smelling strongly of burnt popcorn and the luminescent yellow chemicals labeled as "butter topping," but the job isn't without its upsides. He recently applied to be a cook in the cinema's kitchen, where he would earn fourteen dollars an hour, an enviable sum when factoring in the low teenage overhead of living at home.

As he prattles on about practical matters, what Rhydian really means to convey is that, yet again, his state has broken a promise to him. His ability to get top surgery was already put on hold once, in April 2022, when SB 184 was made law by Alabama Governor Kay Ivey (R).[2] Upon signing the legislation, which threatens doctors with up to ten years in prison for providing gender-affirming care, Ivey claimed the decision was simply "common sense." "If the Good Lord made you a boy, you're a boy," she tweeted at the time. "If He made you a girl, you're a girl."[3] Although portions of SB 184 are temporarily blocked as the result of an ongoing lawsuit from the ACLU,[4] the prohibition against surgical care remains in place—for now—as litigation proceeds through the courts.[5]

"We're looking for alternatives in Atlanta," Mara says in an attempt at consolation, explaining that a new doctor in Georgia would not be bound by Alabama's laws. "We're waiting for the surgeon to call me back."

Mima gives her best effort at providing comfort by relating her experience of a recent surgery to separate two fused disks in her back, which has left her confined to a walker; she receives visits from a team of physical therapists three days a week to help regain her mobility. "Sometimes things happen for a reason, and we don't know why," she tells him. "You remember with mine? How long have I waited for it? Sometimes things you don't understand, but it's for the best." Mima, who was born in Puerto Rico, will tell me later that she was unaware of the term "meemaw," colloquial southern slang for grandmother, when the nickname was bestowed upon her after moving to Alabama two decades ago. The sobriquet was inspired by "mamí," the Spanish slang word for mother, and the coincidence only strengthened Mima's firmly held belief that there's an order to things we cannot see, a blueprint that defies our comprehension.

While everything in their home city of Pelham, with its sundry shopping centers and retail chains, is spread seemingly as far apart as possible, Rhydian's family is as geographically close as one can get in the Birmingham suburbs. He and his parents live next door to Mima in what Mara refers to as their "dollhouse," owing to their home's compact size. Their petite residence's most prominent feature is a school of painstakingly curated fish tanks to which Tom, Rhydian's navy veteran father, tends as an outlet for the hyperfixations he experiences from post-traumatic stress disorder (PTSD). They share the living room with a supply of doggy pee pads claimed by the family's dachshund, Frankie, who is allergic to grass and can't go to the bathroom outdoors without breaking out in a racing stripe of a rash. Sadly for the Gonzalez-Herreros, Frankie usually misses the pads, unable to correctly calculate his own length; the household mop, which is pulled out of the closet upward of three times a day, is so perpetually exhausted that it all but wheezes as it glides across the floor.

Rhydian's oasis within the home is not his bedroom, which he calls "the forbidden room" due to its persistent state of disarray, but rather a playroom that his parents began working on last year that is stocked with video games and children's toys. It's where he seeks repose after learning that his top surgery will be delayed once more, processing this news atop a spartan black futon while twirling a slime-colored fidget spinner. The room, with its peppermint smell and floor covered in puzzle-piece mats designed for preschool classrooms, was envisioned as a space to enjoy the boyhood that Rhydian never got. In rejecting the preteen femininity that was imposed upon him—pink bows, pink dresses, pink everything—he accidentally skipped childhood altogether, serving as the confidant and therapist of the adults within his orbit. Most of the toys he gravitated toward as a child he coldly describes as "educational," such as a plastic tool set that he once used to fix a loose screw on a broken table.

To make up for lost time, Rhydian has become an avid collector of Hot Wheels, favoring the metal cars that he says "go faster on the track" because they're denser and heavier. But he acknowledges that the crown jewel of his collection clashes with his stated taste: a black and white plastic Halloween collectible with skulls on the wheels. His affinity for toy cars is coolly pragmatic—they're cheap to collect, he says, and you can buy them anywhere—but the hobby also serves a therapeutic purpose. "I'm just able to relax and be me, do whatever makes me happy," he says. "I'm just in my space. It's just me and I don't need to worry about what other people think."

Being concerned with the opinions of others and what impact those views might have on his safety has consumed much of his life so far. Students at his former school, a charmless slab designed by an architect who also built women's prisons, would call him a "monster" and punch him in the hallways between classes, often right in front of teachers. Rhydian wasn't allowed to use the men's restroom on campus and was too afraid to use the women's facilities, in fear of further abuse. During band practices after school, he would either ask a friend to guard the door while he went to the bathroom or wait until he got home, developing frequent urinary tract infections as a result. "I felt so tense all the time, and I would come home exhausted," he recalls. "I used to take a nap every afternoon. I would fall asleep immediately because I was just so tired emotionally and physically."

Prior to his junior year, Rhydian transferred to the Magic City Acceptance Academy (MCAA), the only explicitly LGBTQIA+ affirming school in the South, where he is set to graduate in May 2023. With his easygoing confidence, he's arguably the most popular student in school, the kid everyone wants to sit by at lunch, but the adoration of his peers is, in part, a byproduct of envy. He has what so many of them want: a loving family that not only accepts him but even packs him lunch every day. Although he has talked about wanting top surgery for years, Mara was the one who decided that the time had come to take the next step. When he has the legal ability to do so, his mother will be the one to drive him both to and from the surgery, in part because he hasn't operated a car since nearly getting into an accident last month. She has been chauffeuring him sixteen miles to and from school every day while he works on mentally preparing to get back on the road.

But despite the admiration of his classmates and support of his loved ones, Rhydian would be lying if he said he still doesn't fret over how others see him. Throughout the day, he wears baggy clothes to cover his chest—layering a hoodie over his sweatshirt, even in the summertime—and avoids any shirts that might have shrunk in the dryer. He also suffers from what he refers to as the "trans masc slouch." "My back hurts because I'm constantly trying to hide my chest or draw attention away from it," he says. "Normally, if I'm meeting someone new, I avoid letting them see me from my side—because you can tell easier if you're looking at me from my side. I'm scared that if people notice my waist is more feminine, they're going to get upset. I'm just so drained all the time from thinking about these things that other people don't have to worry about."

Rhydian is tired of being scared, tired of waiting, and tired of being disappointed, and he doesn't know yet when the day will come that his fortitude is rewarded. To take his mind off the enormity of even more uncertainty, we walk the sixty feet back to Mima's house, where we raid the stash of games tucked away inside her closet. Before we play Bingo— the low-stakes lottery beloved by drag queens and senior centers—Mara cautions that her mother cheats and yet somehow still always loses, but that does not prove to be the case this time: She plays a clean game but wins all three rounds handily, including the coveted four corners and cover-all matches. I exact revenge by beating her at the murder mystery Clue, although she warns that the reprisal will not be forgotten. "Never make an enemy of a Puerto Rican woman," she cautions with a wink.

Sitting at the glass dinette set in Mima's kitchen among the Gonzalez-Herreros, I feel what it means to be loved: to sit beside one another when things get hard and to still find ways to laugh, to cry, and to be present. Their family shows up for each other in so many ways, whether by dropping off Burger King sandwiches and fries at Rhydian's school because he forgot his lunch or allowing Tom the space in his day to obsess over his newest fixation: the geolocation game Pokémon GO, which keeps him under his iPhone's spell for wordless hours at a time. Part of that love means sharing in Rhydian's hopes and also his fears; Mara and Tom worry for Rhydian constantly, so much so that it affects their health. Rhydian's father will be briefly hospitalized with a panic attack the day after Rhydian learns his top surgery will not be moving forward, and Tom will experience persistent chest pain for the rest of my stay, forcing him to walk and speak slowly. His doctors are concerned that it may be a blood clot, but they won't know for certain without further tests.

Our evening of board games and tough conversations ends with Tom giving me a ride back to my Airbnb, during which we get to talking about his military service, including two deployments to Kuwait. He worked as a hull technician and in customs, where part of his job included processing vehicles that were destroyed during combat, some of which still bore the debris of human remains. Among the more difficult aspects, he says, is a warped version of what his son is experiencing: the hurry up and wait of war. When Tom was on base, there was nowhere else to go: nowhere to take a leisurely afternoon stroll, no corner store to grab a soda. He was alone all day with his thoughts and with the sand, which he says was so thin that it couldn't be used to make concrete. What the sand was good at, Tom recalls, was sticking to absolutely everything in sight—including tabletops, which had to be swept any time the soldiers sat down to eat. To keep his mind occupied, he started playing the World War II shooter game *Call of Duty* twelve hours a day, his very first fixation before he moved on to aquatic dioramas.

Tom retired from the armed forces in 2016 after twenty-three years of service, and while he has struggled with civilian life—the tinnitus he sustained from the restless hum of the base generators, for instance, makes it hard to sleep—the military taught him certain skills in dealing with conflict. When the conversation turns to Rhydian's top surgery, he describes it as just another mission, one that hasn't yet been completed. As someone who was trained in the art of survival, he is deeply committed to ensuring that his team makes it through—at any cost.

"I've seen shit, I've been in the shit," he says, eyes locked on the road in front of him. "Sometimes you just have to embrace the suck, keep on going, and do the best you can. We're going to keep doing the best we can for Rhydian because the mission has to be taken care of. It will be taken care of. Whatever the mission is, we're going to make it happen."

II. GAY SCHOOL

As he lurches toward me, step by ponderous step, Rhydian tries his hardest not to laugh, his smile breaking a little more as he gets closer. In the classroom around him, Rhydian's peers perform the same giggle-inducing task, maintaining strict eye contact as they march on the tips of their shoes. The endeavor is transparently silly, but Rhydian's professor, the affable Mr. Evans, says it serves a purpose: to make his pupils comfortable sharing personal space with one another, in order to teach them how to be part of a community. His goal is to see how close the students can get, whether they can be vulnerable enough to stand within inches of their classmates. Most of the group is successful, although a few grow tired of the prompt and instead doodle a cartoon dog together on the floor. An arrow points toward the hound's long face, along with a cryptic proclamation: "GUILTY."

This exercise, like many performed that day, is adapted from a counseling 101 course that Mr. Evans took in college before joining the faculty at MCAA, a charter school nestled in the Birmingham suburb of Homewood, fewer than five hundred yards outside the city. The students practice active listening by engaging in conversation with three different objectives in mind: summarizing, paraphrasing, and asking questions. Being able to summarize and paraphrase—by parroting back something their partners just said—allows students to demonstrate their engagement, and it's something that people typically do while conversing all the time, usually without realizing it. But many of these students were significantly isolated and detached in their previous communities, rarely having the occasion to practice these foundational social skills. Although Rhydian estimates that 70 percent of his classmates are LGBTQIA+, many came to MCAA because they have other learning needs—such as autism or severe ADHD that makes it challenging to follow along in class, even at a rudimentary level. The school has a high Latine population for the area—at around 20 percent—because so many experienced extreme racism, even violence, in their previous learning environments.

Teaching basic socialization, such as the staring contest that Rhydian loses by blinking immediately, isn't what one might anticipate from a civics course. But Mr. Evans, who students refer to simply by the mononym "Evans," will tell me later that day that he saw the necessity of transforming the class into a life skills seminar after asking his seniors what they'd never learned in their twelve years of schooling. Many didn't know how to pump gas, he says, or even how to scramble an egg. A request from Rhydian, always the first to raise his hand in class, summed up the general mood. "I want you to teach me how to exist in a world that makes me nervous," the boy requested, to approving nods from the room.

The day that I sit in on his lecture, Mr. Evans is wearing a crayon purple blazer as he attempts to get students caught up on everything they missed while marooned in their former schools. His curriculum now includes subjects ranging from how to change a tire and jump a car to what to look for when signing a lease. Later this year, he plans to take the students apartment hunting in Birmingham to show them how to spot potential warning signs—such as black mold and faulty wiring—when surveying prospective rental accomodations. He says he once stopped a class when a student admitted that they felt unprepared for an upcoming job interview. "We did an entire 'how to do an interview' lesson," Mr. Evans will tell me after the students depart for next period. "We actually looked at the job, and we spent the entire class period setting this kid up for the interview."

While most schools prepare students for the rest of their lives, Mr. Evans believes that MCAA has a different mission. Many of the students he teaches didn't think they would live to see graduation—due to violence from others, self-harm, or a mixture of both—and they haven't spent any time preparing for what comes after high school. A transgender student who is currently staying in Mr. Evans's home had, at one time, planned to take her own life on her eighteenth birthday, but when that date arrives later this year, Mr. Evans and his wife are instead taking her to get her eyebrow pierced as a present, in celebration that she is still here. The school's intention, Mr. Evans stresses, is to help students who have extreme mental health challenges and emotional needs with the basic act of survival, a scope that includes life after graduation. "What happens when our students leave us and we can't protect them, guide them, and help them through a day-to-day situation?" he asks. "A lot of our students would be lost. They really wouldn't know what to do. That is irresponsible, for educators to leave students not knowing what would happen tomorrow if they couldn't come to school."

Rhydian might appear to be an outlier in that his career is already mapped out. After graduating from college, he plans to work in civil rights advocacy, whether that means becoming a judge, lawyer, or politician. Alabama has only ever elected two openly LGBTQIA+ lawmakers to its legislature, and just one is currently in office: state representative Neil Rafferty (D), who is a gay man.[6] The Yellowhammer State has never been represented by an openly transgender official, and Rhydian thinks that person, just maybe, could be him someday. Never one to limit himself, he has talked of aiming even higher: of becoming the first transgender Supreme Court justice—and certainly the one with the largest toy car collection.

But even as Rhydian's life leads him toward preeminence, Mr. Evans asserts that the more pragmatic lessons he teaches in class apply to his brightest students, too. "We only had twelve seniors last year," Mr. Evans says, scratching his tight goatee. "I gave them all jumper cables as a senior present. I've gotten pictures from eight of them, saying, 'My battery died, and I knew how to jump the car.' If Rhydian gets stranded on the side of the road and has to wait on somebody to help, there is a good chance that a person stopping to help does not think that Rhydian should exist."

If students' lives are heavy outside of MCAA's campus, you wouldn't know it from spending a day there. After Mr. Evans's class, students sprawl across the floor on purple throw rugs and turquoise pillows as they casually shoot texts to friends. The school's designated support animal, a golden retriever named Firelily who wears "Safe Space" and "Y'all Means All" patches on her harness, causes a minor commotion by rolling around on her back, students crowding around her to stroke her soft belly. Walking the hallways between classes is to witness pure sartorial maximalism: pink plaids that pop like lip gloss, black jeans ripped all the way up, and hair in every conceivable (and inconceivable) color. One student infamously wears "shants" to school: gray skinny jeans with one leg made into shorts, as if their owner were intending to hitch a ride in a black-and-white movie.

The school is a project of Birmingham AIDS Outreach (BAO), the largest LGBTQIA+ resource provider in the state of Alabama. MCAA first opened its doors in 2021, but the idea of a dedicated queer educational facility dates back to 2013. That year, BAO cut the proverbial ribbon on the similarly named Magic City Acceptance Center (MCAC), a drop-in space that operates in a renovated warehouse in Birmingham. The building's initial purpose was to provide HIV and STI testing, but as it grew, Dr. Karen Musgrove, BAO's executive director, tells me that her organization quickly realized its habitués needed profound care beyond its allotted services. Many had similar stories to Rhydian's before he was able to transfer to his new school: They hadn't eaten all day because they were too terrified to sit in the lunchroom with their classmates; many hadn't used the restroom because they weren't allowed to access facilities that matched their identity. Some would come in and sleep for hours because they were so fatigued, and a few would routinely take off their makeup before their parents picked them up each day.

Opening a school where LGBTQIA+ youth wouldn't need to manage daily trauma in order to access education wasn't as easy as simply recognizing a need and meeting it, especially in Alabama. Before the school was able to open, MCAA's charter was denied three times: first by the Birmingham Board of Education[7] and then twice by the Alabama Public Charter School Commission.[8] While the city's reasons for doing so were straightforward—Birmingham doesn't allow charter schools to operate within its limits—the state evidently took issue with the very nucleus of MCAA's ethos. During a series of hearings held over Zoom, Dr. Musgrove says that state commissioners dismissively referred to MCAA as a "gay school" and openly misgendered a transgender child who spoke at the meeting. If that weren't enough already, the testimonies were Zoom-bombed by trolls who flooded the screen with gay pornography, Dr. Musgrove says.

"The kids saw the whole thing," she tells me as we sit in the empty cafeteria before lunch. "It reinforced what they have been telling us all along: *There is no hope, adults don't care, and this is a shitty-ass place to live.*"

After appealing the repeated rejections and threatening a lawsuit, MCAA was finally approved in November 2020 by just one vote—but with a major asterisk: The school had to be ready to open by August, in just ten months' time.[9] "The bulldozers were basically lined up at the building waiting for the vote," Dr. Musgrove says. "That's how serious it was." The construction crew worked three shifts a day to prepare the building, which was once a training center for the BellSouth telephone company, for its inauguration. But for all the chaos behind the scenes of its unveiling, that very first day was completely quiet in the hallways. While parents sobbed as they dropped off their kids at the front security desk, students barely spoke to each other, walking in a daze as if they were afraid the school was a dream from which they would soon awaken.

The August 9, 2021, commencement was particularly auspicious for Rhydian: He had never made it through the first day of school before without throwing up—an annual phenomenon at his prior campus. At MCAA, he didn't have to worry about being outed by people he thought were his friends or about being deadnamed in front of the class. With his pronoun pin on, he could just be Rhydian, and he couldn't ever remember a time when that had ever been true. "It was comforting," he tells me as other students begin to file in for lunch, negotiating the ever-changing politics of which friends they will sit beside today. "Being able to be in an environment where everyone doesn't think twice about your pronouns or your name or the way you look, it clears up a lot of room in your brain to actually learn."

It took two weeks before MCAA students started opening up to each other, before the hallways began to look like an average school campus: new couples walking with their hands in each other's back pockets, friends making weekend plans to play Dungeons & Dragons. (For the truly devoted, the school even has its own weekly club dedicated to the fantasy tabletop game.) To make those discomfiting connections, many students had to overcome their own deeply ingrained fears of letting others in—a defense mechanism developed in response to being let down by virtually everyone they'd ever known. Before enrolling at MCAA, Rhydian's best friend, Zed, had planned to detransition and move in with his father in Texas, thinking that he had no other option but to go along with his father's desires for his life. "His requirement was that I play the 'pastor's daughter role,'" Zed tells me as we eat outside in the parking lot, Rhydian's preferred lunchtime spot. "I would probably either be dead or a shell of a person."

Zed, a fellow senior with a mane of walnut hair, says that he'd never really had a friend before coming to MCAA, and he feels lucky that his first experience with camaraderie was with Rhydian. Rhydian is intensely admired by his peers and viewed by faculty as a leader in the classroom, someone who makes others feel welcome and shows them that it's OK to be visible, to take up space. But for Zed, Rhydian is more than a possibility model: He's been a lifeline, the only person who Zed can spend hours talking with on the phone and not make excuses to end the call. For the only time in his life, Zed feels appreciated and seen for who he is—not broken, but simply pieces of a whole that haven't yet been put together.

"There was one night where I was laying on my bed and we were talking about why we want to be alive," Zed says. "I told him that I have my entire life only been living for other people. By the end of it, I made a goal: that by the end of the school year, I wanted to live for myself. I'm not saying that I would have never got there, but if I did not have him in my life, I don't know how long it would have taken."

As much as others say he has inspired them to be more themselves, Rhydian says that he would never have had the opportunity to be the effortlessly jocular person he is now without MCAA. He remembers his first prom at the school as euphoric. Dressed as elves and lustrous mushrooms to match the enchanted-forest theme, the forty or so students in attendance danced to throwback R&B electronica, including Nelly Furtado's orgiastic "Promiscuous" and Jennifer Lopez's booty-shaker "On the Floor," the latter of which also happens to be Mima's ringtone. Rhydian, who wore a conservative black suit, says the experience couldn't have been more different from his old campus, where he spent homecoming dances hidden in the corner, terrified of being kicked out or even attacked. He could still feel that residual fear inside him even at his new school: muscles tightening over his sternum like a protective shield, shoulders caving in on themselves in an attempt to disappear.

This year's prom theme at MCAA is "starry disco midnight," and Rhydian already has his date lined up: Callaway, a fellow classmate he's been dating for a few months. They go horseback riding and attend parties thrown in deserted houses, and the morning they see *M3GAN* in a crowded theater, Mara and I tag along as the third and fourth wheels on their date.

But for all the eighties teen movie visions in his head of what his last prom will be—celebrating with his friends as he forgets the world for just a moment—a part of him knows it will be incomplete unless he's able to get top surgery before the big dance. While getting ready for prom last year, he cried when he saw the way his suit fit over the curves of his body, a shape that he says is still more womanly than he would prefer. That discomfort makes it hard for Rhydian to embrace gender fluidity on his own terms, whether by wearing heels, painted nails, or jewelry, all of which he would like to incorporate into this year's prom look. The issue is not femininity in and of itself, he says, but rather not being able to be feminine on his own terms; he wants to be the one who draws the lines of gender for himself.

When he thinks about what going to the dance as his fullest self would mean, Rhydian can barely picture it; the thought, after all this time and waiting, is too overwhelming. "I definitely will cry, just out of happiness, trying on the suit for the first time and carrying myself in a way that I don't have to worry about what angle someone's looking at me: *When I'm sitting, does the suit accentuate the fact I have a chest? Does the shirt wrinkle a certain way?*" he says as I devour his mother's leftover piñon, Puerto Rican ground beef lasagna made with plantains. "I just want to be able to enjoy myself and feel good."

The rest of the school day breezes by. Rhydian's next class is theater, where a discussion regarding the philosophy of stage acting leads into a series of games intended to test students' performing skills. First up is Werewolf, in which players must weed out the killer among them before they are all tragically slain, and then a spin on Museum Night Janitor, where the goal is to stand perfectly still while an appointed custodian walks by, trying to catch anyone moving. In this version of the game, the class must pretend to be statues, and the perky Mr. G directs them to hold a series of different poses; they are first instructed to make their arms into a Y shape and then told to stand on one foot. The freeze-frame exercise tests students' ability to react and be present, while Werewolf is acting at its basest level: If the anointed monster isn't able to convince the group of their innocence, the game will be a very short one. Our final stop is math class, where Rhydian is greeted with a pop quiz on fractions, percentages, and decimals. Afterward, Rhydian won't say what he got, except that it was "not 100 percent."

As we walk toward Mara's car at the end of the school day, past the long line of parents waiting to pick up their children, I feel glad that Rhydian was able to find somewhere that he could be so adored, a place that would love him the way he always deserved. One thing that Mr. Evans explained is that the school, which is as much a trauma center as it is an educational institution, isn't a good fit for every LGBTQIA+ student. It's geared toward the most vulnerable, the ones for whom Mr. Evans says the traditional classroom experience "absolutely did nothing." Just seconds after opening the door to his mother's back seat, he is already texting on his phone, slumped over in the dim light. He seems at ease and maybe ready for a nap. He is what so many of these kids couldn't have pictured for themselves even a year ago: alive.

III. GRINGOLAS

A sign warns us to keep away from a swarm of bees collecting honey while Mara checks the blood sugar app on her phone. "Caution: honey bees at work," reads the message affixed to a tiny wooden house. "Enjoy our bees, but remember—bees can sting, so enjoy from a safe distance, and don't swat flying bees!" Mara barely registers the caveat, more concerned with the direction of the arrow on her blood sugar tracker. A sideways arrow means things are copacetic, while an upward arrow signals a potential crash in the near future. If the arrow faces down, that's Mayday: Her hands begin to shake, her vision narrows, and a sudden chill overtakes her. She usually has about a minute to sit down and take a glucose pill before she blacks out, which has happened several times over the past few years.

Mara's hypoglycemia is a rare and unintentional side effect of a gastric bypass surgery from several years back. Although the size of her stomach has been reduced to prevent her from overeating, her body hasn't adapted to the change, continuing to produce the same amount of insulin. She takes two shots in the morning every day to prevent crashes, but Mara's incurable sweet tooth can be her own worst enemy. On the evening I arrived in Birmingham, Mara presented me with a homemade gift basket of gluten-free sweets. The tote bag's contents included two kinds of Mexican cookies, Haribo gummy bears, and a slice of store-bought chocolate cake, along with a bottle of water and antihistamine tablets for seasonal allergies.

Her arrow is pointing down but not at the rapid rate that might suggest an immediate emergency. Mara signals it's time to take a rest, so we walk past the boathouse that nearly played host to the wedding of

Rhydian's older brother, Pablo. As we sit on the bridge, Mara describes the event as one of their happiest days: The nuptials were instead held at a farm on Halloween weekend, and guests were invited to dress in costumes. Among the highlights were a lesbian couple who dressed as Vincent Vega and Mia Wallace from the nineties hipster noir *Pulp Fiction* and an inflatable Patrick Star, the buffoonish cartoon sidekick of aquatic optimist SpongeBob Squarepants. Pablo and his best men, a group that included Rhydian, wore black suits with clip-on ties for the vows before changing into their own costumes for the reception; like many elements of the Gonzalez-Herreros' lives, the proceedings were just a touch on the goth side.

Today Mara is dressed in gold, her sweater so bright that it lit the inside of Mima's car aglow on our drive to Aldridge Gardens, the park where she is currently practicing her breathing while a bale of turtles bathe in the afternoon sun. As she begins to fear yet another unwanted trip to the hospital, these terrible troubles remind Mara of her frustrations with Alabama's refusal to recognize her son's own health care needs: Lawmakers would never deny her access to the medication she needs to keep living, so why should Rhydian be any different?

It took time—and some patience with herself—before Mara was able to see how she could relate to Rhydian, to be the mother and ally that her son needed. That journey meant overcoming ingrained biases from her Catholic childhood in San Juan, where she says she was taught by those around her to be a "come mierda," as she calls it. "It means a 'shit eater,'" she says. "We think we're high class, and appearances were important to me. I want to project that I have a house, kids that are doing great in life and going to college, the things you expect." According to Mara, her concern with surfaces makes her fear others' judgment if her life doesn't reflect what she believes their standards to be, which she has come to recognize is usually her own empty projection. "When I moved to Birmingham, I realized life is not like that. People are people. Now, I just want to be sure that *my* people are happy and comfortable—that they are good citizens, good friends, and good parents, if they want to be."

Mara and Tom relocated to Alabama from Puerto Rico in 1999, and even though it took her time to realize it, the life she has built here includes all of those things that were so important to her. Pablo is happily married to a woman his parents love, and Rhydian is going to the University of Alabama at Birmingham (UAB) in the fall, where he plans to study criminal justice. Rhydian's transition initially caught Mara off guard, an apparent deviation from the plan that her children would be safe and healthy. She struggled with the thought of every possible worst-case scenario: *What if someone hurts him? What if he needs help?* Those fears became obsessions, and they quickly began physically weighing upon her body. Whenever someone would look at Rhydian with an expression she couldn't easily identify, she would become dizzy, feeling her blood sugar beginning to spike from the stress of not knowing what they were thinking. Within seconds, the arrow would fall, and she would faint.

There's a Spanish word that Mara uses to describe this kind of mindset, and although she doesn't know the English translation, she deploys the phrase several times in conversation: gringolas. It refers to the leather cups—commonly called blinders or blinkers—that are placed on either side of a racehorse's head to limit its field of vision during competitions. They are intended to keep the animal from looking to its side or rear, thereby preventing it from becoming injured in a fall and ensuring the horse stays focused on the race ahead. Having a narrow point of view may be helpful on the track, Mara argues, but it's less useful in daily life. "You only see things one way," she says, "and you're not open to seeing the whole picture."

An unlikely loved one was the one to help remove Mara's gringolas: her friend, Terry, a gay widower who lives in the rural outskirts of the coastal city of Mobile, with three cats all named after film stars of Hollywood's golden age: Greta Garbo, Clark Gable, and Montgomery Clift. Terry, a hairdresser who lost his partner to COVID-19 in 2022, unintentionally played a key role in Rhydian's transition by giving him a series of gender-affirming haircuts before he officially came out to his family as transgender. When he was eleven, Rhydian took his first step out of the closet by telling his family that he was a lesbian—writing the phrase "I'm Gay" on red velvet cupcakes—and Mara let him slowly step down to shorter and shorter styles, thinking that she just had a butch daughter. During this process, Rhydian landed upon what has since become his signature hair color: bright green, giving his thick coif the glimmery sheen of either Christmas tinsel or seaweed, depending on the light.

Looking in the mirror and seeing a boy steadily appear made Rhydian more comfortable with declaring that to the world, and Terry explained to Mara that what she perceived as hatred and prejudice from others could just as easily be veneration. "Maybe they're admiring his beauty," Terry had told her of the strangers who sometimes stare at Rhydian. "Maybe they like his skin. Maybe they're looking because they like his nails. Maybe they're staring at him because they would like to have green hair. Some people look at you weird, and what can you do?"

Two years later, Rhydian officially began taking testosterone around the time of his fifteenth birthday, now with his mother's approval. But despite Mara's belated understanding of her son, she has not been made naïve to the realities of Alabama. In addition to the gender-affirming medical care ban, Alabama passed legislation in 2021 that prevents trans students in K-12 schools from competing on sports teams in accordance with their gender,[10] and the following year, it enacted what was then the country's harshest "Don't Say Gay" law.[11] While a controversial statute passed in Florida prohibits discussions of sexual orientation and gender identity in K–3 classrooms, Alabama's version extends all the way through the fifth grade.[12] Since 2016, more than 240 transgender people[13] in the United States have been murdered, and at least three of those homicides took place in Alabama: Jazz Alford in 2016,[14] Dana Martin in 2019,[15] and Jaheim "Barbie" Pugh in 2020.[16] Each of them, like Rhydian, was a transgender person of color under the age of thirty-five; Alford was killed less than twenty miles from the Gonzalez-Herreros' home.

The first time I ever spoke to Mara and Rhydian was over the phone in March 2022, when I was on assignment for *Rolling Stone* reporting on Alabama's then-proposed transgender youth medical care ban.[17] At the time, Mara was so concerned about what would happen to her family if the law were passed that she and Rhydian used pseudonyms in the article: Sofia and Oro, the latter the Spanish word for gold. While she still deals with many of those same anxieties, she can't deny what a difference being able to socially and medically transition has made in her son's life. He's no longer the pensive, withdrawn kid who hid inside his hoodie and wouldn't say hello or make eye contact when he walked into a room. He's charismatic, likable, and funny, although Mara remarks that he has developed a bit of a smart mouth. Later in the week, he will demonstrate the serrated edges of his personality at the Whataburger drive through, playfully teasing his father as Tom stares blankly at the fast-food chain's intercom. As the seconds pass by in silence, Rhydian asks from the back seat with a cheerfully insolent grin across his face: "So, are you going to get me anything?"

Others have also seen a dramatic shift in Rhydian since his transition, now that he has been able to show the world who he really is. A few days after my walk with Mara, I play Candyland in Mima's dining room with Rhydian's preteen neighbor, Julianna, who makes good on her promise to dominate the confection-themed board game, winning three times in a row. Julianna says that Rhydian came out to her as transgender when she was nine; they were drawing with chalk outside in the driveway, and Rhydian sketched a penguin in the colors of the Transgender Pride flag. Unaware of the symbol's meaning, she asked him what the design represented, and she says the answer was easy for her to accept. "I was taught people are the way they are, and that's it," she recalls as she confidently moves her piece, a red plastic man with a cryogenically frozen smile, across the board. "If it doesn't affect you, then mind your business."

Julianna describes Rhydian effusively as the "coolest person" she knows, painting him as a mythic being who "walks on clouds." "Everything bad is down here and then he's up there, just doing his own thing," she says. As someone who is still figuring out who she wants to be, she has gained a lot of insight from observing the way that Rhydian pulls focus in a room, how everyone's eyes are just naturally drawn toward him. She says that it taught her to stick up for herself, to walk with her head held high: "He stands up straight, and he walks with ease. He doesn't walk like he's in a hurry. He doesn't walk slow, though. He walks where it's apparent that he isn't lost, and he knows where he's going."

Of Rhydian's immediate family members, Tom was the first to accept his son's transition—although, being a man of few words, it's tough for him to say why he didn't have the early struggles that Mara did. He compares his son's coming out to acquiring a new language: It requires translating from what you understand into an entirely new lexicon. Adults who are first learning English, he says, might speak with a strong accent or misspeak certain words because they are filtering them through the language they've known their entire lives. And when it comes to respecting his son's sense of self, Tom says that he still finds himself translating before he speaks, even today. "It wasn't easy," he says, watching Julianna take no prisoners from the comfort of Mima's couch. "You have to reprogram. At that point, it was sixteen years of programming my brain that I had a daughter. I have to reprogram that to a son, change names and genders. It takes a minute, but the way I see it, I love my son. If he wants me to call him Alien from the Galaxy of Whatever, that's what I'm going to call him. I need to force myself to relearn."

Mara believes it's important to tell their family's story because other parents need to know that they, too, can become better advocates for their children, she says. Even if they don't get it right away, they can learn. It would be tempting to say that the Gonzalez-Herreros have grown closer because of Rhydian's transition, but the truth is that they've always shared an intense bond. Part of that, Mara adds, is a consequence of the damage they've weathered together, which largely has nothing to do with Rhydian's transition. When Mara was sixteen, her abusive stepfather attempted to murder her after Mima threatened to leave him. She was shot in the back, and her older brother, Carlos, spent three months in the hospital after a bullet punctured his kidney. Today, Mara wears a pacemaker as the result of ongoing complications from her injuries, and she jokingly calls herself a "colander" in reference to the scattering of scars that runs down her body. "I'm full of holes," she laughs, checking her blood sugar app from Mima's crowded couch to find her arrow pleasingly sideways. "Everything is removed. I had a hysterectomy, too, so I don't have any plumbing left."

Nobody understands the relationship that she shares with her brother and mother, Mara says, because they haven't lived through it. But the connective tissue that grows from healing is also what bonds her to the rest of her family members, the thread that has pulled them together so tightly. It's there in the house with Mima as Mara watches her favorite Turkish soap operas with her, along with DVR'd episodes of *Jeopardy!* When I ask about the long-running game show's recent hosting controversies—which have resulted, for the moment, in a pair of emcees alternating duties—Mima says that she prefers the actress Mayim Bialik because she's friendly and warm with the contestants. She thinks that Ken Jennings, seeming heir apparent to the late Alex Trebek, is too smug. "He's so full of himself," she remarks, pinching her face like she just bit into sour candy.[18]

The Gonzalez-Herreros are a family with so many stories to tell—that casually spill out with a backward flick of the wrist—and one day Mima guides me through a tapestry of them during a brief tour of her home. Tossed over the back of her living room couch is a photo blanket depicting many of the most esteemed moments of her life, including Pablo's wedding and Mara's marriage to Tom. One of those portraits is from Rhydian's last birthday before he came out as transgender, in which the family stands outside of an Italian restaurant. Although having a pre-transition picture featured prominently in their grandmother's home might be painful and triggering for many transgender kids—hearkening back to unwanted memories—Rhydian has approved the display because of what it signifies to Mima: that she loved him before she knew that he was Rhydian and that she still loves him now. Nothing is different, not one bit.

While some of his family members feel that Rhydian has become a radically different being since his transition, as if he stepped out anew from the skin he had shed, Mima contests that characterization. She believes that the core of him has remained the same—that he's still the kind, caring person that he was back when he didn't yet have a name for what he was feeling inside. "I don't see a big change because he's always been the way he is," she says, resting in her favorite living room recliner. "I have five grandkids and I say, 'You are Mima's treasures,' but in that treasure, each jewel is a different kind. Each one has different things to bring."

IV. UPSETTI SPAGHETTI

This was supposed to be a joyous week for Rhydian, but instead the air around him is sodden with unspoken thoughts. The Gonzalez-Herreros are sitting in an outdoor Mexican restaurant after driving to Atlanta to see the Greek tragedy-turned-musical *Hadestown* earlier that day, and Rhydian's usual buoyancy has been replaced with a portentous gloom; he has said very little for hours, which could also be the residue of slumber. In accordance with his well-established road-trip routine, he slept straight through the three-hour car ride, only waking up briefly to eat a dollop of cake shaped like a lollipop at a drive-through Starbucks. Rhydian likes to "teleport" on family trips, taking a nap so that when he awakens, he can pretend that his atoms were recombined in a faraway galaxy. Today's reassembly has left him in a daze, unable to fully take in his new surroundings.

Before his appointment was canceled, Rhydian was originally scheduled to have top surgery this coming Thursday, and his parents are hoping that the short vacation acts as a distraction. But unintentionally, *Hadestown*'s plot can't help but feel ominous in context. Infused with New Orleans jazz and just a touch of indie folk by its creator, singer-songwriter Anaïs Mitchell, the musical is a retelling of the Orpheus and Eurydice story from Greek mythology. Orpheus journeys to the underworld to rescue his lover, Eurydice, and Hades lets her go after a wrenching ballad appeals to his better nature ("Epic III," a real showstopper). But the god of the dead puts one condition on his pardon: On their journey out of the darkness, Orpheus must not look back to check that Eurydice is following him; he must instead let faith be his guide. Given that the story famously does not end happily, doubt eventually sets in during their long walk to safety, and Orpheus loses his soulmate forever. The parable was intended as a lesson for Greeks on the importance of trust in relationships, but it has a different allegorical meaning for Rhydian: He knows what it feels like to be so close to the things he wants just to have them taken away.

After wearing out her Rolodex of contacts, Mara was able to schedule an intake appointment a few days from now with a new top surgeon in Atlanta, coincidentally just down the street from the theater. As Rhydian nibbles on a steak and chimichurri taco, which was formerly topped with pickled red onions before he immediately picked them off, he says that he can't let himself be too optimistic about the consultation because he's been in this position so many times before. "I don't want to get excited," he says, looking down at his disassembled food. "My whole transition has been dangled above me. It's like: *Maybe you can have it, maybe you can't.* Why get my hopes up?" He has returned to a familiar defensive posture today, piling clothing on top of clothing to avoid attention to his chest; he is wearing a knit sweatshirt over a black t-shirt that reads "Upsetti Spaghetti" in cartoon atomic typeface. But even under layers of material, he still worries about his bra strap peeking out, he admits.

Should next week's appointment go well, several questions remain. It's unclear whether insurance will pay for the procedure, which Mara and Tom would not be able to afford without financial assistance. Top surgery generally costs between six and ten thousand dollars, and the expense would arrive at a most inopportune time. After driving her mother's car for weeks, the transmission in Mara's old vehicle proved too costly to replace, and she had to get a new car instead. They also have a nonrefundable vacation to Europe planned for March, a trip the family has been saving for four years to take.

If their insurance rejects the claim, the Gonzalez-Herreros would have to either wait until the fall—thus denying Rhydian his dream of going to prom with a body that affirms his identity—or rely on the support of family and friends. Rhydian's former principal at MCAA, Dr. Mike Wilson, offered to help pay for the surgery, but Mara is not sure whether they can accept such generosity. She is used to doing things for others; welcoming kindness is a strange sensation.

The remainder of our last day together is a blur. Following an overnight hotel stay courtesy of Tom's military discount, the morning brings Rhydian's first trip to the Swedish furniture retailer Ikea, where his father takes frequent breaks as chest pains prevent him from keeping pace with the group. After driving back to Pelham for a farewell kiss on the cheek from Mima, we travel to Birmingham for Rhydian's monthly therapy appointment at the UAB children's hospital, where he began his transition three years ago. When we walk into the aquatic-themed waiting area—complete with sailboats and metal fish dangling from the ceiling—the receptionist offers Rhydian a selection from her bounty of toys behind the desk, including a tee ball set, stuffed pigs, and cottony cats with giant dewy eyes. Rhydian declines due to the lack of Hot Wheels, and we play air hockey in the hospital's arcade while we wait. He wins every single time because he keeps his mallet right beside the goal, making it impossible to score on him. Given the week he's having, pointing this out feels unimportant.

The boy that walks into the waiting area that day is not the one his gender care specialist, Dr. Morissa Ladinsky, met five years ago. During their first Zoom call, she remembers how absent he seemed behind the computer screen. "You could see just heaviness in the faces of Rhydian and his whole family," Dr. Ladinsky tells me following an exchange of hellos and hugs with the Gonzalez-Herreros. But after a few meetings to discuss treatment options available to them, that overwhelming resignation she witnessed "began to turn and flip," she adds. "You already saw something that we're tuned in to seeing: a hope returned. The journey was underway. When I look back, I can't imagine where he would be without the hope that our team and this care is able to provide to youth and families."

Dr. Ladinsky remains chipper in conversation despite shouldering the futures of Alabama's transgender youth, as one of the very few medical professionals in the state who specializes in transgender care. Still, she worries that the confusion and profound insecurity that Rhydian has experienced over the past two weeks is not an isolated occurrence. After a district court enjoined the portion of Alabama's transgender youth medical care ban outlawing HRT and other gender-affirming medications in May 2022, many parents were unaware they could still get their children's prescriptions refilled. Families who had been on a waiting list for months weren't showing up to their appointments, thinking they would be turned away.

"We'd have a parent tell us, sometimes even choking back tears, 'We decided that it was better not to come to the clinic and have our son see his hopes dashed than to come and just hear about what he can't have,'" she remembers. In the first few weeks following the partial injunction, Dr. Ladinsky estimates that five to ten pharmacies were calling her every single day to ask: *What do we do? How do we follow the law?*[19]

Even a year later, many doctors in Alabama still don't know what kinds of care it's legal for them to offer. Dr. Ladinsky was the one who had the unenviable task of calling Rhydian's top surgeon to inform him that the procedure cannot be performed without facing the risk of prosecution until Rhydian turns nineteen. The sentence for violating SB 184 is up to ten years in prison, designated as a Class C felony.[20] "I notified him of the details of the law," she tells me alone in the waiting area, after Rhydian and Mara file into her office for their appointment. "He was immensely grateful, but this sadness that my partner, the surgeon, and his nurse coordinator felt, it was a shared depth. We were devastated, but we have to follow the law. We have to do the right thing. That's a promise I make every day: Despite these barriers, I will and I must follow the law."

After finishing the day with sushi at Mara's favorite Japanese restaurant, we take one last trip to my Airbnb, where Rhydian and I hug goodbye with a promise that he will call me with news about his top surgery appointment on Wednesday. As we give each other a studied two pats on the back, I think about how incredibly precarious his world is. SB 184's passage once forced him to miss a prescription refill, and he spent an entire week without his medication before the HRT ban was blocked in court. He describes the ordeal as like being suddenly imprisoned inside his own body, and within that very first day, he began experiencing piercing cramps that prevented him from following along in class. Rhydian sometimes gets hot flashes as a vexing side effect of taking testosterone—he will often walk into the freezer at work when he feels sweat encroaching—but those familiar sensations were soon accompanied by a throbbing headache, skin rashes, bloating, and his period coming back, the latter of which he had feared the most. It had been so long since he experienced a menstrual cycle that he barely remembered how to use a pad, and a single law or unfavorable court ruling stands in the way of that being forced upon him again.[21]

I still have two days left before departing from Birmingham—enough time to let Rhydian mentally prepare for his appointment—and I spend it in the city's downtown district, looking for the renewed hope of which Dr. Ladinsky had spoken. It's there, in unexpected places: in a very queer café where customers can play video games for eleven hours straight and in the most delicious pulled pork at a barbeque restaurant where the waitress immediately clocks me as an out-of-towner. It's there in my coffee date with MCAC's founding director, Amanda Keller, who says its drop-in center now reaches eight hundred LGBTQIA+ youth through Discord, an online platform that allows users to build chat rooms geared toward niche communities. Currently, MCAC serves queer young people across fifty-one of Alabama's sixty-seven counties.

That hope is also present in Rhydian's voice when he finally calls, the phone ringing while I wait for my plane to board at the airport. Even though his appointment did not lead to a scheduled surgery date, he says that he's feeling just a little bit optimistic. They are hoping to get him in next month.

Something shifts in Rhydian during that short conversation. When I first met him in person two weeks ago, Rhydian had a reticence to him, as if he were keeping a heedful distance from the world around him, preferring to hide in the hermetic asylum of his playroom. One of the reasons that he inspires so much admiration in his peers is that he feels younger than he is—as if he has found a way not only to have the childhood that he was once denied, but also a means of staying there. His guarded boyishness, though, has long hidden what he doesn't share with the kids who see him as their personal wish fulfillment: that behind his genial smile, he's as afraid as they are; he doesn't have it all figured out either. But today he is like a cactus at night, opening its stomata to let the world's mysteries in.

Rhydian knows what getting top surgery after all this time would mean to him—the literal difference between life and death—but for the first time in a very long time, he can sense that day is coming soon. If it doesn't happen next month or even the month after, he knows that someday he will know what it's like to be unburdened, to live the life that he wants. "I've been to the mental hospital before," he tells me over the phone, affirming that his resolve to never go back to that place is stronger than ever before. "I've struggled with self-harm in the past, but I have a good support system. I wouldn't want to die before seeing my transition. I want to see myself through. I want to see who I become. That's very important to me."

As the flight attendant makes the final boarding announcement, we say one more quick goodbye, fumbling over the proper words to encapsulate the moment. Reaching into my pocket to grab my plane ticket as we hang up, I instead find a foreign object: a white angel with its tremendous wings outstretched. The plaster Christmas ornament—a last-minute gift from Mima—came with a story. She says her guardian angel appeared to her in Puerto Rico when Hurricane Georges made landfall back in 1989, one year before the family moved to Alabama. She was all alone at the time, and as the gulf winds violently shook the glass doors in her home, Mima was terrified of what would happen to her. She'd experienced so much grief in her life—the shocking acts of violence from her ex-husband, losing her brother to complications from HIV—that she felt as if more sorrow must be near. But suddenly, she could feel her angel with her, telling her that everything would turn out fine.

Mima gave me the ornament so I would be reminded of their story and that she made it through, just as they all have. Thinking of Rhydian as I board, I remember what Mima's angel said to her: *Don't worry. Nothing's gonna happen. You're OK.*

MYKAH

CHARLESTON, WEST VIRGINIA

FEBRUARY 2023

I. ALMOST HEAVEN

Author's note: Mykah uses fluid pronouns and requested that each section of their chapter use a different pronoun—alternating between he, she, and they—to reflect all facets of their identity.

Mykah Smith applies sparkly pink lip gloss seated in the packed balcony of the West Virginia House of Delegates, brazenly unaffected by the room's funereal tenor. Mykah already knew what was going to happen when they showed up to the legislature that morning, their hair clips setting off the capitol building's metal detectors: that despite the testimonies of more than seventy speakers who had driven from all across the state, Republicans were going to pass HB 2007 anyway. With the GOP controlling eighty-eight out of one hundred seats in the lower house of the legislature, its passage was a done deal, no matter how many people begged lawmakers not to move the bill forward. Should the legislation go on to be approved by the state Senate, HB 2007 will make it illegal to administer gender-affirming surgery or hormone therapy to transgender youth, although the parameters of the exact punishments for medical providers remain unclear.[1]

Among today's assembled speakers protesting the bill are doctors, teachers, and local leaders, both religious and political. Morgantown mayor Jennifer Selin notes in her brief remarks that the progressive college town, which is home to West Virginia University, is one of the few cities in the state that is growing, a fact she ascribes to its robust support for the LGBTQIA+ community. Morgantown, which sits just below Pennsylvania's southwestern border, was the second of three municipalities in West Virginia to ban the harmful, discredited practice of conversion therapy, in which doctors or faith-based practitioners attempt to "cure" LGBTQIA+ youth of their identities.[2] The treatment has been condemned by every leading medical association,[3] as well as human rights experts with the United Nations,[4] but it remains fully legal and unrestricted in nineteen states,as well as nearly all of West Virginia's other cities and counties.[5]

The most emotional testimonies come from parents who say their transgender kids blossomed when they were able to see their true selves in the mirror for the first time. Without access to the medications that made such transformation possible, opponents of HB 2007 fear that their children will choose death over the chance that they may lose the ability to see a person they recognize staring back at them. "It feels like this bill is trying to make it so trans youth don't exist in West Virginia," says Paula, who pointedly introduces herself to lawmakers as the "*Christian* mother of a *Christian* child." "Since there's an extraordinarily high suicide rate among trans youth who don't have access to gender-affirming care, this bill might just succeed. The bottom line is this: I would rather have a live daughter than a dead son."

The legislation's grave stakes are a recurring motif of the morning's speeches, which are periodically interrupted by the echo of dry February coughs and the banshee bellow of cell phone alarms. Kris, a pediatric chaplain at a children's hospital, says that on the two-and-a-half-hour drive over from Morgantown, her transgender teenager had expressed concern about the potential impact the bill would have on their friends. "I will have to walk through a field of the corpses of my friends," her child had told her, "because some politicians decided to impose their trans-phobia on the rest of us." Nicki, a nonbinary college student, fears that they personally wouldn't survive if a medical care ban were to be signed into law. "If you pass this bill, you will be subjecting thousands more to violence, thousands more like me," they say. "If this bill passes, you will not only have multiple people's blood on your hands, but mine as well."

Of the few conservatives to speak up in support of HB 2007, one says what no one else will acknowledge out loud: that the hearing is a poignant formality, staged more for the benefit of those testifying than their elected leaders. "Despite the crowd opposing this bill, this is a red state, and there's a big push in the conservative movement for this bill," says a right-wing activist who compares gender-affirming care to a patient electing to have their arm cut off. "If you don't vote for this bill, we will vote you out." Fewer than a dozen West Virginia House lawmakers are even present to hear the blunt admission; the only empty seats in the entire room are their wooden desks, an abandoned ampitheater arranged in a semicircle.

Mykah had planned to speak this morning alongside fellow campers from last August's Appalachian Queer Youth Summit (AQYS), a summer camp for LGBTQIA+ teens hosted by the ACLU of West Virginia, but time runs out before they get the chance. The hearing clocks in at under two hours due to the stringent restrictions placed upon speeches: If orators talk for more than sixty seconds, their microphones are shut off. The draconian rules result in surplus remarks shouted in vain to audience members, who lean over wooden pews with ears cupped while muttering their discontent to one another. While Mykah had hoped to talk about their experiences in West Virginia as a Black and biracial person, their nonchalance becomes its own form of protest. In contrast to the lobbyists seated down below with their perfectly parted hair and neat blue suits, Mykah is wearing casual ripped jeans and a brown argyle sweater—a melanated homage to Cher Horowitz, protagonist of the nineties teen social satire *Clueless*. With their lips pursed and Dalmatian-print headphones in tow, Mykah's personal presentation is a thinly veiled message to these people, the kind they have been dealing with all their life as a queer person of color in one of America's whitest, reddest states: Mykah is, like, *so* totally over this.

"You hear older people in West Virginia who say, 'Our state is dying. Everybody's leaving. We need the youth to stay,' but it's like our state is giving us no other option but to leave," Mykah tells me later that day in a crowded apartment on the outskirts of Charleston that they share with their mother, Dawn Paxton. "West Virginia does not care about trans kids, they do not care about LGBTQIA+ people, and they do not care about people of color. They just don't care, and that sucks. Because it's like: If you want me to stay here, there needs to be an incentive. Why would I stay here when I could go to New York and find five of me if I throw a rock?"

Mykah has wanted to leave West Virginia for such a long time that it's become a defining feature of their personality. Now eighteen and in their senior year of high school, Mykah used to collect *Vogue* magazines as a child, and one of their earliest acquisitions featured a Black model on the cover, her lambent silhouette set against the opulence of New York City at night. The city's silken lights and infinite skyscrapers represented everything that Mykah's home state was not: a place where dreams are realized, where all that you desire is just a cab ride away.

While West Virginia tourism bills the state as "almost heaven," the implied separation from nirvana, for many of its residents, is a consequential distance. Mykah's state has long been exploited by outsiders for its natural resources—its mines ransacked for coal, its mountaintops stripped and leveled—until there was nothing left to steal. That sordid history has played a major role in contributing to the nation's second-lowest life expectancy[6] and sixth-highest infant mortality rate.[7] West Virginia also ranks forty-seventh of the fifty states in education,[8] fiftieth in health care,[9] and fiftieth in infrastructure.[10] West Virginia's rate of opioid deaths is so much higher than the next closest state that it got its own color—a foreboding dark green—on the Centers for Disease Control's 2020 fatal drug overdose map.[11] More than six thousand children are housed in the West Virginia foster care system, the largest number per capita of any state in the country.[12]

In response to those generational challenges, young people like Mykah are leaving the state en masse. West Virginia saw the largest net migration from any state between 2010 and 2018,[13] and it boasts the nation's third-oldest population, behind the retirement-friendly hubs of Maine and Florida.[14]

Feeling that their state has no resources left to plunder, Mykah has kept their eyes trained all these years on a single goal: attending New York University (NYU). I first met Mykah at AQYS in 2022, while I was covering the camp for the Canadian LGBTQIA+ magazine *Xtra*, and soon after we started talking, they took me on a scenic tour of their envisioned future.[15] Sitting on the floor of the main cabin as fat streamers and rainbow tinsel dangled from above, they told me that they intended to major in musical theater at NYU and minor in political science, en route to a formidable career on Broadway. In addition to winning enough Tonys to fill a cement truck, they also planned to be the first Black transgender designer to present a collection at Paris Fashion Week. Although it was unclear how those disparate threads would eventually become entwined, Mykah's complete and total belief in their talent sold me on the reverie's eventuality. *This is a kid*, I thought, *who is going to make it happen, no matter what.*

But by the time my plane lands in West Virginia in February of the following year, those lofty aspirations now seem unreachable to them: Less than a month ago, Mykah bombed their NYU audition after coming down with COVID-19 on the week of tryouts. They were unable to hit many of the high notes in "Oh, What a Beautiful Mornin'," one of the signature numbers from the Rodgers and Hammerstein musical *Oklahoma!*, and the disasters further accumulated during their second solo. Convinced they were blowing the one shot they would ever get, Mykah started to cry while attempting to sing "Not My Father's Son" from the stage adaptation of *Kinky Boots*, an elegiac ballad about the elusiveness of familial acceptance that is a tearjerker even when it isn't performed under duress. When the Zoom call was over, Mykah immediately began sobbing and didn't get out of bed for three days.

Ever since the audition, Mykah has been struggling with depression, and today's trip to the capitol building is the only time in weeks they've left their apartment or allowed others to see them. Their viscous sorrow has exacerbated preexisting conditions: Mykah hasn't attended school in person since November following a series of devastating panic attacks. While Mykah wouldn't admit it to me, Dawn says the isolation of being trapped alone in their room all day has caused her child to fall weeks upon weeks behind in their coursework. She fears that Mykah is on the verge of failing to graduate. For work completed at home to count toward graduation, a mental health professional needs to sign off, and finding someone new has been a struggle after a previous therapist decided that she wasn't able to offer the specialized care that Mykah needs. If Mykah doesn't catch up and can't find a psychologist to help, they might not be eligible to attend NYU at all—or any other college, for that matter.

Mykah still holds out hope that everything will work out in the way they have pictured ever since they were a toddler, stomping up and down the stairs in high heels while singing word-salad covers of their favorite songs from the radio, but the darkness has crept in. Their downward spiral has confirmed all of their worst suspicions about themself: that they aren't lovable, they aren't unique, and they don't have "that 'it girl' factor," as Mykah calls it. If their talent and self-worth are immutably intertwined, it's because the theater has given Mykah some of the few opportunities they've had to feel celebrated, to feel like they matter. The rapturous applause they earned for portraying the Cat in the Hat in their high school's production of *Seussical,* a musical amalgamation of Dr. Seuss stories, was one of the high points of Mykah's life, and they have been chasing that rush ever since. "One of my biggest nightmares is that I'm just a run-of-the-mill . . . guy. I don't want to be that. I want to be spectacular, show-stopping, amazing, never been done before," Mykah says, incorrectly reciting an oft-memed quote from the pop star Lady Gaga as their voice turns to despair. "I need this. There's no other option for me. It would be like my whole world being taken away from me."

Although their current predicament has left Mykah feeling abandoned, as if the world has given up on them just when they needed help most, a cheering section has rallied around them: the other kids from camp, who are also navigating their persistence in a state that's increasingly hostile to their presence. Less than twenty-four hours after the hearing, the West Virginia House passes HB 2007, and as anticipated, the legislation is approved along party lines: Eighty-four Republicans vote in favor of outlawing transition care for minors, while ten Democrats oppose the measure.[16] The campers, much like Mykah, are used to this by now, and they realized a long time ago they shouldn't have to be.

Following the hearing, Mykah grabs a personal pizza at the popular local gastropub Pies and Pints with a cavalcade of campers, who are in good spirits despite everything. Erin, who recently aged out of AQYS and hopes to come back as a counselor, is wearing a "She/They" pin over her sweater following a mix-up. "I have the wrong one!" she laughs as she looks down. "Somebody else has a 'She/Her' pin on!" Since last summer, Lloid has acquired a metal tongue piercing that flutters as he speaks; the steel sheath feels an appropiate thematic match with his washed-out aquamarine hair. Although Lloid had wanted to testify during the hearing, he dreaded that his irksome childhood stutter might prevent him from expressing himself accurately, so the camp's rainbow-bespectacled director, Mollie Kennedy, had read the speech on his behalf. "You are killing my friends and family," Mollie said, clutching in her hands a slip of paper with Lloid's words written on them. "You are taking away their hope and their will to live."

Despite the impassioned warning, Lloid still maintains a steadfast optimism, for the moment, that HB 2007 won't actually pass. The GOP boasts all but three seats in the West Virginia Senate after a near–clean sweep in the 2022 midterms, a once-unthinkable outcome for a state that voted for the Democratic presidential candidate in all but three elections from the end of World War II to Y2K.[17] "They wouldn't dare kill a child," Lloid tells me over pizza, trying to convince himself as his smile tightens. "Sorry, no way. How could they? How could they at all?"

In spending the afternoon swapping camp stories and catching up, Mykah finds everything that they have been missing—a reason to keep going, despite life's unfortunate setbacks. Of the more than two dozen kids who had spent the previous summer canoeing and making buttons together, today's cast of characters includes camp heartbreaker Abby, nonchalant behind her overgrown mushroom cut; shy Ren, whose rainbow "Loud and Proud" t-shirt strikes an ironic juxtaposition to their gentle demeanor; and lesbian couple Savannah and Catie, a matching set in identical tie-dye. Mykah spends so much time feeling alone in a state where it seems as if there are so few people like them, but they have forgotten that they don't have to do all this by themself. They have people in their life who love them, who will lift them up, and who will help carry them when they can't push themself any further, if only Mykah would allow themself to be carried.

Although Mykah tries to cling to their air of self-assuredness, they admit that it's difficult to accept that other people could care for them. Mykah has withstood so much rejection in their lives—whether it's the estranged father who they believe never liked them, the state that is trying to give them no choice but to leave, or the college that's on the verge of laying waste to their dreams—and those experiences have taught them they're better off alone. "The world has proved to me that acceptance is very rare," Mykah tells me, hands somberly folded on the table as others chatter excitedly around them. "Everything I've been through has prepared me for being alone, so it's hard to go from always being alone to finally having people try to come inside. They're trying to knock down those walls. It's going to take a lot of work."

ii. APPALACHIAN VALLEY GIRL

Walking into Mykah's apartment is an overwhelming sensory experience: a clamor of barks and yelps followed by a tumult of tiny paws rushing to the door. Panda, a Siberian husky with albino eyes, is usually the first to reach the entrance, followed shortly after by Bentley, a mini-Schnauzer with an intense, focused disposition. The horde's more lackadaisical representatives are a Jack Russell terrier named Buddy and a lone cat, Vex, whose short list of hobbies includes leaving exactly one drop of feces in the exact same spot each day. The dogs' leashes always remain attached to their collars to stop them from escaping into the complex's parking lot, although that strategy is sadly not foolproof. On one unlucky occasion, Bentley's jailbreak necessitates a madcap chase scene and a half-hour search—followed by a scolding that, due to the language and species barrier, he ignores in favor of licking his hindquarters.

The dwelling itself resembles a well-curated rummage sale, with "Simply Blessed" and "Thankful for Every Moment" signs covering every available wall. Above the giant, squishy living room couch are detached window frames decorated with spraypainted wreaths, and next to the door is a wooden box for prayers, although there are currently none to be found inside. Dawn's dedication to an ambiance she describes as "shabby farmhouse chic" is admirable, if borderline obsessive. Mykah's mother works hard to keep the apartment in order, joking that something must be wrong if she's not following its other dwellers around with a handheld vacuum, but all the "Choose Happy" tchotchkes in the world can't disguise the fact that they are barely staying afloat. Although Dawn is employed at an agency downtown that provides work-based training for senior citizens—a job she loves and is good at—she frequently has to borrow gas money from friends to afford the daily commute to Charleston. They are currently on food stamps, a meager stipend that is invariably gone almost immediately after its monthly disbursement, and Mykah lives in fear that any day could bring the piece of paper slipped under the door making them homeless. Their landlord has already tried to kick them out on at least two occasions.

Mykah, now several weeks into her cloister, is spending her afternoon rewatching *Sex and the City*, and it's easy to understand her fixation on an escapist sitcom about sophisticated girls about town. *Sex and the City* is the platonic ideal of her New York fantasy, where men are in endless supply and friends are forever. Mykah is currently binge-watching the HBO show's sixth season, during which the nouveau riche aspirant Charlotte has divorced her impotent ex-husband just to stumble into a hasty cohabitation with her ill-mannered divorce attorney, and bon vivant Samantha has begun dating a wannabe actor many years her younger. Uptight attorney Miranda is in an interracial romance with the hunky team doctor for the New York Knicks basketball team, while narcissistic sex columnist Carrie is upset that her five-hundred-dollar shoes were pilfered at a party.

Although Mykah has the brash pomp of a Samantha—with her all-eyes-on-me energy—she is a Carrie by necessity: Mykah would *never* let someone else be the main character. She hasn't yet seen the 2021 reboot, in which Carrie and Samantha are no longer close, having long drifted apart, but I tell her not to rush into watching it, not wanting to spoil her cosmopolitan dream.

It's difficult to say when exactly Mykah's existential nosedive began, when her world became so small; she traces it back to the early days of the pandemic, when she lost the daily socialization that was vital to her mental well-being. Although Mykah had often felt pigeonholed and tokenized by her peers—seen only for the color of her skin and the swish in her walk—being the most visibly queer person in school brought her a certain level of notoriety. Her fashion choices elicited no shortage of stares and side-eyes in the halls, but they also won her praise. The first time Mykah wore lipstick and mascara to school, she was terrified that she'd be taunted or shoved into the hallway lockers—that is, until some girls in class asked her to do their makeup for homecoming. That early embrace encouraged her to always be herself, unapologetically, and she was more than glad to take the note; these days, she sports cat gloves to go to the supermarket and dresses in skimpy tank tops in all manner of weather conditions.

Mykah had always been a straight-A student (well, with the occasional B), but her grades began to slip in an all-virtual learning environment, just as the disappointments began to pile up. She struggled to get cast in shows that would broaden her portfolio, often forced into offensive parts: *Would you be willing to do an ethnic dance? How about a Jamaican accent?* In a knife twist of foreshadowing, Mykah hoped a local *Kinky Boots* production would change her luck; the role of Lola, a drag queen who helps to rejuvenate a struggling shoe factory by producing a line of high-heeled boots, seemed tailor-made for her. The actor Billy Porter, whose larger-than-life red-carpet looks majorly influenced Mykah's fashion choices, had won a Tony Award in 2013 for his stirring performance in the Harvey Fierstein-penned musical. When Mykah didn't land the part, it felt like there was something wrong with her and that there always would be. Mykah feared that she suffered from incurable mediocrity, as if the casting directors had looked directly into her soul and recoiled with boredom.

But at the apex of Mykah's pyre of woes is the recent and sudden realization of how very frangible her life is. If the fear of eviction looms large, it's because she's already been through it once before: Mykah and her mother were kicked out of their previous home last year, separated for months while they searched for a new place to live. Mykah was forced to stay with her older brother, and feeling suffocated in a house they shared with seven other people, disruptive questions flooded her mind: *Would she ever be truly happy? Would life always be like this?* "I had everything going for me and then it abruptly changed. This person that's been in your life for the past eighteen years is suddenly not there," she tells me as Carrie waxes poetic over a "woman's right to shoes." "No matter how good I do, it's all overshadowed by negative things. I feel like there's always this overwhelming cloud of negative energy."

As we sit in her living room after the episode ends, Mykah's competing traumas are palpable. Her box braids have begun to grow out, leaving a short Afro underneath a knotty web of frayed cords, a topic about which she is highly insecure. One of the many reasons that she rarely leaves home these days is that she doesn't want others to see her this way. During one of Mykah's few trips outside, a kind woman who specializes in styling Black hair approached her with a business card and the offer of help, but even at a discounted fee of one hundred dollars, the cost was much too steep for the family's tight budget.

The Mykah of February 2023 starkly contrasts with the person I met at camp: a plus-size Appalachian valley girl whose airy demeanor disguised a piercing intelligence. Mykah was both the camp's queen bee and its conscience, leading the other youth in a two-part intersectionality workshop to teach them about issues facing people of color, including everything from structural racism to redlining. The latter, as she explained, refers to a system of rampant housing discrimination that kept Black families from moving to America's then-novel suburbs in the fifties, and its legacy is still felt today. Some of Mykah's peers had never heard of these concepts, and what's more, many had never met someone who was both Black and LGBTQIA+ before. West Virginia is America's second least diverse state, with a population that is more than 89 percent Caucasian.[18] If every single Black West Virginian lived in the same city, its population would still be less than half the size of Kanawha, the county that Charleston calls home.

Mykah admits that she was nervous when she and her mother first arrived at the camp two summers ago, unsure if she even wanted to get out of the car. This was August 2021, when the camp was about half its current size, and a small group of kids sat in the grass making friendship bracelets. They invited Mykah over to join them, but she was reluctant, thinking the gesture precipitous. *We're not friends!* she thought to herself. But she was able to let her guard down when she spotted an unexpected vision among the grass: a face like hers. One of the first campers to arrive at that year's retreat had been Markus, whose billowing Afro wobbles every which way when he walks. Dawn waited in her truck while Mykah surveyed the landscape, deciding whether this place was the right fit for her, but after seeing Markus, she told her mother that it was OK to drive away. "I'm fine," Mykah said, with her trademark flippancy. "I see a brother."

The ACLU of West Virginia created the camp to be a training ground for the next generation of young activists; by participating in storytelling workshops and know-your-rights trainings, tomorrow's leaders would be able to learn how to organize and engage in political lobbying efforts. Mykah's first camp featured a panel of out LGBTQIA+ elected officials led by Wheeling city councilwoman Rosemary Ketchum, the first (and to date only) transgender woman to hold public office in West Virginia. But while its overarching goal is to give young people tools and skills to bring back to their home communities, AQYS is also about letting LGBTQIA+ kids experience the queer camaraderie and belonging they might otherwise lack. The camp's daily schedule also includes canoeing, ropes courses, movie nights, pool parties, and all the little moments that can't be planned in advance: impromptu late-night slumber parties, bonding over s'mores, and sharing secrets its young attendees never thought they'd ever be able to give to another person.

For Mykah, camp is the only time that she has ever felt like anyone really listened to her or cared what she had to say; it's a place where her peers value her input and are willing to learn from her unique experiences. So often in her life, Mykah has felt that she must hide herself away, thinking that solitude was the only way to survive. Her father had forced her to play football when she was younger in hopes of raising a "strong Black man," she says, but she often broke off from the other athletes during games, making forlorn crowns out of flowers she picked off the field. At camp, Mykah doesn't have to code switch or worry about pleasing anyone; the space it provides encourages her to express all parts of herself in their beauty, their rawness, and their contradictions. This is what emancipation feels like, she thinks: to wear what she wants and talk in whatever pitch of voice she likes without being worried that she might literally be killed for it.

"I don't think I'm ever truly my authentic self unless I'm home," Mykah says of the other eleven months of the year when she's not at camp. As she confesses this, she is burning incense in her room in hopes of finding spiritual balance in its peppery scent. "I feel like I always have to be poised. I always have to be smarter. I don't go to parties because as a Black, queer teenager, that's not smart for me. My teenage experience is so different because I can't do the other stuff that my peers do."

Returning home to the Charleston suburbs each year after camp is where Mykah loses the unconditional acceptance she experiences so briefly, and those transitions have jerked her out of rhythm. Because she has no other public spaces where she really feels safe to be herself, Mykah has chosen to stop giving the world the opportunity to hurt her, filling the newly vacant spaces with the music of her preferred divas. She wakes up each morning to the sounds of British torch singer Adele's nurturing alto and randomly belts out pithy snippets of the R&B wünderkind SZA throughout the day, occasionally pausing mid-sentence for an impromptu solo. The jarring arias are intended to preoccupy her disquiet, to stop herself anytime she begins to peer too far into the void.

While the campers keep in touch through the occasional group text and supportive social media comment, many of Mykah's closest friends live several hours away—on the wrong end of the country's most moun-tainous state, a hazardous terrain that complicates day trips.[19] Some have immigrated to faraway colleges. She's looking forward to this year's camp, which will be its largest ever after the ACLU of West Virginia secured a grant totaling a quarter million dollars to expand its programming, but surviving off the hope of one single week a year, as she points out, is no way to live. "At camp, we're family for a week," she says. "I feel like I'm in perpetual high school reunion hell. It's like, 'Oh, I love you guys so much. Let's meet back here ten years later and do the same thing over again.'"

Mykah doesn't know how to get out of the dreadful hollow that has swallowed her whole or reclaim the voice that was once so strong. It takes a week of Mykah sleeping through her 7:30 a.m. alarm—as well as Dawn's furious pounding at her bedroom door—before she can be con-vinced to leave the house with any regularity. Our first full day out in the world together begins with 8:30 a.m. tea at Taylor Books, a beloved café and bookstore in Charleston that boasts an independent movie theater in the basement. We then hail an Uber to the ACLU of West Virginia's headquarters, where Mykah has come seeking a volunteer opportunity. For once, timing appears to have worked out in her favor: The office is aflutter with activity for the first time since before the pandemic. The state legislature only meets for the first sixty days of the year, and lobby-ists have until March 11—currently less than a month away—to prevent lawmakers from discriminating against the LGBTQIA+ community.

Every single hand at the ACLU of West Virginia is occupied when we arrive, and Mykah is quickly tapped to stuff donor packets for an upcoming fundraising dinner. Filling the pile of identical white enve-lopes is like a course in intermediate origami, in which Mykah is tasked with twisting events calendars like winding staircases, and among the calamity of triangles and squares is an advertisement for an upcoming internship she hopes to land. Mykah just wants something to be excited about again, and as the application date nears, she intends to lend a hand a few days a week, hoping to rediscover her sense of purpose.

No one understands the frailty of Mykah's existence better than she does. All the major decisions about what happens next in her life are presently being made by other people, and that limbo has left her feeling powerless. As she tells me back home in her apartment, what she longs for more than anything else is consistency: the routine of going to the same place every day or having the same people in her life. Seated on opposite sides of her bedroom, Mykah expresses her increasing aware-ness that my stay is already halfway over, the end nearing day by day. In these daily chats, she has found some of the orderliness for which she has been searching, and she is desperately worried that she is going to spiral when I am gone. Without someone to listen to her and help tidily arrange her days, she could lose herself again, this time for good. "I don't think it's going to hit me right away, but I think I'm gonna dip once you leave," she says, looking at me directly. "I feel it coming like a storm."

I try to remind Mykah that she is her own best advocate: She has the power to get back up when she is down, to be the person who fights for herself. But the words mean little when it feels as if another squall is just over the horizon and there's nothing to do but wait for it to raze everything all over again. As is very often the case when she doesn't know what else to do, Mykah puts on music, this time the funk-pop artist Lizzo's self-empowerment anthem, "Special." She has the lyrics, which encourage listeners to find those unspoiled places within themselves and protect them at all costs, memorized by heart, and they are better solace than any person could offer. When Mykah closes her eyes to harmonize, using the swaying of her hands to guide her through, I wonder what she sees through the darkness. I hope it's something good.

III. THE STRONG-WILLED CHILD

Dawn offers me a lesson in the proper pronunciation of West Virginia lingo as we sit alone in her living room at the end of yet another long day. In acting out our own regional spinoff of the Lerner and Loewe musical *My Fair Lady*, Mykah's mother is thanklessly cast in the professorial Henry Higgins role. "*Hur-ick-ane*," I say, the unschooled Eliza Doolittle attempting to fit my cockney mouth around the sounds of Dawn's youth. "*Hur-ick-un*," she corrects, advising me to drop the "a" and the "e" from the word one might wrongly assume is spoken like the violent ocean winds that lend the town its name. Hurricane is among a plentitude of hamlets in southwestern West Virginia that have made bygone destruction part of their brand—a list that also includes Cyclone and Tornado, both of which were named for disasters that befell their towns in the nineteenth century. These small nuances in pronunciation are the quickest way to spot outsiders, a phenomenon familiar to New Yorkers and Los Angelenos, who know the thoroughfares Houston Street and Cahuenga Boulevard as *How-ston* and *Cow-eng-uh*. It's the little details that separate the natives from the interlopers.

Dawn was raised in Tornado, which is pronounced with an *uh* affixed to the end, giving it a little extra oomph. Home to around a thousand people, the town was recently mired in a surprisingly bitter dispute over its distinctive moniker. The area was briefly known as "Upper Falls" following a 2010 mandate from the United States Board on Geographic Names; the selection was a nod to the Upper Falls of Coal Post Office established in 1851, but residents vehemently rejected the imposed name change. Following a 2013 petition by the Kanawha County Commission, Tornado was officially restored to its original nomenclature.

This brief history necessitates its own teachable moment in linguistics. "*Kuh-nahhhh*," Dawn instructs, to which I ask: "Where did all the letters go?" The proper elocution of local geography, as it turns out, can be a bit like French: The more consonants you drop, the closer you are to getting it right.

Dawn liked growing up in Tornado, the kind of place where you never had to worry about locking your doors and everyone knew their neighbors because there weren't all that many. She was the superior of any boy when it came to riding motorcycles, feeling most at ease when her body hissed through the air like a javelin. Still, her upbringing had many drawbacks: Her family was so poor that when they first moved to the area, they didn't have plumbing or running water. She wore the same outfit every day, and because they couldn't afford cereal, Dawn's mother whipped up her patented homemade Frosted Flakes every morning. The dish was prepared by tearing slices of toast into tiny bits, smothering them in sugar, and serving them in a bowl with milk.

Her mother stayed at home to raise the children while Dawn's father painted bridges, a profession that brought a financial windfall in the summer and grim doldrums during the colder months, when he was unable to work due to seasonal hazards that made his vocation more treacherous than it already was. Dawn's father was frequently hurt on the job, the regularity of his injuries attributable to his daredevil nature: He was the painter who took the risks no one else would. "He wasn't afraid of anything," she tells me as we sit in her living room, which is presently enjoying an uncommon moment of bark-free silence. "He fell so many times, had so many accidents. He was hit by a train once."

In a household where they had so little, Dawn learned to put others' needs before her own and never to want for herself, to take only the bare minimum of what she needed to get by. When she moved out as an adult, Dawn had to shoplift to make sure that she had clothes to wear, and she used to keep an inventory of everything she stole, thinking that she would eventually pay it all back. "I just never did," she says. "I just decided somewhere it was OK for somebody to help me, and that was my help." But despite Dawn's begrudging acceptance that having needs and agency is part of living, she is hesitant to assert herself or claim her space. Before she cut her hair into a dour bob, Dawn used her thick sheet of raven tresses to cover her face, shielding herself from a world that she thought would judge her harshly if it were to get a close enough look. She is barely visible even now; dressed in an oversized nightshirt that swallows her tiny frame, she sits on the couch with her hands on her knees.

Despite appearances, those who have known Dawn for a long time say that she is so much more confident than the person she once was, a progression that Dawn attributes to Mykah's own flourishing. Her child, she says, helped give her the courage to be who she was, living openly and proudly as a queer woman. Dawn spent most of her life a closeted lesbian—in denial most of all to herself—and the one evening she spent with Mykah's father at the age of thirty-seven represented a last-ditch attempt at heterosexuality. She hoped to prove that she could be straight if she just wanted it badly enough. "Mykah's never known me in a heterosexual relationship, ever," says Dawn, who is now fifty-six. "I haven't been with a man since. I had never felt less myself than that act right there, and I never looked back."

From the earliest of ages, Mykah represented everything that Dawn was not: courageous, defiant, comfortable in his own skin. Although terms like transgender and nonbinary weren't part of Dawn's vernacular eighteen years ago, her youngest was not shy about telling her who he was, repeatedly demanding a sky blue "frincess dress" in the style of Tiana from the Disney animated fairy tale *The Princess and the Frog* until he eventually got one for Christmas. While attending local Pride events with his mother and whomever she was dating at the time, he would get on the festival stage and perform alongside the drag queens entertaining for the screaming crowd. "He would show them up!" insists Mykah's older sister, Cassie, who stops by for a brief visit with yet another pet in tow, a slobbery rescue dog named Reese with one disfigured ear twisted into the shape of a clover.

While Dawn says that she always embraced Mykah for who he was, she couldn't relate to his inborn fearlessness, which both delighted and terrified her. As a white lesbian raising a Black child, Dawn spent so much of Mykah's early adolescence feeling as if she needed to constantly be on guard, worrying what would happen if she slipped up or wasn't careful enough. If she went to the grocery store with a female partner, they would immediately split up to avoid being seen together, pretending they didn't know each other until they were back in the safety of their car.

Being queer herself doesn't mean that Dawn is without reproach when it comes to acknowledging Mykah's personal conception of his own gender. Mykah describes himself as feeling equal parts masculine and feminine, and he instructs others to use visual cues to determine his pronouns for the day: a do-rag paired with a muscle shirt would suggest that Mykah be greeted with a "he," while a fuzzy fleece sweater and sparkly butterfly necklace might indicate that "she" is most appropriate. Dawn finds these guidelines confusing and solely refers to Mykah using masculine pronouns, as do the other members of his family, even the most affirming ones. While Dawn wants to respect his wishes, one of the aspects that makes it difficult for her is that she struggles with memory loss as the result of a 2017 car accident, in which her truck skidded down the side of a mountain after she hit a patch of black ice. "I have never fully recovered from brain injury," she says. "It has truly changed who I am."

As much as she wants to, Dawn says that she just doesn't remember to use anything but the pronoun she has used since before Mykah was even born. Aware that this bothers him, I ask Dawn whether she has ever considered leaving a note for herself on her bathroom mirror, so she can wake up to a reminder when she looks at herself each morning. Even if Dawn slips up, perhaps a Post-it inscribed with "he/she/they" would show Mykah she's trying, I delicately suggest. But inadvertently, I have touched one of Dawn's softest spots, a tender place that she tries to protect from others' fumbling hands. She begins to stammer as tears rise to the surface, our conversation seemingly one more indication to Dawn that she is deficient, bad, and worst of all, imperfect. "It's hard," she says. "I have a hard time with it. I don't know why. It's not really something I do on purpose because I would never purposely make him uncomfortable or hurt him."

Although she knows that other parents may judge her for falling short of flawless allyship, no one is harder on Dawn than herself. She has spent her whole life wanting to be perfect—the perfect daughter, the perfect wife, the perfect mother—and she has never felt that she measures up to her own impossible standards. When her children were still young, Dawn used to read self-help books to learn how to be a better parent; a dog-eared copy of *The Strong-Willed Child*, a treatise on tough-love discipline authored by James Dobson, founder of the conservative anti-LGBTQIA+ group Focus on the Family, was a permanent fixture on her nightstand during Cassie's teen years. In the kitchen at least, Dawn's zealous ethic has paid off: Her homemade fajitas, which drip voluptuously down the edges of their hard corn tortilla shells, are without equal.

But Cassie says that what's so ironic about Dawn's fruitless quest for faultlessness is that she has always been a great parent, the mom that all her childhood friends wished they had. Cassie says that during her youth, her friends wanted to hang out at her house instead of their own, and many have kept in touch with Dawn over the years, regularly sending her updates on their family's health and day-to-day developments in their children's lives. While Cassie's friends may have thought of Dawn as a second mother, her daughter thought of her as something even more than a parent: Cassie, a domestic violence survivor, says that Dawn was her role model, proof that she could live through anything if she kept fighting. "My mom is a tower of strength, knowledge, and wisdom," says

Cassie, who keeps her short hair pulled back in a calico ponytail of faded purples and blues. "I know that she doesn't see herself that way. She doesn't really say that she is beautiful or amazing or powerful, but it's because of her that I am still here, literally. She showed me that I could make it because she did."

After surviving more than her own share of suffering, Dawn is ready to move on and to let herself be happy. She has recently rekindled a romance with her ex-wife, Jean, who pays a visit to the apartment a few days later, arms tucked inside the sleeves of a hooded sweatshirt as she stands in Dawn's kitchen. The two first met thirteen years ago in a Charleston gay bar that had at one time housed a funeral parlor; drag queens who performed at the establishment would use the basement area, where morticians formerly washed the deceased for viewing, to hose themselves down at the end of the night. Jean, who was just twenty-seven when they met, was by her own admission too young and too immature for real commitment during their first go at romance, still lacking the ability to give fully of herself. But Jean, now forty, wants to prove to Dawn that things have changed and, more importantly, that she has changed. "I am crazy about her," she says, eyes wide and unblinking. "We've never not loved each other. I want to give her the forever that I wasn't capable of giving her back then."

When we are alone, Dawn admits to me that she isn't sure what she wants yet or whether her definition of fulfillment includes a life growing old with Jean. After everything they've been through together and all the times she's been hurt by the people she loved, Dawn doesn't know if she has room to let another person in. The other night, she says, Jean turned to her in bed and told her, "I promise you with everything in me that I am not going to hurt you," but Dawn can't let herself believe it. She feels as if she's lived her life like the titular Giving Tree from the Shel Silverstein children's book, stripped of everything others can take from her until all that's left is a stump. "You just can't give yourself away like that," she says. "People do not appreciate it. They just take and take and take until there's nothing left." Jean has given her a week to make up her mind, and Dawn doesn't know her answer yet.

If Dawn has no idea what to do about her personal life, that is doubly true when it comes to loosing Mykah from his stubborn rut. She has done everything she could for her children; she worked two jobs to buy Cassie the shoes she needed for cheerleading and waited for hours in the car—every day for a *week*, she stresses—so Mykah could finish his marathon of auditions for *Kinky Boots*. But after thirty-nine years of raising children, she wonders if she has anything left for anyone. She doesn't have the energy to force Mykah to do his homework when she's already working overtime to keep them from being evicted. For all the parallel pains and worries they share, the two seem to have lost the ability to communicate, with most of Dawn's commands greeted by some combination of a sigh, an eye roll, or the closing of Mykah's bedroom door. Occasionally, she gets the entire trifecta.

For most of my time with the family, they have spoken to each other from other rooms, rarely occupying the same space. When I propose that all three of us watch *The Woman King*, a swords-and-sandals epic starring Dawn's celebrity crush, Viola Davis, as the leader of an army of African warrior women, the suggestion to gather in the living room violates an unspoken demarcation of boundaries. It takes us two days to view the film in its entirety due to a series of interruptions: texts, phone calls, and a knock at the door, followed by each of us falling asleep, one by one. Mykah and Dawn love each other so much, but in all the rawness that love entails, it can hurt to be around one another. Each wants nothing but what's best for the other and hopes to spare their loved one the sight of seeing them in pain; that emotional calculus results in Mykah shutting himself away from the world and Dawn spending the weekends with Jean. Dawn believes that she is giving her son the space he says he wants, but what she doesn't seem to realize is that Mykah needs *less* distance between them. He needs to know his mother will be standing right beside him no matter what tomorrow brings and that she will still love him even if he isn't perfect, much like the indefatigable woman who raised him.

More than anything, Dawn wants her child back: the little kid whose effervescent joy showed his mother that her own queerness was something beautiful, that she was still the person God meant her to be. Despite her own trepidations about sharing so much of herself with an outsider, she believes that being part of this project will reawaken Mykah, show him that he can again be that person who inspires others to be their best. She says that it doesn't matter to her if Mykah is a globally recognized superstar, whether his future holds a spot at NYU, or if he ends up "a freaking pea farmer," so long as he is content. "I think he has so much potential," she adds. "He's so smart. I just worry about him. He's sad a lot, and I don't know how to help him. I've tried everything. I've tried to be loving. Just because you're a parent, you don't automatically get a manual. You don't know exactly what to do."

Dawn pauses for a moment as she releases one last fear: that the thing that's holding him back is some personal shortcoming of her own that she hasn't considered. "I do not want to be the mother that he has to survive," she says, a clipped shiver blowing through her voice. "I don't want to be something he has to survive."

IV. OOH-AH-AH SENSATION

Mykah is greeted with an enthusiastic squeal as they walk inside the West Virginia Black Pride Foundation, stepping through its paint-chipped front doors to a decibel-splitting embrace. The eager hugger is the organization's founder, Kasha Snyder-McDonald, a local drag legend and the reigning Miss Gay Pride West Virginia, famous for whirligig performances that utilize every bend and snap of which the human body is capable. "She is *that girl* when she's on stage," Mykah explains before paraphrasing Mo Heart, an alum of the ever-expanding *RuPaul's Drag Race* reality competition franchise. "She really gives you that *ooh-ah-ah* sensation." Mykah notes that she and Kasha share more than just mutual adoration: Kennedy Carmichael, Kasha's drag mother, was the first queen to ever put Mykah in a full face of makeup, at eleven years old. "I am from the House of Carmichael, so that makes Kasha my drag sister."

We have come today for a tour of the Black Pride Foundation's community space, which remains a work in progress since its soft opening in December 2021. A compact one-story house obscured by a tempest of weeds, the building doesn't look much like an LGBTQIA+ center from the outside. If its sparse lawn appears unkempt, that's because the Black Pride Foundation is a two-person operation; its only other employee watches the surprise family reunion unfold with a smile from the comfort of a black leather armchair in the corner.

Kasha is doing everything she can to manifest her dream of a safe space in West Virginia for Black queer people, but it's clear that two people can't do it all by themselves. The walls long for an extra coat of paint, and temporary rugs mask wooden floors that have scuffed with age. A timeline of Black LGBTQIA+ icons drawn onto the wall in permanent marker ends in 1966; this is not because of a lack of available trailblazers born after the poet Audre Lorde and choreographer Alvin Ailey but the result of sparse free time to honor their achievements. The Black Pride Foundation's proprietor keeps a busy schedule of peer mentorship programming, fish fries, book drives, and job trainings, and she even hosted an Easter egg hunt at the center last year. This summer, Kasha intends to hand out free sack lunches to low-income youth.

As we stand in one of the center's barren rooms, which are waiting to realize their purpose, Mykah doesn't see all the work that remains to be done. They see love all around, staring right back at them: in the portrait of Kasha right by the front door, the hanging wooden spoon painted in rainbow, the quilt portraying woven figures riding horses that hangs on the wall. The blanket's familiar thickness reminds Mykah of ecstatic summers at their grandmother's home, where every single day was spent playing outside with their cousins as if nothing else in the world mattered. Those memories are precious, they say, because they were among the best moments of Mykah's childhood—a rare time in which they felt no judgment, free to live and free to flourish. "That's what Black houses are like: the blanket covering the window, the chairs, the smell—there's a fogginess," Mykah says, although they know the portrait isn't universal. "Even the faint smell of weed is bringing back a memory that I did not know was inside of me."

If the Black Pride Foundation reminds Mykah of what it feels like to be cherished and cared for, it's also proof that the world is so much bigger than New York, bigger than anything they could have possibly dreamboarded. Earlier that day, Mykah visited the offices of Fairness West Virginia, the state's largest LGBTQIA+ advocacy group, to discuss getting involved in the organization, whether that means testifying alongside other activists at Lobby Day or traveling to school districts across the state to help make them more inclusive for queer students. Fairness is currently working to raise funds for a new advocacy position, for which Mykah is invited to apply, and while that opportunity would be several months away, even the discussion alone provides a glimmer of the deliverance they so badly need.

Kasha knows exactly what Mykah is going through because she experienced the same hardships before finding her place in the world, one she had to create for herself. When she first moved to Charleston, she was temporarily unhoused after being evicted from a relative's home, and she had nowhere to go. "I wish that I had some place that I could have went to, that could have said, 'Hey, come on over here, we got you,'" Kasha tells me. "But I didn't have that. I had nothing."

The Black Pride Foundation is a testament to what Kasha has been able to build in a state where few even thought that was possible, and it's a model of what Mykah could achieve if they were to stay in West Virginia. Charleston's annual Pride festival didn't have a Black emcee until 2022—a subject of much controversy—and when Kasha first unveiled the Black Pride Foundation a year and a half ago, some accused her of attempting to divide the local LGBTQIA+ community. That didn't stop her from doing it anyway, she says, because she knew the community needed this. She, too, needed to feel tethered to the earth after so many years of rootlessness. "When Black people try to do something for themselves, people think we're trying to divide, and we're not," Kasha asserts as Mykah snaps in fierce affirmation. "I was looking and seeing that everyone was marching and screaming 'Black Lives Matter,' but nobody was screaming 'Black Trans Lives Matter.' I decided to open up a place where trans people of color can meet and feel safe."

Kasha believes that she has achieved that. The center is, for many Black transgender people in Kanawha County, their first stop after they come out, a place to get hygiene kits or gender-affirming clothing for a job interview. Kasha's dream is to create a Black Pride pageant in West Virginia as a platform for Black excellence, a stage where the Mykahs of the world can prove wrong everyone who ever counted them out.

It's my last week in Charleston, and these passing moments with Mykah feel sacred, each one another chance to turn it all around. I can't help but want for Mykah the same thing that everyone else in their life wants for them: the superstardom they so badly crave. Mykah knows they have something special to offer, but they wonder if anyone will ever let them give it. Watching them turn Dawn's truck into karaoke—a little bit of Motown queen Tammi Terrell here, some Donna Summer disco fever there—it's clear that the passion in their voice comes from a belief that they could follow in the footsteps of the pop legends. I wish there was someone who could help reignite their belief in their gifts, tell them that the opinions of one college do not determine their worth, but maybe that isn't necessary after all.

When we arrive back home, with the mail comes an acceptance letter from West Virginia State University, a historically Black college less than fifteen minutes away by car. It's now the second school to admit Mykah after Marshall University in Huntington. Although Mykah had never seriously considered going to college in West Virginia—both applications were nothing more than backups for NYU—they are starting to think differently, that there might be something worth staying for.

We spend my final days in Appalachia visiting with Mykah's closest friends from camp, beginning with a bus trip to Morgantown to catch what they thought would be a drag show at Vice/Versa, one of the only two gay bars in the state. But instead of its weekly Saturday revue of drag performers, the eighteen-and-up establishment is hosting an event blending Cirque du Soleil with a carnival freak show, one not for the squeamish. A man describing himself as a "human pincushion" inserts needles into his arms, cheeks, and eyelids as "Bad Moon Rising" by the swamp rock band Creedence Clearwater Revival blasts from the speakers. Several performances prominently feature open flames, which makes one question how fire code regulations work exactly, specifically during a number in which a performer twirls a hula hoop lit like an eight-sided candle. Their eyes wide with wonder but also a hint of terror, Mykah sits right next to the stage as the force of the hoop's gyrations extinguishes all but one of the flames by the end of the number.

Among today's cast are Markus and Lonnie, who happen to be the only other Black campers who attended AQYS over the past two years. Each describes the camp's impact as life-changing and transformative, and they partially credit Mykah for making the space feel like home. Lonnie, whose coffin purse perfectly matches the mausoleum elegance of his black lace outfit, says that Mykah was always the first person to enliven a room, sometimes by force. "I think my favorite memory was when Mykah cleansed the whole cabin with essential oils, like a priest with holy water," he says, fighting for space in the packed crowd of bargoers in overalls and "God Hearts Fags" t-shirts. Ana, with her bare midriff defying the atrocious cold, says that it was seeing Mykah be so brazenly themself that gave her the courage to tell people outside of her close circle that she's a lesbian. Although her friends and family members have known for years, she never would have shared that information freely unless she'd met Mykah. "Mykah has taught me to be more bold about myself," she says. "That's something that I really admire about them: They do what they want. They say what they want. They wear what they want."

That otherworldly self-possession extends to the powder-blue tube top Mykah wears to the bar, a handmade design that appears to have been cobbled together with dental floss and coffee filters. Mykah wears the paper-thin ensemble with such poise that they look like a luxury Rolls-Royce convertible with hair extensions, and I see a glimpse of that famous wit when I ask how they aren't "absolutely freezing" in the prickly mountain air. "Hoes don't get cold," Mykah shoots back, flashing the glint of an opalescent crystal bonded to their left incisor. "Every time I wear this top, I get into trouble—good trouble and bad trouble."

Fortunately for all involved, the evening is only the good kind of trouble. Before the bar is overtaken by fiery spectacle—the performers spinning upside down upside down on giant rings—the campers dance on the crowded stage in a thin mist of Axe body spray. If Mykah was the one who showed everyone at camp that it was OK to be themselves, that they could be whomever they wanted, Mykah's freshly resurgent composure has a similar effect on the dance floor. They teach everyone the Wobble, a synchronized dance involving gyrating one's body like a vertical worm. When "My Humps," the Black Eyed Peas' paean to the female posterior, plays in the bar, the floor squirms in time with the writhing crowd.

Our bus ride back to Charleston the next day is quiet aside from the low murmurs of fashionable Amish teenagers, and in the hush, I question if this trip will, paradoxically, worsen Mykah's depression—the high before everything bottoms out. It's a phenomenon that the campers describe often: the fleeting bliss of having a space where you are unconditionally loved and understood, followed by the intense withdrawal of having that acceptance taken away. While getting to be in the physical presence of the people who know them best was a temporary endorphin rush, I wonder how it will affect Mykah to go cold turkey and whether one great day is enough of a reason to live again. Maybe it is; they have already begun making plans for another expedition to Morgantown, which they note is just nineteen dollars on the thrifty Greyhound bus line, to catch the drag show that they all missed. Tentative dates are thrown around, along with the exchange of photos and nascent remembrances of yesterday's visit.

Buzzing with energy, Mykah takes a break from their correspondences to read aloud to me the speech they would have delivered to the West Virginia House two weeks ago, the words they never got to say. An incurable theater kid, they stiffen their posture before beginning, shoulders spread apart. Mykah tells their imagined audience that what's made them the person they are today is the support they've had from their mother and their community in all the choices they've made—including the decision to delay medically transitioning until they are ready, if they are ever ready. They still aren't sure yet whether they want to begin taking medication, but that's a decision that they (and every other young person) should have the freedom to make, Mykah asserts. "I can't speak for all trans people, but not everyone wants or needs to transition or have surgeries," they say, voice unwavering. "Knowing that we can at any time is enough for us. I know you probably don't care, but listen to me when I tell you my community is strong. We are powerful. We are resilient."

Here, Mykah is in their element: They are most alive when they are perceived, when they can bask in the glow of performing for others. The spark of a crowd—even if it's a gallery of one—jolts Mykah from their prolonged stupor, as if they can look outside themself for a moment and see the potential that everyone else does. The astral projection puts them in a reflective mood. When they look back on this time in their life a few years from now, Mykah predicts that these experiences will feel surreal to them, as if they happened to someone else. To make sure they remember, Mykah has started keeping a daily journal, and each morning begins with the same question: *What good are you going to do today?* At night, they check back in on the deeds they were able to accomplish, an exercise that is for their own sake as much as it is humanity's. If they ever get to a point in their lives when they don't need to answer the question anymore—because their existence is good enough—Mykah thinks they won't feel so crushed anymore.

"I'm trying to work on stuff," they say. "I'm doing a lot of self-work and trying to get to know myself better. I'm trying to learn to just exist. I'm trying to spend more time just by myself, with nothing going on. It's really, really hard for me because I have a hard time keeping my mind clear. I'm struggling to do it, but I'm trying."

RUBY

HOUSTON, TEXAS

MARCH 2023

I. THE SAMARITAN WOMAN

The walls of St. Mary's Episcopal Church in Houston are bare as a padded cell as the Reverend Marquita Hutchens, wrapped in purple cloth, delivers the weekly homily. In today's address to the congregation, she asks churchgoers to rethink what they know about the Samaritan woman from the Gospel of John, with whom Jesus shares a drink of well water before revealing himself to be the Messiah. Identified only as a resident of Samaria in central Palestine, she has for centuries been cast in a bad light on account of her marital status: She's a serial divorcée cohabitating with a man who is not her husband, approximately two millennia before the socialite Zsa Zsa Gabor would make five failed marriages look unambitious by comparison.

The Samaritan woman has alternately been described by biblical scholars as an "adulteress" and a "woman of shame," but there's nothing in the Bible to suggest that, Reverend Hutchens says. If the average lifespan in the single digits of BCE was just thirty-five years, she could have been an extremely unfortunate widow or simply doing what she needed to survive during a time in which women weren't permitted to work outside the home. Hutchens urges the congregation to instead look at the Samaritan woman as Jesus sees her, calling her a "striking example of a faithful woman." "The Samaritan woman goes on to become an enthusiastic evangelist, a witness to the transforming power of faith," she says. "She uses her voice and her experience to gather more believers to Jesus."

The sermon is a statement of purpose for the LGBTQIA+ affirming St. Mary's: If women are rarely given a fair shake in mainstream Christianity—dating back with Eve, shackled with the blame for man's fall from grace—neither are queer people. The message on this particular morning, however, is hard to hear over a toddler's determined jabber, made ever the more piercing by the removal of crosses and other sound-absorbent décor in observance of Lent.

Next to the young girl is Ruby Carnes, who sits patiently as the child takes thick plastic zebras and giraffes out of a Ziploc bag, loudly introducing Ruby to the members of her zoo one by one. A tranquil hush falls over the room when the child is mercifully led away to Sunday school, but as the older girl notes, her former charge had some trouble with taxonomy. "She got the names of the animals wrong every single time," Ruby says, shaking her head in mock disapproval as the child is escorted through a tiny door at the back of the church. "Every *single* time." Despite the factual errors, Ruby had listened calmly to the child, warmth radiating from the porcelain skin she diligently keeps out of the sun. Here in this blank space, she looks beatific, attired like a film noir blonde in a black sleeveless turtleneck and burgundy nails that match the pew cushions.

Like all of Ruby's sartorial choices, the synchronicity of hues is not an accident but rather the result of assiduous planning. She puts a great deal of thought into what she wears, whether it's a thrifted polka-dot tank top featuring a cartoon bee exclaiming "Sting me!" or a simple red dress. It's, thus, not terribly surprising that she can quote by heart the entirety of *The Devil Wears Prada*, a dishy workplace dramedy that's become its own sacred text for aspiring fashionistas like herself. A famous speech in which Meryl Streep's imperious magazine editor witheringly humiliates her reluctant protégée, played by a very bang-forward Anne Hathaway, by educating her on the history of cerulean is recited verbatim on a near-daily basis.

So much of Ruby's life is determined by her costume of the day, her attire representing one small thing in the world she can control. When thinking back on her coming out at St. Mary's almost exactly two years prior, Ruby remembers not how she felt but what she wore: a blue sundress with green strappy heels and gold wire earrings shaped like flowers. "I should have gone with different shoes, but I didn't own any other sandals," she tells me after today's sermon ends. "And I would have gone with a necklace and little earrings instead because I had big hair that day. It didn't make sense to also have big earrings."

In June 2021, St. Mary's hosted a renaming liturgy for Ruby, a ceremony in the Episcopal tradition that marks the riddance of a transgender individual's birth name in favor of the person it was their destiny to become. As bursts of late afternoon sunbeams streamed through the skylight on that momentous Sunday, the church's wooden pews teemed with masked faces, many of which belonged to family members and longtime friends. Just as some young women have cotillions to mark their entrance into society, this rite of passage served a similar purpose: Surrounded by her dearest relations, Ruby would claim her womanhood for her own. She announced to the world not only a new name but also her true self after so many years of hiding.

The hour-long liturgical ceremony began with parishioners standing for an opening hymn and a song of praise before joining in a series of scriptural readings, including Corinthians 3:12–18, a promise that those who accept God's love will be lifted toward the divine. "Now the Lord is the Spirit, and where the Spirit of the Lord is, there is freedom," the passage reads in part. "And we all, with unveiled face, beholding the glory of the Lord, are being changed into his likeness from one degree of glory to another."

Episcopal rites are characterized by their soothing sameness, the comfort of already knowing the major plot beats. Worshippers have sung these exact numbers and read these parables aloud together dozens upon dozens of times throughout their lives, but placing Ruby's journey at the center gave those familiar words new meaning. Leading the church in a reflection, Ruby said that the verses from Corinthians represented being able to embrace herself fully and, by doing so, allowing those around her to embrace her as well. Following a process of becoming that had sometimes proven turbulent, she proclaimed to her fellow churchgoers that the gospel offers a "message of peace."

"It says that I shouldn't worry about my body or what I wear, that I should just be who I am and be at peace with God," Ruby said in her speech, towering above the altar as she addressed gatherers. "I think that message is something we all need to hear every day. So often we worry too much about things that don't matter, no matter how real they may seem to us. I was so worried about what other people would think of me when I came out, but I really just can't care about that. Jesus loves me, and he loves you, too. Frankly, that's the most important thing to me."

The history of queer people within Christianity is too often one of rejection and persecution, but that hasn't been Ruby's story. Her family compares their experiences to the television show *Schitt's Creek*, a riches-to-rags hangout comedy set in a fictional small town where homophobia doesn't exist; the titular hamlet is a place where a down-on-his-luck former heir to a video store fortune can rediscover his purpose without prejudice standing in the way. And outside of a few congregants who quietly stopped coming to St. Mary's following Ruby's renaming ceremony—for reasons that, it should be noted, could have been entirely unrelated—the rest of the church has treated her exactly as they always have: as a loved child of God.

Every Sunday morning, Ruby's family is still greeted with hugs and caffeinated pleasantries as soon as they step inside the church's doors, and they remain among the most active parishioners at St. Mary's; in fact, they have been fixtures in the church for much of their respective lives. Her mother, Molly, whose feathery haircut frames her face in golden waves, was the first-ever youth pastor at St. Mary's; she later worked in the church's welcome ministry. Her father, Ryan, is more of the journeyman type, moonlighting in a variety of posts; a lack of transferable experience, though, prevented him from serving as the church's organist or its music director. Ruby's older brother, Benjamin, was raised in the church as an altar boy and credits his faith as instrumental to his recovery. After falling into drug addiction early in high school, he reached his hundredth day of sobriety before he could even drive a car. For Ruby, the unconditional embrace she has found at St. Mary's has played just as critical of a role in her life, showing her that she doesn't always have to think the worst of others' intentions. There she has learned that people can occasionally surpass her expectations.

Three days after I arrive in Houston, something very unexpected happens: the boy Ruby likes asks her out. Cooper, a member of the tech crew in her community college's theater program, invites Ruby to accompany him to a friend's birthday picnic in the park following weeks of mutual flirting. Ruby says that she knew she liked Cooper when she met him, and her reasons were exceedingly logical: He is soft-spoken and has long hair, and she likes guys who are soft-spoken and have long hair. "I found that those two specific groups of men are usually very respectful and kind, especially to women," she says, before recalling a specific experience chatting with a man on Tinder who did not match those aesthetic preferences. "I've never seen a man with long hair who is practically whispering say, 'I think all women over 145 are elephants, and they should lose weight.' I tend to make very snap judgments about people, and 99 percent of the time, they turn out to be true."

Ruby has high hopes that Cooper, unlike the partners who have rejected her in the past when she told them about her gender history, will be different. But the romance may prove short-lived, as the world is unfortunately not a Canadian sitcom fantasy: In August, Ruby is transferring schools to pursue costume design at a college in southern California, and she has no intention of ever coming back to Texas. The move was planned after Governor Abbott issued an executive order in February 2022[1] ordering the state's Department of Family and Protective Services to investigate parents who allow their children to medically or socially transition for "child abuse," which has since led to child welfare agents knocking on the doors of more than a dozen families across the state.[2]

Although by then Ruby was already a legal adult, her parents worried they could still be persecuted under a clause that allows state agencies to open retroactive investigations for medical care administered before a transgender person reached the age of eighteen.[3] When the governor won reelection in November 2022, defeating former congressman Beto O'Rourke (D) by eleven points, the outcome only confirmed for Ruby's parents that no help was coming.[4] The only way they could ensure Ruby's safety was to get her as far away as possible.

Ruby is excited for a fresh start in a new place, describing her soon-to-be college like a diver uncovering a sunken city. She is simply awed by the school's sea of food trucks and its prestigious faculty members, who she says actually want to know how you're doing when they ask. "There's a planetarium with a gift shop that sells Paul Frank merchandise!" she breathlessly informs me back at home. "They have a Starbucks and a botanic garden on campus to sit and study in!" But at the heart of her move is an unfortunate binary of options, one which has placed her at a crossroads of surviving and thriving. She turns twenty in a few months, and this may be her final chance to enjoy her passive teendom, to finally have the transcendently mundane experiences she's craved for so long.

Cooper, a boy she hardly knows, isn't enough of a reason to stay behind, but the possibility of what could be makes leaving complicated. When I first meet Cooper, he is sitting at a table outside their campus auditorium before rehearsal, and his connection to Ruby perfuses the air even more strongly than the greasy odor of his Chick-fil-A fries, for which he apologizes immediately. "It's the one way in which I'm not an ally," he says with an embarrassed chuckle, referencing the restaurant chain's well-documented history of donating to anti-LGBTQIA+ causes.[5] They smile conspiratorially as they talk about the play they're working on, their second modernized Shakespeare adaptation in a row; they laugh at their own in-jokes as if they already have their own lexicon of references and shared experiences. They haven't even gone out yet, but it feels like they've been together for years.

Although Ruby and her family know that her imminent escape is for the best, the blunt force of that sacrifice is felt at every moment, as everyone around her reckons with the fact that these next few months could be the last time they are all together. Ruby's grandmother, Mimi, is ninety-four and has lung cancer, likely the result of her late husband's dedicated smoking. Her cognition is very poor due to her medication and old age, and she spends her time on the couch struggling in vain to follow the plots of women-in-peril films aired on the cable network Lifetime. She is a particular fan of the *John Wick* series, starring Keanu Reeves as a retired assassin on the run, she tells me, because she relates to the plight of a man who is just trying his best to stay alive. "I think he's a good person, and he has had some hard things going on in his life," she says, adding that she is looking forward to the forthcoming fourth installment of the franchise. "He works very hard to beat it and then he has a lot of problems with people trying to kill him."

It is Mimi who is most excited when Benjamin visits to announce that his wife, Hannah, is pregnant with their first child, joking that the presently untitled offspring will be named either Astrid or Nebuchadnezzar. But the reality is that up to two members of the household may no longer be there when the baby is born.

Ruby and her loved ones are making do with the time they have left, whether it's going to church on Sundays, eating discount burgers from their favorite local pub on Mondays, playing board games, or watching movies. Our time together begins with a family Oscar party and ends with everyone gathered in the living room to watch *The Palm Beach Story*, a classic Claudette Colbert/Joel McCrea farce about a woman who concocts a wild scheme to help her broke architect husband build his dream airport: She will dump him, marry a rich guy, and get her new beau to give her old one the money he needs. Ryan's booming guffaw pounds against the living room walls as the film's many complications—among them a put-upon manservant hailing from a fictional European country and a lustful princess with one thing on her mind—resolve in a surprise triple wedding. The ceremony, naturally, includes two sets of identical twins.

While it feels strange to laugh so hard when so much is at stake, Ruby says the joy I hear is not just the terms of her survival but an act of protest. "Trans happiness is subversion," she explains. "I think we're just supposed to sit down, be quiet, and disappear. I tried to force myself into a box. I tried to make myself what I think people would want me to be, and we saw how that worked out. It didn't. So I am who I am because I don't have a choice."

ii. RING FOR A HUG

When Cooper arrives to pick up Ruby for their first date, she greets him in the foyer by knocking a framed photo off the wall: a geometric sketch her grandfather made as part of a drafting class in high school. The artifact is but one of many mementos of days past displayed throughout the Carnes household, which is as much a family museum dedicated to nearly every significant memory from their shared history as it is a habitable living space.

Also on display in the museum's permanent collection are Ruby's first pair of ballet slippers, the handkerchief that Molly carried on her wedding day, a "third in class" award bestowed upon their former automobile by a Corvette enthusiast magazine, and a cup filled with tongue depressors that a young Ruby gave Molly as a gift. Each oblong stick is an IOU inscribed with a different pledge in blue permanent marker, and the array of wooden coupons includes a "shoulder massage" and the promise of "no annoying-ness," although the exact terms of the latter are left undefined. On the posterior of each voucher, the message "I love you" is scribbled in now-faded ink—a promise that technically remains in effect as the timber objects do not list an expiration date.

The family is meticulous about the many exhibits on display for visitors, and so when the marked photo smashes against the floor, glass shards flying in every direction, Ruby winces as her mother rushes for a broom. Cheeks flushed with mortification, she grabs Cooper's shoulder and whispers to him, "Oh my god, I can't believe I broke it." Her disbelief is inspired less by a fear of what Molly will think than what her longtime crush will. Ruby tends to create a distance between herself and the world around her by, for instance, slipping into an Australian accent in conversation or throwing in a quote from the famously unbothered supermodel Naomi Campbell. But her air of calculation slips when she's near Cooper, for an obvious reason: She really, really, really wants to impress him.

Despite the literal mess she has made, winning him over probably won't take much effort. She became aware of his feelings toward her one day after class when Cooper, who is a few inches shorter than Ruby, was standing on a platform above her, staring with a grin so winning that he looked as if he had several rows of extra teeth. When she informed him that he was, for once, her vertical superior, Cooper's ill-fated attempt to return her playful banter unintentionally revealed his longings. "I like tall women," he said. When he invited her over to "meet my dog" in an equally unsubtle text message a few weeks later, she called out what both already knew to be true: "Are you asking me out on a date?" He was, and he had wanted to since nearly the first moment he saw her.

The sight of Cooper in his everyday uniform of jeans and a t-shirt does little to ease Ruby's nerves, but they slowly find their way into an uneasy rhythm, the turning of wheels steered by his quiet confidence. Molly and Ryan instantly responded to Cooper's willingness to come meet them; there were no old clichés of a father crouched over a porch chair with a shotgun in hand, prepared for an interrogation. Ryan would be poor casting for the stern patriarch role; his casual demeanor is a mixture of televangelist Joel Osteen and the motor-mouthed gumshoe from the slapstick comedy *Ace Ventura: Pet Detective*, although he does have experience with crotchety fathers. "The first time I picked Molly up for our first date, her dad answered the door and he said, 'No,'" Ryan tells me later. "I could tell he was just trying to mess with me."

Although Ruby and Cooper haven't left yet—later, they will share lemonade and barbecue chips as they sit on park blankets with his friends—there's already an ease and familiarity in the way they lean into each other. Cooper, with his thick, wavy hair that smells of coconut shampoo, fits nicely in the family museum, seeming at home among its displays. He looks as if he could be the next exhibit, arranged neatly alongside ornaments from Mimi's childhood Christmas tree and the silver watch Ryan wore when he was five years old.

The date itself goes much better than its shattered introduction might predict, but later that evening, their fledgling romance is unexpectedly interrupted when Molly calls Ruby to ask that she come home, in fear of the violence the world inflicts upon transgender people, especially women. Molly doesn't know where Cooper lives or how to track down her daughter if something were to go wrong. She and Ruby didn't even have a code word in case the girl called because she was in trouble and couldn't say it. Cooper, ever the courteous suitor, takes the news that he will have to drive Ruby home well, remarking that it's nice her parents care about her that much, although she is much too furious in this moment to see it that way.

Her mother's abundance of caution pulls Ruby temporarily out of her paradise. Sitting across from each other on Cooper's bed after their picnic, they had talked for hours, about both everything and nothing. She had hoped to stay in his guest room for the night, a first for her so early in a relationship; she had been feeling comfortable and couldn't bear the thought of her perfect night coming to a premature end. She had wanted to coast on bliss a little while longer. "I knew that there wasn't anything wrong because I've known Cooper for months, and he would never do anything bad ever," Ruby tells me the next day, excitedly recapping every twist and turn in the night. "I think I'm a good judge of character. I knew what to expect, and I felt very in control of the situation. I was not concerned at all."

Fortunately for Ruby, Molly changes her mind after seeing her daughter step out of Cooper's car, the sublime lightness in her stride reminding Molly of the days when infatuation was an elemental force. She immediately knows that this isn't a girl who needs rescuing, who has spent her evening wondering if she'll end up deadnamed in the local papers; this is a girl who is beginning to experience an emotion that it will take weeks, if not months, for her to allow herself to name, a vibration that feels something like what she imagines love to be.

After Molly gives her blessing for Cooper to whisk Ruby away once more, their overnight date ends the following day with lunch at a sushi restaurant, where Ruby confesses something over the California roll they share. "I never thought I would have this," she tells Cooper. "I never thought I would see someone that I wanted and go on a date with him, someone who would be honest with me and appreciate me. I just never thought I would have that." But what Ruby does not address during the recounting of her evening is how much she has chosen to share with Cooper about herself, whether he was made aware of the full significance of the fleeting bliss she hoped to savor. Finding the right moment to reveal all of oneself is always unnerving in its vulnerability, but that's particularly true for Ruby who, having struggled with suicidal ideation before she became herself, never thought she would live to see this moment. Given that the subject of disclosure is not mentioned, I assume it has been delayed for a later date.

Before she transitioned, Ruby had planned to take her own life at sixteen, convinced there was no way out of the enclosure that she had built around herself. Early in their daughter's life, Molly and Ryan thankfully realized that they were either raising a gay boy or a transgender girl, and so they did little to force normative gender roles on her, allowing her to shop in the bright pink aisle at their local Toys "R" Us store and buying her tutus at Christmas. After Ruby learned to sew at the age of six, she and her mother started a regular tradition of watching the fashion competition reality show *Project Runway* together, and Molly made a tireless habit of pointing out all the queer and gender nonconforming contestants; she wanted to ensure that her youngest had a plenitude of possibility models. "Oh, look at this person!" Molly would say. "They're gay and they're doing great!"

But despite the occasionally over-exuberant affirmation that Ruby experienced at home, a part of her felt like a failure for not living up to the stereotypical expectations of manhood—as if her inability to conform meant she was somehow defective, fundamentally broken. She initially came out to her parents as transgender at fourteen but quickly took it back in favor of forcing herself to be male. She began walking differently and lowering her voice to mask—as best she could—the recently stated fact of her gender difference. She was so used to hiding that the thought of being herself, the emotional risks that accompany being truthful about who you are, shook her already brittle foundations. "I was stuck in the rut of trying to be someone else, and I was scared to be myself," she tells me. "Trying to be someone else was 'more comfortable,' even though it wasn't."

Ruby attempted to furnish a distraction by burying herself in extracurriculars, staying so busy that she wouldn't have time to ponder the reality of her womanhood. But she was overworked to the point of exhaustion, piling trips to church conferences on top of 3 a.m. study sessions and four-hour rehearsals of her school's production of *Oklahoma!* One day, Ruby came to her mother's bedroom and told her, after bursting into tears, that she wanted to die.

From there, things moved quickly: Her parents collected in a shoebox every sharp object in their house, and Ruby began intensive therapy. Molly and Ryan had already been through this with Benjamin, driving him back and forth between rehab and twelve-step meetings every night for months while he got sober, but the COVID-19 lockdown in March 2020 offered them an unexpected helping hand. Within the remove of Ruby's own home, away from others' judgment and opaque glances, she felt free to wear what she wanted and to be who she wanted. "It felt like I was finally putting on my clothes, not someone else's clothes," she says of those early experiments with heels and vintage mini dresses. "I was on autopilot for months, years." After years of spinning out of orbit, she felt newly aligned, fully in charge of a liberation that could take her anywhere.

Although Ruby underwent a series of gender-confirming surgeries after she turned eighteen, hoping to lessen unwanted scrutiny by making herself less visible, an even more important step in her transition was deciding what kind of woman she was. As someone who idolized Barbie, Ruby says the appeal of the iconic Mattel doll is its many variations—from the 1959 original billed as a "teenage fashion model" to the astronaut Barbies produced in the sixties and eighties who traveled to space in go-go boots and puffed pink neon sleeves. "You can put on who you want her to be, because she has had, like, one hundred and fifty different careers," Ruby says, although some estimates put the number at over two hundred. "It explains how she can afford all these clothes and several dream houses."

Ruby found pieces of her feminine ideal in her idols: the ethereal platinum blond curls of proto-bad girl Jean Harlow, the boldness with which Naomi Campbell commands a runway, the airy innocence that Marilyn Monroe projected in her films. But if Marilyn's frothy persona disguised that she was a woman riddled with deep insecurities forced to live under constant surveillance, Ruby can certainly relate: Like the actress herself, she wears her glamour as a suit of armor, hoping to make herself impenetrable. But instead of shielding her from a fifties-era America that wanted to exploit her until there was nothing left, Ruby's delicately applied makeup and the careful softness in her voice is protection from a state that never wanted her to be authentically alive, that would rather see her dead than live her own truth.

Meeting Cooper hasn't necessarily given Ruby the comfort to tear down the defensive walls she built to survive in Texas, but it has been a relief to be able to let down a drawbridge and allow visitors at last. Even by her own admission, she and Cooper are galloping through the early days of their relationship at an exquisite velocity, going on three dates in twenty-four hours. Within less than a week, they've each met each other's families, although being introduced to Cooper's mother put Ruby in the awkward position of pretending that she hadn't already been a guest in their home. (On the evening of their first date, his mother was out of town.)

In fact, Ruby's new suitor actually meets her family *twice* that very first week. Her parents invite Cooper over for an evening of barbeque and board games that he and Ruby spend whispering together in their corner, sharing mumbled commentary between bites of three-bean salad and Molly's wonderfully crumbly homemade berry crisp. We begin the night's entertainment with Catchphrase, a handheld electronic game in the vein of charades at which Mimi proves uniquely terrible, describing every word that flashes across her screen as "popular" or "interesting," a list that confoundingly includes both Native Americans and supermarkets.

But when it comes to narrating What Do You Meme?, Mimi is unrivaled. In the game, players are asked to pair ribald prompts to a series of famous Internet memes, such as David After Dentist and Side Eyeing Chloe, and Mimi scores the game's biggest laugh by announcing the winning card for an image of a woman sobbing on her bathroom floor. "When you wake up with gum stuck in your pubes," she says in a fey southern lilt akin to a parakeet with a full tank of helium.

Although Molly will eventually become passively vexed by Cooper's ubiquitous presence in her home, muttering to herself *he's here a-gain* as they dart up the stairs each day after class, seeing her daughter rest her head on a boy's shoulder validates everything they've been working toward. When Ruby was younger, she was intensely affectionate, once telling her mother that she needed "ten hugs a day to be happy." Among the Carnes household antiquities is a bell that reads "Ring for a Hug," but as Ruby got older and less comfortable in her skin, the bell fell progressively silent. "She did not want anyone to touch her, and we would have to ask, 'Can I hug you?'" Molly tells me after the games are packed away for the night. "Very quickly after she came out, she became like the child that we once knew."

Almost two years later, Ruby is effusive in showing her love for those around her, braiding her fingers tightly around Molly's during church sermons and leaving a kiss on Mimi's forehead before she goes about her day. "We hold hands and we hug because for so many years, we didn't have that," Molly says. If Ruby once feared that she wouldn't ever get to experience a week like this one, her mother worried, too, that she might lose Ruby before she knew how sweet life could be.

The evening ends with Ruby and Cooper sitting on her bed and playing tic-tac-toe as they continue swapping confessions and previously undisclosed bits of personal trivia: Cooper and his older brother bonded in their youth by watching the seventies space-opera *Star Wars* on repeat, and Ruby has an entire drawer filled with nothing but tank tops in different colors and styles. On their first date, she wore her favorite sleeveless white lace shirt, which she paired with Dr. Martens boots and the baggy jeans her mom hates. While Ruby is horrified to learn Cooper doesn't have a favorite color, what she likes so much about him is that he draws out the honesty from her, giving her a space where she feels safe to be her full self. Cooper calls when he says he will, he shows up on time, and he's emotionally transparent, a combination worth its weight in platinum. "That's why we've been moving so fast," she tells me. "We communicate with each other. We trust each other. I don't play games, so it's really nice to meet someone else who doesn't do that."

When they shared their first kiss, sitting on Cooper's bed, he requested permission before leaning in. He could have already inferred the answer, but it was wonderful to be asked.

III. LITTLE MIRACLE

The bluebonnets are in full bloom as Molly makes the long drive from Houston to Austin, a gleaming centipede of cars stacked alongside the road while their occupants stomp through the grass in search of the perfect selfie. Bluebonnet season usually begins at the end of March, but climate change has brought them to central Texas early this year, brightening the fields with inaccurately named stalks of tiny velvet bells. Indeed, some of these delicate flowers are blue, but others are a variety of glowing purples and pinks. The distinction matters little, though, to the tourists indulging in the time-honored custom of smashing them until they are flatter than this stretch of highway.

Molly has made this round trip, which clocks in at around four and half hours, countless times throughout her life, and she has these signposts thoroughly memorized. Among them is the billboard advertising personal injury services from "the attorney that rocks," whose dreadlocks and leather jacket are surely meant as confirmation of his rock 'n' roll credentials. There's also the restaurant where Molly orders chicken salad to go and then cries in her sensible SUV if things don't turn out the way she had hoped. She has spent weeks dreading this journey, with the pressure of knowing it was coming wrapping itself around her like a tight vest. Last night, she hit a breaking point: Sitting in her bathrobe, Molly kept repeating to herself, *I shouldn't have to do this,* as she shook her head in disbelief. "This isn't normal," she told me in her living room. "I can't believe I have to do this all over again."

Molly is, yet again, on her way to the Texas capitol to lobby for the rights of Texas's LGBTQIA+ community—a fight which, for her, began with SB 6, a 2017 bill seeking to force transgender people to use public restrooms that align with the sex they were assigned at birth.[6] If SB 6 had been signed into law, schools and other governmental entities would have faced a maximum fine of more than ten thousand dollars if they did not refuse transgender people the right to use the restroom that corresponds with their gender identity.[7] Proponents of the measure claimed that it was necessary to prevent predators from preying on children, a decades-old argument relying on at least one of two myths: 1) that transgender people pose a danger to kids and 2) if they aren't themselves harming children, granting them equal access to public life is a slippery slope to pedophilia.[8]

Amid fears that overtly targeting transgender people would result in financial backlash against the state, the bill's proponent, state senator Lois Kohlkorst (R), opted for the latter of those tactics. "I have to say that while many have made this about a transgender bill, it's more about someone that will use this bill as an excuse to go into the most intimate places we find ourselves in," she said during debate over SB 6.[9] The lawmaker was sensitive to criticisms of transphobia after the passage of North Carolina's bathroom bill—HB 2, now defunct—resulted in millions of dollars in lost tourism revenue.[10] Concerts and sporting events canceled in protest, while major corporations pulled planned expansions in the Tar Heel State.[11]

Texas's SB 6 ultimately did not pass, but lobbying and meeting with lawmakers offered an early lesson in what Molly has come to recognize as "emotional whiplash." Although she initially came to the Texas capitol years ago with visions of moving people's hearts and stirring their souls, just as a great sermon does, the legislature is dictated not by the will of its citizenry but by decades of entrenched politics; that bureaucratic tyranny is embodied by the white men whose portraits line an interminable hallway in the building's basement. Those who built the system don't want it to change, especially if that change is being driven by people it was never designed to benefit, Molly says.

"You have no control over the process," she says of testifying. "They'll tell you the hearing is going to be that day, but they don't tell you what time. They'll put a million things ahead of you so that you have to hang around all day, hoping that you'll leave, and then some of these people don't treat you very respectfully. You're feeling powerful because you're doing something, but then at the same time, you're constantly reminded that you are not in power, and you have no power here."

So much in Molly's life has changed since that first trip to the capitol, years before her daughter was ready to become the person she had previously been reluctant to be. When Ruby came out to her mother as transgender for the second—and final—time in May 2020, Molly had spent eons preparing for that very day. In a state like Texas, she had no choice but to be ready; she knew what was coming. When lawmakers reconvened for the following year's legislative session, they pushed seventy-six bills[12] that sought to take from LGBTQIA+ people the basic rights and protections that others freely enjoy every day, such as the ability to receive health care that meets their specific needs,[13] fully participate in school programs,[14] and have birth certificates that reflect who they are.[15] That number represented what was then, by far, the most massive slate of anti-LGBTQIA+ legislation to be introduced by a single state in one year, and yet it now seems quaint by 2023's standards. As of April of this year, more than 130 such bills have been introduced, with the same goals in mind.[16]

So while Molly was more than ready to learn that she was raising a seventeen-year-old daughter, what startled her was Ruby's choice of venue to make this announcement. They were waiting to order chicken nuggets—which felt, to her, anticlimactic after so much toil and anticipation. "You're telling me *now*?" she had asked, her voice peaking like a tea kettle. "In the Burger King drive-through?"

Traveling to Austin time and again has become the collective millstone around their family's necks, their spirits weighed down by the frank indifference of politicians who have little understanding of or regard for the populations they hope to discriminate against. Ruby testified before a Texas senate committee in July 2021 wearing a green dress that matched the chamber rugs—that time a coincidence, she swears. "I silently struggled with depression and anxiety for years because I didn't feel comfortable to be who I truly was," Ruby told the legislature, elbows perched on a wooden desk as she leaned into the microphone. "Having to wake up each day and shove down my identity was enough to make me suicidal. Every day became a struggle to find the will to live, and coming out finally helped to lift that burden. Being transgender is the only way for me to stay alive." Molly says this moment was a high point of her career in motherhood: Her daughter, who had spent most of her life cowering in the shadows of others' perceived judgment, was now declaring herself to the world.

Although Ruby's reminiscence began with chiding Texas Republicans for legislating against transgender people when very few of them had even met someone from the community, GOP lawmakers didn't take the opportunity to prove her wrong. Despite the courage it took to challenge them, few of the conservatives in the room actually listened; instead they checked their phones, stared at the ceiling, and refused to make eye contact.

By the time Molly got up to speak, her patience had been smoothed by wear. She wanted to confront senators directly and force them to look her in the eye, but instead she collected herself and addressed them as a Christian, one who shares the same core beliefs as the people exploiting religion to take away her daughter's rights. "The beautiful thing about transgender people is that they understand at a very deep level that their soul, not their body, is truly who they are and who we all are, and that is the foundation for dignity and respect," Molly said, as if she were preaching from the pulpit. "I believe they are God's messengers, who are teaching us a very important lesson, perhaps one we should have learned as children."

The bill that Molly and Ruby fought against, which forces transgender student athletes to compete on school sports teams in accordance with their "biological sex," would be signed into law a few months after Ruby's testimony.[17] Three special sessions of the legislature were mounted to ensure the legislation's passage, costing the state more than four million dollars in tax revenue.[18]

Ruby chose not to attend the 2023 legislative session, unwilling to continually put herself out there for the benefit of politicians who haven't earned her vulnerability. A black blazer now sways from a hanger in the back seat where Molly's daughter would normally sit, obscuring our view of the black and brown cows in the fields outside the car's tinted windows. What keeps Molly coming back is the certainty that this is her calling: a belief that the whole of her religious life has prepared her for the work of advocating for her daughter's rights, as well as the rights of other transgender youth. Even when it feels like things will never change and there's nothing they can do, Molly has faith that this is where she is supposed to be, that she is fulfilling the purpose that God has intended.

"I really liked it better when my purpose was to be in parish ministry and help other congregations be welcoming because that call is super easy and fun," she tells me as we cross Austin's city limits. "But I know I'm not called to that anymore. I did lots of good things there, but they say that a very mature Christian does their ministry outside their congregation because you've been prepared. You're supposed to go."

After finding a parking spot near the capitol building, Molly checks in at Equality Advocacy Day, a frantically paced lobbying boot camp hosted by the ACLU of Texas and Equality Texas, in partnership with a multitude of other civil rights groups. The annual event allows community members to put their newly learned skills into practice by personally interfacing with lawmakers. Molly is hastily shuffled into a cabal of folding chairs filled by other parents of transgender kids, along with a sardonic gay rabbi in a rainbow yarmulke. As they pick through ready-made boxes of wizened turkey sandwiches, our group listens while the moderators attempt to quell the thunder of the crowded gymnasium long enough to narrate their PowerPoint presentation. The partially audible seminar contains the same tips and tricks that Molly has heard repeatedly over her years of attendance—*look lawmakers in the eye, say your name, personalize your story*—and she is hoping this time they work.

The training ends in a rally at the capitol steps where around seven hundred protesters gather in support of the LGBTQIA+ community, holding signs that read "Trans Kids You Are Loved" and "We Deserve the Same Rights as You." Of the assembly's celebrity cameos, a sparkly Cynthia Lee Fontaine of *RuPaul's Drag Race* fame lip syncs in gold sequins to the Gloria Gaynor cover of "I Am What I Am" from *La Cage aux Folles*, a drag musical satirizing conservative hypocrisy. Dressed in a rainbow poncho, Jonathan Van Ness of the inspirational makeover show *Queer Eye* urges protesters to talk about taboo topics like religion and politics in their everyday lives. "You do not let anyone silence the things that move your life . . . because let me tell you something: These people on the right, they are not silencing their faith to legislate your lives," says Van Ness, whose own sign declares that "Trans Is Beautiful."

But the weight of living this day over and over again is evident in the faces of the crowd. Next to an inflatable orange dinosaur, a protester weeps as an anti-LGBTQIA+ activist breaches the barricades, ready for a confrontation. As the man repeats *it isn't natural, it isn't natural*, preaching the gospel of a ruthless God driven to acts of genocidal spite, the protester holds their sign high to block the unrequested sermon from others' sight. "I Am Not a Mistake," the poster board reads.

A mother who stands in the back of the rabble, arms tucked inside her "Free Mom Hugs" hoodie, tells me that she is planning to leave the United States after too many years spent shielding her transgender son from people who want to brandish their religion against him. After her family's photographs and personal information were shared on the

Internet, picketers protested outside their house and chased her to her workplace with illegal firearms in the back of their truck. Fearing they wouldn't be safe in Texas much longer, her family began immediately making plans to seek refuge in New Zealand, where her son is now attending college. While she intends to follow him later this year, a part of her worries that she won't make it, that she won't be able to run fast enough. "If these idiots kill me for being your mom, I need you to be safe," she told him before he left. "That is priority number one."

The crowd eventually disperses, and Molly's group hobbles into the Texas capitol to speak with the three lawmakers they have been assigned, each of whom are Democrats on record for supporting LGBTQIA+ equality. The majority of the group is brand-new to lobbying, having signed up for the event out of the same desperation that has led other families to flee Texas. A woman with periwinkle fingernails and Converse sneakers is nervous to tell her story, having shared it with few people outside her immediate family. Her son used to experience such deep suicidal ideation that they would cry on the floor together while she cradled him, but since he came out as transgender, she is no longer scared that every time she holds him will be the last. "If they knew the lengths we went to to save our kids, no one would accuse us of abusing our children," she tells me.

Molly, in contrast, is a natural—telling her story as if she's been doing it for years because, well, she has. As our gaggle of eight stands huddled in the office of Texas state representative Ray Lopez (D), Molly explains that she can see the light shining in her daughter's eyes again ever since she began receiving the medications and gender-affirming surgeries that made it possible for her to be herself. "She is funny, ambitious, and kind, and she doesn't want to live under the cloud of wondering if the life-saving care she received is going to go away one day," Molly says, as the former San Antonio city councilman patiently listens in his tan suit. "That's why I'm here." Notably, she omits mention of Ruby's planned exodus from the state, hoping that the story of a stalwart Texan will resonate with him more deeply.

Despite her apparent polish, Molly feels off her game, and she will realize why during our commute back to Houston later that day: She had forgotten to pray before the meeting. "I usually pray before I go into each office and then my words just flow," she will tell me. "I just call on the Holy Spirit to come upon me. I take deep breaths, and it comes on me. It sends chills down my body and it fills me up. Sometimes if I pray with people, I feel it come out of me. One time I put my hands on someone to pray with them and I almost fell over because I felt it in my body so much."

Molly sometimes prays with the Republican lawmakers she meets to show them that Christians can affirm transgender people just as they are, that religion doesn't have to be synonymous with hate, but Lopez is in no need of the message. He is a member of the LGBTQIA+ caucus in the Texas House of Representatives and a vocal opponent of legislation seeking to prevent transgender girls from competing on school sports teams in accordance with their identities. He tells the group that a Republican colleague once attempted to get him to sign on to a transgender sports ban by telling him that it was a "pro-lesbian bill." When asked to explain that characterization, the GOP lawmaker claimed the majority of women's athletes competing at the college level are lesbians. "The issue is about equality," Lopez tells us, clutching a Diet Coke. "The issue is about doing the right thing for everyone. That's our chore, right? That's what the Lord tells us to do."

Conversations like these are rare, and even those who are new to the political process feel that charge in the room. The other meetings that day are with young legislative aides in oversize sweaters, each of whom is tasked with dutifully explaining that their boss is currently in a meeting and, no, they don't know when the lawmaker will be back. They jot down constituents' concerns on a notepad while expressing heartfelt regrets. In contrast, a placard on the wall of Lopez's office indicates that we are welcome here: "If You Attack One Texan, You Attack All Texans."

The surroundings are filled with posters boosting San Antonio tourism and advertisements for a march honoring the labor activist Cesar Chavez, along with copies of Lopez's own calendar.

Throwing water on the group's shared excitement, Lopez admits that he is worried LGBTQIA+ allies don't have the numbers to stop the flurry of bills targeting transgender people in Texas right now. In 2021, Democrats delayed the vote on a transgender sports ban by walking out of the capitol building in protest, but he fears they can't hold the legislation back forever. "Things don't look good," Lopez says. "The stakes are high. I don't want to sound naïve or Pollyanna, but maybe cooler heads will prevail."

Throughout the day, Molly looks for reasons to keep coming back to the capitol, some sign that all the exhaustion and heartbreak is worth it. After Governor Abbott issued his executive order targeting families of transgender kids back in 2022, her family started writing things they were grateful for in white pen on a wall in their home, just to remind themselves that their happiness is not dependent upon the opinions of Texas's political leaders. Messages included "the perfect rug," "my new haircut," "passed driver's test," and "found the keys," the latter probably the biggest relief to all involved.

But while Molly may have forgotten her prayers today, they were answered anyway: When we return to Houston, she telephones her local state representative, Mike Schofield (R), after she sees that he was one of the few GOP lawmakers not to co-sponsor anti-LGBTQIA+ legislation this year. When his aide learns that Molly has a transgender child, she quickly pencils in a meeting for the following week. "I'm *sure* that he will want to hear your story," the young woman says emphatically. Molly immediately begins to feel the presence of the Holy Spirit within her, that ethereal force embodying the fulfillment of her purpose. This is what she needed today: a reminder that even if the Texas Legislature isn't on her daughter's side, God is. "It feels like a little miracle," Molly says. "It really feels like an opportunity, a crack in the door."

iv. THE LADY EVE

Driving around the neighborhood with Ryan is an immersive experience in déjà vu. The subdivisions in their quiet suburb, where the traffic glides like silent Velcro, are virtually indistinguishable—endless rows of taupe dominoes equipped with air-conditioning and two-car garages. The Carneses have spent most of their lives in Houston, with its enormous tree-ring metropolis and highways that levitate overhead like haunted noodles, and it's simultaneously surreal and comforting to think that their time here may be nearing its end, both for Ruby and the people who raised her.

Molly spent much of her early childhood in Minnesota before moving back to her home state at ten years old, and Ryan's family has sweet tea coursing through their veins: His mother's side hails from Louisiana, and his father's people settled in Mississippi after immigrating to America in the 1630s. While Molly has long resented Texas's repressive conservatism, Ryan speaks of the state with a detached warmth. This is the place, after all, where his son and daughter were born, where they would line up at the neighborhood pool on summer mornings before the acrid heat turned the water into a lukewarm stew of unhappy customers. Houston's ubiquitous man-made lakes act as concrete buckets designed to keep homeowners' living rooms from flooding, and when Hurricane Harvey hit Texas in 2017, Ryan took solace in knowing his family would be OK.

"It just rained as hard as you can imagine, where you'd have to pull over because you can't even drive," he says. "It just went on and on and on. You kept wondering, 'Is it ever gonna stop?'"

If these are Ruby's waning days in "Generica," the less charitable phrase that Molly uses to describe their suburb's anywhere-USA homogeneity, her parents aren't sure how much longer they will stay either. Molly, who was once an aspiring actress, pines for the brief period she spent in California in her twenties, and they have also discussed starting over in Colorado to escape a state that feels less and less like home with every passing legislative session. Even Ryan views the McMansions that have swallowed their suburb over the past decade with skepticism: If you have that kind of money to spend, he wonders, why would you do it *here*?

But finding their ticket out is proving to be a chocolate bar in a million: They can't afford to move anywhere they would want to go. For instance, the annual cost of living in Sacramento and San Diego is, respectively, 16.7 percent and 58 percent higher than Houston.[19] Other pragmatic concerns include Mimi's health, which could be imperiled by relocation, and Ryan's sister, who has severe developmental disabilities and lives in a group home nearby. As her guardian, Ryan visits regularly to listen to her sing children's nursery rhymes and repeat fragments of commercial jingles she heard on TV. "Diet Coke," his sister repeats to herself, liking the way the words feel on her tongue.

Despite the many challenges they have faced, the Carneses have had a good life in Texas. Ryan and Molly met in their midtwenties at a now-defunct local dive called Bayou Mama's, where Ryan recalls that his future wife "was looking for a guy with a ponytail" while he was searching for a "good time." "We both got neither," he laughs with the kind of faint chuckle that indicates he's rhapsodized over their meet cute many times before. They collided on the dance floor and Molly let him buy her a drink, thinking that a blindfolded bowler was more likely to score that night, but as it turned out, they had much in common. They were Episcopalians and members of churches that were just miles apart. Both had parents who traveled often: Ryan's father was one of the top college textbook salesmen in the country, and Molly's dad was an influential leader in the local Republican Party.

Six weeks after trading pager numbers outside the bar, Ryan and Molly realized they were falling for each other. On a party bus their friends had rented, Ryan tested the prospects of their blossoming courtship with some sweet talk. "Do you want something, *baby*?" he asked, and they both immediately felt that that term, in all its uneasy newness, fit like an old sweater.

What Ryan wants for his daughter is what he and Molly were lucky enough to have: the kind of nostalgic love story that feels comforting to revisit, like a dog-eared photo album stashed inside a coffee table. Ryan says that he was so scared to ask Molly to marry him that he panicked at the white tablecloth restaurant to which he had taken her for expressly that purpose; it took until later that evening, when she begged to know if she had been gaslit into believing herself a bride-to-be, for him to gather his gumption. "I don't know what happened here, but I kind of thought you were going to ask me to marry you!" Molly said, the exasperation heavy in her voice. She had already known this dinner was coming because Ryan had visited Molly's father to ask for her hand in marriage; true to the churlish character he took vast pleasure in portraying, he had initially turned Ryan down. "I know what you're here to ask me, and the answer is no," her father had said with a contrived gruffness, knowing that he ultimately had as much say in the matter as the pope.

It's much too soon to know if Ruby has found someone to fulfill her dreams of five tow-headed children and her own house filled with antiques because, after all, she's only nineteen. But Ryan hopes that someday, Ruby will find that perfect person willing to scale the walls of others' disapproval for her, who will adore her no matter what lies on the other side. "I just want her to be happy," he tells me. "This young man seems to be very nice. He always looks me in the eye and shakes my hand with a firm grip, which I appreciate."

Later that day, Ruby and I decide to resolve a disagreement over whether Mimi looks more like Ginger Rogers or Barbara Stanwyck by watching the lightning-paced forties screwball comedy *The Lady Eve*, in which the latter of the two midcentury starlets plays a stylish con woman who decides to give up the grift after falling for an absent-minded ophiologist. (Her grandmother is, in fact, more of a Ginger.) Settling in for the film in Ruby's parlor with its leopard-print couch and assemblage of gadgets—the weathered metal spindle inscribed with Tibetan prayers, a drum on a stick the family bought from traveling acrobats—it occurs to me that the film's themes unknowingly play out a trope of which transgender women are very frequently accused. In thirty-five states, it's legal to use a transgender woman's identity in court as a defense tactic in a homicide case: to claim that she is a swindler and a trickster and that her alleged lies justify lessened punishment for taking her life.

Looking over at Ruby as she watches the movie, I wonder if she is thinking about her own coming moment of revelation—when she feels comfortable and safe enough to tell Cooper everything about who she is, who she has always been. I wonder if she worries that Cooper will be her next disappointment, that his rejection will reinforce the false notion that she could never possibly find in a partner the unequivocal affirmation that she's found in her church and her family. But Ruby has forgotten to disclose to me a critical detail of their meet cute: He already knew about Ruby's gender history when he picked her up for their first date. She told him in a text message two days after he asked her out, and he responded that it didn't alter the course of his feelings in the slightest. When Cooper joins us now in the parlor, he sits next to Ruby, locks his hand in hers, and tells me that the unexpected divulgence only made him respect her more.

"The bravery that it took for Ruby to tell me that she was trans, I don't know if I've ever experienced that before, the maturity and the trust: *I am trusting you and sharing this information with you*," he tells me, looking over at Ruby from the corner of his eye. "It was very moving. It was very powerful. I felt honored."

143

Ruby, however, was not immediately aware of the irrelevance of her transness, as he had hesitated for several minutes before replying to her text. Cooper didn't want to sour the moment by saying the wrong thing, so he called a friend to ask the most appropriate way to tell her that he didn't care, that he liked her anyway. Making matters much worse, Cooper responded obliquely with a thumbs-up emoticon while Ruby waited by the phone for him to say something, anything at all, staring blankly at his read receipts as the minutes passed with excruciating lethargy. "I was so confused," she says. "I didn't know what to do. I was like, 'What now? Where do we go from here?'"

As we sit together, Ruby is dressed down in a baggy black t-shirt depicting a three-headed Cerberus as if it were the subject of a Scholastic children's book. "Mommy, can we keep him?" asks a young girl as flames engulf the canine guardian of the Greek underworld. Considering how fashion-minded Ruby is, it would seem to be an odd choice: the kind of graphic tee that used to be sold at every mall in America, so seemingly passé. She has worn it several times throughout my stay—including to an oddities festival promising a "100 percent real mermaid" and a "six-foot man-eating chicken"—and I will later ask her why she's so fond of this particular shirt. Ruby says she wears it when she feels at her most comfortable; she attended the expo with one of her oldest friends, who knew her even before the world knew she was Ruby. Taking in the happy couple's presence, the look on her face right now reminds me of the girl I saw in church when I first arrived in Texas: perfectly placid, like there was nowhere else she could possibly want to be.

Ruby does not know what will happen next, as the passing days until her departure evaporate like smoke rings, but she is trying to focus on being here now, anchored in these moments she had never thought would come to pass. "I'm trying not to think about it right now," she says, throwing her legs over Cooper's lap. "I'm just trying to have a good time while it lasts."

While her California voyage is still weeks away, my departure is much nearer. My flight is due to leave in the morning from an airport that is much like Houston itself: a sprawling puzzle of false exits and hallways that end right back where they started. As I prepare to leave her, I have a vision of what Ruby is yet unable to see: that she is one of those lucky people who will be loved her entire life, just as she has been loved every single minute preceding this one. Molly shows Ruby that she loves her through that affectionate nagging specific to mothers and daughters—a constant, low-stakes vexation regarding Ruby's choice in shoes—and Ryan's love is expressed by killing all the grass in their front yard in an attempt to rid their lives of weeds.

Mimi's love is the most straightforward because she has little time for subtext. Sitting in the living room in her trademark pastel velour tracksuit, she tells me that seeing her granddaughter live the life she was meant to is what gives her the strength to get out of bed when she feels like she has nothing left. "That's enough right there to make you want to live for something," Mimi says. "I want the best for my babies and I'm hoping that she has a good life. She has worked so hard to get there."

When I ask Ruby if the sacrifice feels worth it—leaving behind the boy with the naturally crimped hair, who is so obviously falling for her, and forfeiting the nearness to virtually everyone she knows—there's not a doubt in her mind that she's made the right choice. Cooper's nuclear-grade adoration doesn't change the fact that she has no future in Texas, no way forward, and they both accept that. Cooper intends to come visit her at school over break, and although he insists that he won't chase her, there are more than a hundred colleges in Southern California to which he could transfer if he changes his mind.

Their trial separation will begin four months from now, when Molly will make the twenty-three-hour drive to move Ruby into her dormitory, plus a few pit stops. First, there will be Buc-ee's, the chain of enormous Texas gas stations with hypnotically clean bathrooms fronted by a cartoon beaver, and then the Rainforest Cafe, the endangered species of mall restaurants specializing in jungle kitsch. "There are so few of them left," Ruby says. "I have such good memories there, and it's going to be so magical to smell that fountain water again. It's the start of something new." The girl looks over at Cooper and smiles in that strictly confidential way that they often do, sending him a message intended for only him to decode. He smiles back, and it's a great smile.

CLINT

CHICAGO, ILLINOIS

APRIL 2023

I. CONGRATS, IT'S A BOY

The front row is the place to be as Muslims gather at a Chicagoland mosque for the Saturday evening call to prayer, rushing past with their complementary dates and bottles of water clutched tightly in hand. The sounds of newly satiated hunger—appreciative gasps and groans—echo around us as a man in a navy-blue hooded sweatshirt offers a freshly opened delivery box of cheese pizza that vanishes almost instantly. The sacred practice of salat requires Muslims to pray five times a day, the routine punctuations intended as a cue to always stay oriented toward Allah. According to scripture, Allah originally mandated an ambitious allotment of fifty daily prayers until the Prophet Muhammad—at the urging of the ever-rational Moses, who pointed out that no one has the time for that—requested a more user-friendly five. The briefest of the daily prayers, known as fajr, takes place before sunrise, and those scheduled in the afternoon and evening typically take between five and ten minutes to complete. The current prayer, the fourth of the five, is known as maghrib, and during Ramadan, it also coincides with everyone's favorite time of day: the breaking of fast at sunset.

The month of Ramadan, in which Muslims are obligated to abstain from food and drink during daylight hours, can be a difficult time for seventeen-year-old Clint Ahern, who gobbles up his oozing pizza slice before helping himself to a second. Among Ramadan's many terms and conditions, participants aren't allowed to drink caffeine during their fasts, which can begin as early as 4:30 a.m. "I'm a very different person without coffee in the morning," says Clint, who is currently wearing a pair of diminutive pearl earrings, each barely larger than the sharp end of a thumbtack. "I've shown up five minutes late to school every single day. I don't talk. I just sit there. I passed out in my TA class. My teacher was like, 'Good god, what's wrong with you?'"

Clint is joined in worship by his father, Joe, who struggles with stinkier predicaments during Ramadan: He gets a bad case of what's called "faster's breath." "Being a teacher, I'm trying to talk to the kids, and you squat down next to the desk," says Joe, outfitted in a short-sleeved button-up and a plaid newsboy cap. "But I'm like: *You don't want me over there.*"

Joe and Clint await the beginning of prayer as their row inches closer and closer together, shoulders nearly touching. With an impish smirk, Clint whispers to me that the closing of gaps between congregants leaves no space for the devil to get in, explaining that worshippers at some services will push their feet out until they resemble a chain of paper dolls. Our tightly bound mass is attired in a jarringly eclectic blend of the formal and casual: The businessmen in their Nike athleisure, highlighter-green polos, and camouflage cargo pants clash sharply with the more traditional members in their monkish brown cowls and silken jet-black thobes, which flow with the ease of a conductor's hands as they reach for the floor.

The imam, in his blue suit and argyle scarf, trots over before prayer begins to invite us to stay for the iftar, which would normally be the meal to break the group's fast if it hadn't already been usurped by junk food. "I will lead the prayer now," he says, putting a delicate hand on my shoulder to indicate that I'm new here. "After we finish, we have food. You can eat." The warmth of his greeting is a surprise to Joe, who had incorrectly predicted that the worship leader wouldn't speak to us directly, as the imam rarely mingles with guests. "I'm always wrong about everything," he laughs with trademark self-deprecation. "*You're not going to get greeted at the mosque,* then the imam comes and says hi. Of course, we do stick out a little like sore thumbs."

Although our formation would be ideal for line dancing, Muslim prayer instead requires an intricate waltz of repeated bowing accompanied by chants. Muslims are instructed not to break from the rite prior to its completion, and when Clint's older brothers, Idris and Hud, were younger, they would constantly test their father's devotion by creating as much chaos as possible, such as pulling up a chair and attempting to pull the fire alarm. Today, two girls race back and forth across the green carpet patterned in a repeating alcove motif, which gives the room the illusion of falling through an endless door. Despite the flash of their robes speeding by, not a soul flinches during the day's prayers. The company's steps end with a parting plea to Allah asking to watch over Muhammad and his followers, followed by a glance to the right and then to the left. "May peace, mercy, and blessings of Allah be upon you," the room chants.

Before he came out as transgender, Clint would worship in the women's section, a modestly sized enclosure overlooking the more spacious men's prayer space. Located up a flight of stairs, the women's area always smelled like samosas and was packed with fidgeting toddlers, emergency binkies, and overly friendly maternal figures. "We had aunties who'd give you candy, totally negating that 'don't take candy from strangers' lesson," he says. After today's prayer ends, we are shuffled to a basement cafeteria where we join the women for steaming servings of goat biryani piled up like halal mountains, peppered with the thinnest blanket of cumin.

Clint told his family about his gender in the eighth grade by giving his mother a baby shower greeting card reading, "Congrats, It's a Boy," and to his pleasant surprise, that's exactly what he was treated as during worship. He immediately began praying alongside his father down in the men's section, and the feverish euphoria of that unexpected validation only further strengthened his connection to his faith. Clint has never felt as if being transgender presented a conflict of interest. Of the ways in which he feels as if he doesn't measure up to Muhammad's example, he believes his fits of road rage are a much bigger issue, as anger is considered a fast-breaking act during Ramadan.

"I've never seen being trans as making me a bad Muslim," he says. "Being trans is not in the Quran, and I don't feel like it affects me. In a lot of ways, going to the mosque helped me to affirm my identity."

While Islam is frequently painted as uniformly intolerant of LGBTQIA+ people, Clint has largely flown under the radar at his mosque, where the other congregants either haven't noticed or have kept their opinions to themselves. He and his family practice the Sunni tradition of Islam, and their mosque tends to espouse a markedly liberal worldview. Although imams at neighboring congregations are prone to lengthy diatribes lecturing women for being improperly dressed—critiquing the length of their robes or the wanton patterning of their floral print head scarves—Clint's imam tends to focus on more universal themes: being a good person and caring for humanity.

Clint is also able to slip through the cracks because no one ever assumes he's anything other than the boy he is. After he began cutting his hair short, strangers would praise him as a *polite young man* when he would hold the door open for them. He experiences the same invisibility at his high school, where the other guys on his swim team have no idea that he's transgender. When a few teammates innocently inquired about the twin scars flayed across his chest, Clint said they were the result of a childhood "lung surgery," a response that was not met with scrutiny. It's not that he's keeping his identity a secret, he clarifies, but that few people ever ask; even the kids who knew him before his transition have a habit of forgetting.

Honestly, though, Clint prefers to be unseen: to live his life without explanation or correction, to not have to constantly fight to assert his right to live as himself. His mother, Maha, is a dedicated advocate for LGBTQIA+ equality—a former member of the Human Rights Campaign's

Parents for Transgender Equality National Council and a current facilitator for Desi Rainbows, a support group for South Asian parents and
their LGBTQIA+ children—but Clint has no interest in activism or being
a voice for others. Although Joe wears an ally pin on his lanyard during
his day job teaching English, Clint won't allow him to fly a Transgender
Pride flag in the front yard. That symbol, for all its ferocious beauty,
doesn't resonate with Clint's cardinal mission: that others know him
not as a transgender boy but simply as a boy.

"A lot of people in the community really advocate for people being
out, owning who they are, and spreading awareness," he says. "If I was
out all the time, I would feel more dysphoric than if I'm just able to live
my life as a guy and not have to worry. I don't think it's a selfish thing
to want to live a life that would make you happier. The whole reason I
transitioned was so that I could be happier. In the end, it's everyone's
own life. You've got to live it the way you want."

Clint lives life on his own terms, almost to a fault. When I first arrived
at his family's home on the far outskirts of greater Chicago, his parents
cautioned that Clint can be brusque and bracingly direct in conversation; he always speaks his mind, even if it occasionally rubs people the
wrong way. Shortly after our meeting, Clint attempted to suss me out
by making me play a song for him, a common test to which he subjects
newcomers. I selected "When the Sun Hits" by the nineties ambient rock
band Slowdive, which filled his car with a wailing wall of sound, and
Clint responded that distortion-heavy cough-drop ballads aren't really
his thing. He prefers country music because it doesn't take itself too seriously and privileges storytellers: troubadours like Merle Haggard, Willie
Nelson, and even a young Taylor Swift before the one-time Nashville
ingénue code switched to pop.

But as much as he fashions himself an iconoclast—a suburban cowboy
in hand-me-down t-shirts—Clint is also thoughtful and extraordinarily
conscientious toward the world around him. He usually bags up his iftar

leftovers to avoid food waste, but today he has forgotten to bring a box of Ziploc pouches with him; he hasn't been to the mosque in years, due to the pandemic, and is admittedly out of practice. Because it would be next to impossible to consume the mound of biryani laid out before him, he puts the styrofoam plate holding the discarded remains of his father's meal over his own, to hide his shame.

If Clint does not foresee making LGBTQIA+ activism a habit, many of our conversations during my time in Illinois center on the future he pictures for himself: a remote existence akin to the pastoral refuge of nineteenth-century transcendentalist author Henry David Thoreau. Twenty years from now, Clint envisions a life lived as a forest ranger and conservationist, dedicating his time to preserving America's national parks. His free moments, he imagines, will be spent hanging out with his partner and children, going on walks with the family dog, and playing banjo on his porch while drinking a cup of coffee—except during Ramadan, of course. "I want to run away to the woods, live there, and be independent, like Teddy Roosevelt," he will tell me a few days after worship service.

At the time of this confession, we are sitting on a turquoise sofa in his mother's front parlor, and I'm making chemtrails in the velour with my fingernails as he waxes philosophical. "Nature is the way humans want to see ourselves," he says, sitting cross-legged with his elbows on his knees. "We'd like to believe that we're indestructible and ceaseless, like we're always going to be there, but the only thing that really can do that is nature. It's interesting that we like to try."

Clint will finish his senior year of high school in May 2023 and plans to attend university this fall on the West Coast, where he will pursue a degree in marine biology or environmental science while he strives for infinity. He may be ready to take the next step in becoming the lone adventurer of his wildest manifestations, but Maha and Joe are not quite there yet. In the weeks ahead, their family will celebrate not only Clint's prom and his graduation, but also Eid al-Fitr, one of the most venerated days of the Muslim religious calendar. Colloquially shortened to "Eid," the feast marks the close of Ramadan, in which worshippers rise for morning prayer at the mosque and then spend the day breaking fast among their loved ones.

This will be Clint's last Eid before he goes off to college, and for his parents, that finality is a reminder that soon their bull-headed son will no longer be there to pray with Joe in the saggy-eyed mornings or snuggle up for a movie with Maha at night. These coming days, in many ways, are the last of Clint's adolescence, a farewell to the creature comforts of childhood in favor of the uncharted mysteries of adulthood, and the Aherns will spend them as they always have: as a family.

II. PEACH BLOSSOM JELLYFISH

If dinner is a hallowed time during Ramadan, when the daylight hours are marked by irritability and unrelenting headaches, Joe takes his evening meals even more seriously than most. Juxtaposed with the stacks of recently graded tests and assembled LEGO bonsai trees is an absolutely staggering library of cookbooks; the collection reads like a United Nations roll call, with the national cuisines of Thailand, Malaysia, China, and Indonesia represented several times over. That's not to mention the four Italian cookbooks and twelve Indian cookbooks—because eleven books on the correct cheese-to-spinach ratio in saag paneer simply wasn't enough—or his guides to cooking with a wok and the dos and don'ts of pan-Asian fare.

The most controversial entry in his ever-growing ragbag of recipes is a set of instructions on making Greek kykeon pulled from a cookbook devoted to ancient cuisines, some of which have gone extinct for good reason. Referred to as the "drink of heroes" in honor of the small supporting role it played in Homer's post-Trojan War epic *The Odyssey*, kykeon is blended from a lugubrious mixture of wine, barley, honey, and—most bafflingly—goat cheese. The final product looks like bubblegum mixed with yogurt, and it has the texture of vomit. Even Clint, who hates wasting food, took just one sip before pouring his mugful into the garbage.

Although Joe has always been a whiz in the kitchen, food became one of his key coping mechanisms following his divorce from Maha, a breakup that was anything but mutual. "The divorce was hard for me for a solid three years," he confesses to me. "If you go to the bathroom, I still have a shower curtain with all these motivational phrases on it.

I had these phrases above the door: 'This Is a Place for Happiness and Love,' 'You Don't Have to Be Perfect to Be Good.' Looking back, all the signs for our divorce were there, but I was in denial, so I didn't see them."

Joe converted to Islam before marrying Maha, a Pakistani woman whose conservative parents already didn't like that she was marrying a white man, so a nonbelieving white man was fully out of the question. What he liked about his adopted faith was that being a believer wasn't a prerequisite to achieving salvation, thus resolving a riddle that Catholic school had left unanswered: If someone born in a remote village never has the opportunity to accept Jesus as their savior, are they automatically doomed to hell? Rather than dealing in irresolvable paradoxes, Islam teaches that entrance into heaven is a question of moral character, how one spends their time on earth.

Years after the split, Clint divides his evenings between his parents, who live in adjacent Chicago suburbs connected by a silent river, one which never seems to reap bounty for the patient fishermen loitering on its shores. A few days after the service at the mosque, it's Joe's night; before our dinner begins, the two excuse themselves to the sitting room for hasty prayers, the prostrations and rhythmic murmurs expedited to bring the day's sacrifice to a temporary close.

Our meal begins with a series of appetizers: the standard fast-breaking dates followed by Arab guacamole, a whip of sesame seed and sumac that we consume by breaching its lime green swirl with cauliflower and French bread. Joe's cooking style is that he whips up just about every-thing stocked in his pantry and dines on leftovers for the rest of the week. Tonight's main course includes chicken kottu, a Sri Lankan blend of chopped roti, onions, and scrambled egg, and keema, a minced beef dish with onions and tomatoes that is popular in Pakistan. For dessert, there's the sweet Indian yogurt smoothie mango lassi, a pale yellow confection whose dulcet flavor is mercifully free of cheese wine. No one is more pleased by our abundant spread than Moxie, the family Maltese, who sits at a chair by the table resting on her hindquarters, waiting to be served like any other hungry diner.

Our opulent meal is paired with a film: the Bollywood sports drama *Lagaan*, a winning anti-colonialist fantasy in which a group of villagers resists white supremacy by playing cricket. Clint says he selected the movie, despite its three-and-a-half-hour runtime, because it features everything that makes popular Indian cinema so special. "It's quintessential Bollywood," he says. "They've got the songs, the girls-versus-boys dance, the evil British people. Aamir Khan is awesome, and he's got the muscles. It's really great."

The plot is strikingly similar to the 2022 Telugu-language box office smash *RRR*, a violent revenge fantasy à la American grindhouse maestro Quentin Tarantino wherein two revolutionaries stage a revolt against the British Empire. Clint disliked the garish jingoism and CGI tiger punching of *RRR*, preferring instead *Lagaan*'s equally far-fetched liberalism. "It's not realistic in any way," he says of the latter film. "They'd *never* let an untouchable on the team. They'd never *touch* an untouchable! It's a caste system! That was kind of dumb, but it's a nice thought."

This seemingly straightforward evening—a father and son sharing a meal and sitting down together to enjoy a film they both love—would have been unthinkable prior to Clint's medical transition. Back then, he was struggling to just make it through the day. He received top surgery at sixteen, a rare occurrence for transgender youth who haven't yet reached the age of legal adulthood. While much legislation seeking to restrict transgender youth health care focuses on what opponents of LGBTQIA+ rights claim are "irreversible" surgeries, these types of operations are only performed in exceptional instances where a minor's well-being is deemed at severe risk unless they receive medical treatment.[1]

Before he was able to get the surgery that helped him become the wily kid he is today, Clint was one of those emergency cases. He needed help he didn't know how to ask for; a ghost in discount Wrangler jeans, he would only talk to people if they initiated, never going out of his way to make a new acquaintance or let someone in. Clint had a few friends, but he would never hang out with them outside of class. Instead he would bound directly up the stairs to his bedroom after school each day to avoid being seen by others, his best attempt at disappearing completely. Like a preteen cat, he would stay in his room for hours upon hours at a time, only coming down to grab something quick to eat before retreating to his void.

Clint's formerly antisocial tendencies were rooted in his severe discomfort with the size of his chest, which he attempted to conceal by wearing compression binders intended to flatten what he perceived to be a feminine shape. When worn correctly and fitted appropriately, these Spandex and nylon garments are considered a safe means of alleviating the gender dysphoria that some transgender people experience around their figure, but Clint neglected to follow proper procedure because he was so worried about his appearance.[2] He began wearing binders in the eighth grade and would squeeze his body into two at the same time, despite strong caution against doubling up.[3]

The intense pressure on his ribs left him with purple and green bruises on those long days where he would have no opportunity to take the binders off—such as during weekend hiking trips with his father—or when he would ignore prohibitions against binding while exercising. "I was doing track with a binder on," he tells me while we pause the film for bathroom breaks and chai refills. "It was like being swaddled in Saran Wrap. Because of binding the wrong way, I'd get random shocks of pain." He hid in his room so much because it was the only place he felt safe, where he didn't have to worry about others' perceptions of his physical form.

In high school, Clint finally got a single binder that was properly sized for his short, spindly frame, and while he no longer had to structure his day around when he could at last unbind, the lack of physical discomfort didn't address a much bigger problem: He still couldn't be the boy he wanted to be.

Clint had always wished to try out for the men's swim team at school, and he couldn't do that with a binder on, which felt in the pool as if he were wearing a sheath of armor. Even a well-fitted binder meant that going kayaking or running up a hill was out of the question, making it a strain to participate in the routine activities of a family that spends so much time outdoors. Joe drives around with a canoe in the back of his SUV, and walking into his modest two-story home means navigating a faintly pungent palisade of hiking boots and Converse sneakers. In the living room is a map of all the states they've visited, each distinguished by its own commemorative magnet: a red hot chili pepper for New Mexico, a portrait of Tupelo native Elvis Presley for Mississippi, an orphaned sandal drifting off into the ocean near the coast of New Jersey. They've visited every national park in the continental United States save for two: Isle Royale on Lake Superior and the Dry Tortugas in the Gulf of Mexico.

But Clint was fortunate in being able to make his dreams reality: He doesn't live in a state that has made it illegal to live his life in accordance with his gender. As of April 2023, Illinois is one of twenty-two US states with comprehensive civil rights laws fully prohibiting discrimination on the basis of LGBTQIA+ identity,[4] and in January, Governor J. B. Pritzker (D) signed legislation to protect necessary health care for transgender youth.[5] Under the new law, Illinois courts will not be required to comply with subpoena requests from jurisdictions that attempt to punish transgender minors and their parents for traveling out of state to seek gender-affirming medicine.

With no legal barriers in place, Clint's medical team at Lurie Children's Hospital of Chicago, one of the nation's top pediatric care centers, felt that he was a strong candidate for top surgery due to his difficulties with binding, as well as the positive impacts that hormone replacement therapy had exhibited on his mental health. He received his first shot of testosterone at Lurie's when he was fifteen, requesting that the theme music from the underdog boxing drama *Rocky* play as the doctor adminis-tered the medication. Only one of his parents could be in the room, so Joe filmed the moment—Clint climbing the stairs of self-actualization—for posterity while Maha waited in the lobby.

Getting officially cleared for top surgery, even considering the demon-strated need, was a taxing, tiresome process that included at least a dozen trips back and forth to Chicago—an hour's drive each way—to meet with surgeons and other assorted medical professionals. It took a year's worth of appointments with a therapist to get the formal diagnosis of gender dysphoria that would clear Clint for surgery. And even after that, he still needed to meet with Lurie's own in-house psychiatrist for evaluation. "It was a whole thing because scheduling with Lurie's, just trying to call them, was a nightmare," the boy says. "It took a while to even get them to call my insurance, and then I had to be on testosterone for six more months."

The night before he was scheduled to undergo the procedure, at long last, Clint was so nervous that it wouldn't actually happen that he had to tranquilize himself with melatonin to fall asleep, terrified there would be yet another hurdle at the last minute. But fortunately, any fears of disap-pointment proved unfounded: The operation was such an unmitigated success that he individually thanked each nurse after it was over. "You guys are so nice!" he said, slurring through anesthetic somnolence. "I love you." He fell asleep in the car and slept the rest of the day—but not before his parents recorded a video in which he adamantly denied that he was high on post-surgery medication. "I'm not on drugs!" he squealed into John's iPhone camera.

It's been over a year since his top surgery, and Joe says that the brash, outspoken boy that Clint is today barely resembles the shy kid that he was just a few years ago, the child who was afraid to live, hiding away under layers of hooded sweatshirts. After the operation, his father was struck by how newly comfortable Clint seemed with himself and his body, ripping off his shirt at any potential opportunity. "You ask him to cut the grass?" Joe says. "He's taking off his shirt. It's getting hot outside and you're walking Moxie? Pulls the shirt off."

Clint had to wait for an entire year after the operation before he was allowed back in the pool, but right in time for his senior year, he was finally able to join the men's swim team at school. When his body sliced through the water's surface, Clint felt free of his prior barriers—finally able to do what he'd wanted for so long. After everything he's been through, he hasn't thought much about telling the other boys on his team about his gender, deeming the gesture beside the point. "If I told them that I was trans, I don't think any of them would care," he says. "I know that they would have been understanding, but it's just something I didn't want to have to deal with."

Being stealth, to Clint, means preserving that endorphin rush of freedom: a liberation from others' expectations or their opinions about the choices that have made him the happiest he's ever been. He describes this year as the best of his life so far, and it also happens to be the year that he's had to think about being transgender the least. "Sometimes I forget that there was ever a time that I wasn't like this," he says. "It's hard for me to go back and think about when I was still binding because this feels right. This feels like the way it always should have been."

If he doesn't talk about being transgender much and doesn't make it a point to tell other people, it's because he doesn't want to be reminded of how hard it was to get here, to a place where he no longer has to confront his own body on a daily basis. Obsessing over his gender would make him dysphoric, sacrificing the many labors it took to reach this dreamlike idyll where he can just be. "I'm happy that I've had this journey," he says, hesitating before confessing something he hopes isn't received in bad faith. "It's really taught me a lot about being human, but if I had a magic button and I could be cis, obviously, I would take that."

I fall asleep three-quarters of the way through our screening of *Lagaan*, which stretches well past midnight due to its absolutely excruciating length. The film ends as one would expect: with the defeat of British imperialism and an epic dance number in the rain, the torrential ecstasy especially sweet after a prolonged drought threatened the village's crops. It occurs to me that the scene must resonate with Clint, who spent years wandering the desert, isolated from even himself, until the rain came.

Earlier in the day, Clint had told me that once, on a kayaking trip with his father, he saw a school of peach blossom jellyfish, an invasive species from China with bodies the size of a quarter. In those waters, the sighting was exceptionally rare: Peach blossom jellyfish attach themselves to the bottom of the lake for years on end, only swimming to the surface to mate, but that day Clint saw hundreds of them in bloom. "You could be going to that lake for forty years and never see the jellyfish there," he says, the satisfaction glowing from his cheeks. Some things in life, he has since realized, are worth waiting for.

III. SALAM ALAYKUM

For Muslims, the coming Eid is a time for communal joy: the anxiously awaited end of a month's worth of spiritual prudence, with the aim of cleansing the mind and body in order to reflect on what is most important in life. On the day of Eid, many mosques around the country host carnivals with pop-up henna tattoo parlors, dunk tanks, inflatable bounce houses, and even theme park rides, although the thrills tend to be limited due to liability concerns. If there is a Ferris wheel on the grounds, it's rarely much taller than a lanky barn.

The decorations in Maha's home, a statuesque tan brick McMansion with a rear patio overlooking a vast golf course, reflect that same air of makeshift celebration. Bespangled by the light of a two-story cathedral window, a gold party store banner displayed over the living room fireplace reads "Ramadan Mubarak" in anglicized Arabic, a literal congratulations for a successful month of hunger. Underneath the banner are this year's Eid baskets in green paper bags, each curated with a sensible eye: soup and chai for Hud, who is always forgetting to feed himself; bergamot-scented soap for Idris, who works up a sweat at his day job as a paramedic and firefighter; and a gift card for Clint, who will need to furnish his dorm when he goes off to college.

Baskets are not a traditional component of Eid, during which adult relatives customarily give money to children, a convention that Maha compares to the red envelopes handed out on Chinese New Year. When she was growing up, Eid meant a day of driving from the home of one relative to another to be force-fed a punishing parade of custards; their sickly sweetness was only improved by the fact that a young Maha generally accumulated quite the stack of cash by Eid's end. But when she had her own kids, Maha was insistent upon creating traditions they could all enjoy, rather than reliving memories of smiling politely as the grownups around her engaged in the same dull conversations they did every year. When Clint and his brothers were younger, she would let them have virtually anything they wanted on Eid, whether it was patronizing the Muslim-owned halal KFC restaurant after worship service or going out for ice cream. "Hud always got the SpongeBob ice cream that looked so distorted," she tells me, referencing the frozen dessert's misshapen oblong teeth and beady gumball eyes.

Maha's heterodox approach to Eid resulted in her pilfering choice elements from other religious traditions, such as the not-Easter baskets that have since become a staple of the family's annual gathering. When the kids were little, their baskets would be filled with gifts to keep them busy on the family's frequent and protracted car trips: coloring books, crossword puzzles, blank tic-tac-toe sheets. A big hit among the group was the Wooly Willy game, in which the player uses magnetic shavings to sketch eyebrows and facial hair on a cheerful cartoon man whose face is completely bare aside from, for undeclared reasons, a bulbous red clown nose.

Although Maha remains a devout Muslim, her divorce from Joe has allowed her to luxuriate in the guilty pleasure of Christian holidays: After moving into her own apartment for the first time in her adult life, she bought herself a Christmas tree. When she was in elementary school, Maha wanted to celebrate Christmas so badly that one year, sick of hearing her friends extol the virtues of gingerbread cookies, she took matters into her own hands. "I got up on Christmas morning, and I strung popcorn on a piece of thread using my mom's sewing needle," she says as she rests on the couch, relaxing into her reminiscence. "I put it around this plant that wasn't even real in our living room. I took my dad's cologne from his bathroom and wrapped it up, and when they woke up, I said, 'Merry Christmas!'"

For Maha, bucking convention isn't just about sidestepping the unique traumas of her youth but also claiming her religion for herself—owning that she still has the right to call herself a Muslim even though her life hasn't taken the traditional path that her parents planned for her. After her family immigrated from Pakistan in the seventies, her father became the director of Houston's first-ever mosque, a major hub for what has since become the largest Muslim diaspora in the South. Maha being his only daughter meant all eyes were on her from a young age; her parents controlled what she wore, how she cut her hair, who she was friends with, and whom she dated. She estimates that her parents invited to their home a minimum of forty suitors—including a distant cousin—on stilted dates where she would pour them tea to prove what a docile wife she would be. It was a sham pageant that they all knew, deep down, was destined to end in tragedy.

"Since I was six or seven years old, my parents always told me that I was making bad choices: 'God doesn't like the way you're dressed. God doesn't like the way you put that makeup on,'" Maha says. "Since I went through my separation seven years ago, it has been about trying to relearn how to love me. It's about accepting that God loves me. That is a foreign concept to me right now."

Following her divorce, Maha would learn that she wasn't the only person who worried that her life didn't measure up to the immovable standards of everlasting judgment. After Clint came out to her as transgender, she joined the online support group Desi Rainbow, which hosts workshops and discussions for LGBTQIA+ South Asians and their families. Some parents in those meetings said they felt as if they were breaking under the weight of an assignment for which they were unprepared, desperately wanting to affirm and support their children but not knowing the right thing to do or what to say to relatives and friends. In a recent meeting, a seemingly put-together couple with a transgender nine-year-old broke down in tears as they confessed how horribly alone they felt; they were profoundly terrified of what they believed the world has in store for a child who never asked for the untold burdens they will be forced to bear. "We cry on each other's shoulders," they told the group. "The rug's been pulled out from under us. We don't know if it's going to get worse, and we're just scared of something bad happening. In front of our child, we may look like we have it together, but inside, it's tearing us to pieces."

Three years after her initial meeting, Maha is now a facilitator with Desi Rainbow, and she's become such a fixture of the organization that many of the young people refer to her as "auntie," a term of respect for one's elders that is typically used in an affectionate, even playful, way in Pakistani culture. The first time she led a discussion, she says the kids were shocked to see a parent present; too many had been conditioned to expect heartbreak from the adults in their lives. "Most of the ones that come to the LGBTQIA+ group are ones that don't have that support from their families," Maha says. "It gets very emotional. There's a lot of tears. I do my best to motivate them, to love them, and to tell them how amazing they are."

Desi Rainbow holds a virtual Eid celebration every year for those without family to share it with, although they usually draw low attendance due to the near-impossibility of scheduling a single time that works for a regionally disparate bunch. For the few who do partake in this year's reflection, Maha plans to present a tutorial in creating your own Eid decorations, thereby hoping to show others that they can make the holiday what they want it to be, that they can be Muslim on their own terms. Not every Muslim shares Maha's singular grief over Eid, and members of the group could have an entirely positive relationship with the holiday, just as many of the 1.9 billion faithful around the world do. But for those who may be mourning their own private sorrows or do not have the privilege of celebrating with their families of origin, having that space is critical.

Although Maha still has her own personal struggles with Eid, they do not stem from internal conflict over Clint's identity—as she has embraced him as her son since the moment she opened that climactic faux baby shower card. She keeps the card on a desk in her study, and inside its front cover, Clint's handwriting reads, "I hope your [sic] OK with this because I know you always wanted a girl, but that's just not who I am." The implication took her aback, she says, because any residual attachment to having a daughter was immaterial; what mattered most was that her child was happy and healthy, especially after a difficult pregnancy that resulted in her hospitalization. Being pregnant with Clint was completely different from how it had been with her other boys: She could barely eat without vomiting her food back up, and she would dream at night of sleepwalking around her home, only to find herself in the kitchen when she awoke. "I was always in a different plane, a different level between Earth and something else," she says.

Fortunately, Clint was born in fine physical condition, weighing in at a typical seven pounds, and when Maha held him in her arms, the first thing she told him was: "Salam alaykum, I love you. You're here to make the earth a better place." She wanted for her child what every parent wants: to see him happy and thriving, reaching for his goals and aspirations without letting fear hold him back, and making the most of a life that is simultaneously very long and much too short.

Maha says she learned a lot about raising children from her relationship with her own parents, which she functionally ended three years ago. She did so by letter, the gravity of which makes her gently quiver as she reads it aloud to me. She hasn't perused these words in years, and she is suddenly living those old betrayals all over again, among them her parents' rejection of her soon-to-be-fiancé, Keith, whom she met on the dating website Match.com shortly after her divorce. Keith was raised Jewish but converted to Christianity as an adult after being baptized in a pond, and her parents outright refused to meet this Jesus-worshipper who was dating their daughter. "We're all hurt," she reads, gripping the four pieces of paper tightly in her fingertips as if the loops of cursive might fly away. "I'm hurt. We're all tired. I'm very tired. I've had to force my boundaries with you all because the truth is, you don't get to tell me whom I can love, how to raise my kids, where I can go, and what my beliefs are on a personal level."

Before writing the letter, Maha had visited her father and begged him to accept her relationship, lying recumbent at his feet as she asked for his forgiveness or merely to demonstrate even the faintest flicker of paternal compassion. Even as Maha's mother pleaded with him repeatedly to hold his daughter, her father had walked away from her, leaving her to sob on the floor.

What Maha is still learning, even now, is that there is nothing for which she needs to apologize: She has a wonderful life with a kind man who cooks for her every evening and children who bring her incredible happiness. She loves the person that Clint has become since that day in the hospital where she first wrapped his tiny body in her own, the gifted artist whose portraits of wheat fields so impressed his middle school teachers that they called her personally to deliver their adulation, the wise philosopher who teaches her as much as she does him. She says her youngest son reminds her of a poem from the early twentieth-century Lebanese-American writer Khalil Gibran: "You are the bows from which your children as living arrows are sent forth."

"As a mom, I don't want to have control over every little aspect of my children's future," she tells me. "It would make my relationship with my kids miserable. You don't get to plan for them. They're from you, but they're not you. If I did what my parents did, that would destroy me as a person. I would never be happy. I can't imagine doing that."

Even as Maha remains resolute in her decision to sever any semblance of a relationship with her parents, she is slowly coming to accept that her children have not made the same choice. She has come to appreciate, for instance, that her parents are making an effort with Clint, that they are working to extend to him the unconditional love that Maha so rarely saw when she was a teenager.

Back when Maha originally told her parents that the child they thought was their granddaughter had never been so, they didn't initially understand—due, in part, to the multitude of terminological nuances lost in translation. Maha didn't know the correct words in Urdu to explain the feelings that Clint had experienced all his life, and as she fumbled through her improvised Trans 101 presentation, her parents mistakenly assumed that he was just sick and needed to go to the doctor. But then her father sat up straight with his eyes wide, suddenly grasping what he was being told. "We need to fix this," he repeated to himself. When Clint underwent top surgery at the hospital, Maha's mother called Joe's cell phone over and over in a desperate attempt to talk them out of it, to convince them that Clint was still too immature to fully recognize what a big decision he was making.

But things have changed now that her parents, who are in their eighties, are rapidly growing older and have come to recognize how few opportunities they have left for recompense. Now that they've moved away from Texas to be closer to their grandchildren, Clint sometimes goes over to their house after school to pray or read the Quran. When he was younger, his grandparents would give him ten dollars for every book he was able to read in the original Arabic, which would have been a solid rate if he were more fluent. After years of tension and hard discussions, they now use the masculine Muslim name Clint chose for himself upon beginning his transition—or at least they try to. When Maha's father inevitably slips up, which happens almost every time, his family members firmly correct him in unison: "Yusuf!"

Years into their estrangement, Maha isn't yet at the point where she's ready for amends of her own, but on the night before Eid, she decides to return one of the numerous voicemails her mother has left on her answering machine. Maha had hoped her mother wouldn't actually answer the phone, fearing that she would scream at her or commence with the usual accusations, but their brief conversation is cold and calculatedly civil, each of them trying their best not to say what's actually on their minds. "I just want to thank you for being so respectful and for accepting Yusuf," Maha tells her, sitting up in her bed as she pauses her evening turndown routine. "You use the right name and the pronouns. That means so much." Her mother responds that Clint is a "good boy," before illustrating that bad habits are not easily broken by slipping in one implicit comment about Maha's personal life: "I really hope that you find the right path."

When she was in high school, this was around the time of day that Maha's mother would be spreading sugar and lemon juice on her daughter's arms to darken her henna tattoos for Eid; the girl would stay awake all night with her hand on a pillow to make sure the design didn't smear. There's too much history for the two women to ever share such tenderness again, but as they say polite goodbyes, Maha is glad they can agree on one thing: Her son *is* a good boy.

iv. **BLINDING LIGHT**

The mosque on Eid morning has the feel of a rock concert but with even less parking. The limited number of spots in its humble lot go to the truly devout and those fortunate to share the congregation's same zip code. Although it's not formally included in the Quran, the apparent punishment for latecomers and the less geographically blessed is being forced to park on the adjacent street and hike to the mosque, leading droves of unimpressed children behind. After trudging past the foot-washing stations, the delinquent parties are then shepherded into a low-ceilinged basement for the overflow prayer service. This is where we find ourselves during my second and final trip to the mosque, watching the imam's address from a trio of flatscreen television sets arranged like our own miniature jumbotrons—except that, in this case, the nosebleed seats aren't even in the same stadium as the headliner.

Our lateness is not the result of indifference but overbooking. This is Clint and Joe's second Eid service of the day after attending an 8:00 a.m. prayer with Maha's parents, who reasonably insist upon a bit more elbow room when proclaiming the name of Allah than the 10:00 a.m. crowd allows. Clint is wearing an emerald-green kaftan ordered online that his mother frantically hemmed when it arrived a foot too long. His bright ensemble blends well with the other men crowded around us: the worshipper whose coil of dark curls flow seamlessly into the wave of his electric-blue thobe, the father in a pink suit who clasps both of his arms with his hands as he stands for worship. Clint and Joe snap a selfie just as service begins, by which time every single foot of available space in the room is occupied by tardy congregants, many of whom save face by bringing their own mats with them.

The three of us are positioned toward the back of the basement—about twelve rows from the television sets—which means that we have missed out on both the implicit bragging rights of having a better view and the doctrinal bonus points awarded for being down front. Rewards are said to be given to those closest to the imam, thereby lauded as the most pious, but the exhortation does not specify as to whether watching him from a different room would lessen the extra credit.

Considering that the general vibe of Eid is similar to Thanksgiving, it's fitting that the imam's sermon concerns the necessity of thankfulness. As he switches back and forth between English and Arabic, he tells the faithful to "be happy, be joyous, share happiness, and share joy in your community." "This is the grace of Allah," he says, with the digitally flattened backdrop of a gray marble altar behind him. "Ramadan was a grace of Allah. The blessings that we have are from Allah." The imam proceeds to remind listeners to follow Muhammad's example by always believing the best in people, to see others for more than just their shortcomings and mistakes, and to focus on the positive. "Remember, all of us are going through challenges. All of us are broken. Ramadan was a means of healing for us. Many of us may not have been completely healed yet, and we are here for each other to ensure that we can guide ourselves and our communities along this process of healing people."

The simplicity of his message is a welcome change of pace from the earlier service at a more reactionary mosque preferred by Clint's grandparents. The imam, who is prone to fits of bloviating, had launched into a diatribe admonishing parishioners for spending too much time on their phones.

The celebration of this year's Eid is more loaded than most: Clint has openly admitted to his family that after he goes off to college, he's unlikely to fly all the way back to Illinois just for a single weekend. Because the start and end dates of Ramadan shift back two weeks each year, due to the gap between the Islamic lunar calendar and its Gregorian equivalent, he can't even be sure how the timing of Eid will line up with his school breaks. He also doesn't foresee himself pilgrimaging home for the Muslim holidays as an adult, meaning that this could be the last one he ever spends with his parents.

The slow-footed epiphany that she may never get to take another photo of all her sons together on Eid has been painful for Maha, who is already dealing with the leftover teen angst of feeling like an outsider in her own family. Although she is supportive of Clint's continued relationship with her parents and immensely grateful for the strides they've made, everyone—even her ex-husband—being together at the mosque without her has triggered in her an irresolvable longing. Maha is the one who made the decision to cut off contact with her parents, and she shares too much sour history with organized religion to ever go back to a mosque. A part of her, though, still yearns for the good memories that so often eluded her.

But despite her fears of time slipping away, Maha will find no shortage of souvenirs from this particular day to preserve for the family's historical records. After we weave our way out of the congested mosque—Joe leading Clint through the inching throng by guiding his shoulders, just like he did when his son was little—we drive to Maha's house to meet up with Idris and Hud. Today marks the first time since the divorce that the boys have simultaneously been home for the holiday and the first they have gotten to spend together with both Maha and Keith.

While their mere presence would be present enough for Maha, Clint one-ups his elder siblings with a special Eid care package for his mother, who has never received her own basket before. The focus has been always on Maha's children rather than herself, but grasping the symbolic import of his final Eid at home, Clint figured it was time for certain traditions to change. The evening before, Clint had stopped by a nearby grocery store to purchase a bouquet of red roses, gardenia-scented hand lotion, and Maha's favorite chocolates. She cries tears of shock at the basket's reveal, which Clint presents on behalf of the group. "Thank you," she says, hugging her boys one by one as they tell her how much they love her. "I'm so happy you all are here. I'm so proud of you."

The holiday unfolds as Eids so often have in the Ahern household, but this time unaccompanied by the ceremonial airing of grievances that sullied so many celebrations prior. There's the usual food and drink, but rather than the custard dirge of years past, the spread includes four boxes of pizza and—for the adults who imbibe—colossal wine glasses the size of softballs. Conversation throughout the day often turns to family lore, such as the time that Hud started his own religion in middle school, an adorably eccentric enterprise until the eponymous "Hudism" accidentally caught on among his classmates. Although its core tenets taught followers to be true to themselves and not go along with the crowd, some mixed signals resulted in other students continually standing up to bow to Hud during the middle of class. The frequent interruptions led administrators to shut down the upstart faith, but Hud's entrepreneurial spirit had some positive externalities: Clint's brother was so popular at school that after the boy transitioned, Hud told friends to watch out for his younger sibling, thereby preventing any bullying before it even started.

"The best family can do is just try to understand and accept, always be supportive," Hud tells me, fastening a wayward strand of shaggy hair behind his ear. "If you love someone, there shouldn't be any conditions attached. Clint has prepared me a lot for just dealing with people in general. That was an entirely foreign situation, but now I understand. I'm very blessed to be able to have experienced that in my own life."

Our merry band expands as the day goes on: first with Hud's loquacious ex-girlfriend, with whom he has remained close following their amicable split, and then Clint's best friend from school, Judy, an amateur paleontologist in whose eccentricities he immediately found a kindred spirit. They had first met in gym class, as he recounted earlier in the week, when Judy had approached him wearing a raccoon necklace and broke the ice by talking about collecting specimens. He would soon realize that he had found in her a funhouse mirror image of himself. "She's into all the weird things I'm into," he told me. "She likes niche country. She wants to run away and live in the woods."

Clint didn't initially come out to her because Judy talked about her brother being transgender so much that he assumed she already knew; he figured that she was demonstrating her allyship. Still, like with nearly all the relationships in his life, the delayed revelation changed almost nothing. The two are still platonic soulmates and now soon-to-be prom dates, as Clint surprises Judy upon her arrival at Eid with a promposal perfectly tailored to her taste for the outré. During one of his hikes, he had found a deer's thigh bone in a scorched prairie and taped its lightly crispy remains to a poster board that reads: "Throw Me a Bone by Going to Prom with Me?" She accepts with a squeal, just in time for the commencement of Ahern family karaoke.

The group crowds into Maha's scrupulously furnished basement—with its foosball table and indoor putting green—for the opening number: "Only the Lonely," the Motels' new-wave reimagining of Roy Orbison's classic rockabilly torch song. Several wine glasses in, Maha hits most of the notes while cavorting in a blonde Halloween store shake wig, but the hairpiece proves not long for this number; she rips it off and begins swinging it around during the song's anthemically mournful chorus. Clint, the biggest supporter of her inebriated musical ambitions, yells "Yass, vibrato!" as the oscillating wig glows gold in the disco lights.

The evening's set list includes a Clint and Judy duet of the Johnny Cash outlaw country landmark "Folsom Prison Blues," an all-hands rendition of Train's metaphysical mad lib "Drops of Jupiter," and Keith nasally singing the kiss-off ballad "Like a Rolling Stone" as if he were an off-duty caricature artist, although Bob Dylan's croaky vocals surely invite such parody. Idris, the family's most reserved member, is the only partygoer not to participate, but he does indulge in some good-natured brotherly hazing by grabbing Clint's leg and attempting to brand it with permanent marker. "I don't want anything written on it!" Clint yells, jerking away his limb before it's inscribed.

The evening ends with a series of drowsy adieus as Hud and Idris, holding their mother close, promise that Clint's impending absence doesn't mean they won't join to butcher more pop standards on future Eids. Despite the odds stacked against it, this emotionally perilous day has turned out so well that the family is already plotting a sequel but with a slightly different principal cast. A few days from now, Idris will propose to his longtime girlfriend, who couldn't make Eid proper but visited earlier in the week, and they will marry soon after in a small ceremony.

Things went fine, just as they are always ultimately fine, because what's most important is not entrenched disagreements or old hurts but that their family loves each other the most, past the religious and even political differences that might otherwise divide them. Keith, who is slowly making plans to marry Maha, is the household's sole Republican, but he has been supportive of Clint's gender journey since the day that he came out, seeing how much happier Clint was when he was able to be himself. "He knew exactly what he wanted," Keith told me earlier in the week as we ate Chinese takeout in Maha's kitchen. "I had not one inkling of thinking that top surgery was not the right thing for him. What I respect the most is his understanding of himself. He makes his own decisions, and he's very independent."

All Clint wants, really, is to continue having the freedom to maintain that maverick spirit: to be the kid who watches deep sea documentaries in his free time, loves trivia about ancient Egypt, and can effuse endlessly about trees. He sometimes thinks about a gaffe from former Utah senator Mitt Romney (R) during his 2012 presidential run, wherein he praised

Michigan trees as the "right height."[6] Although the remarks baffled journalists at the time, Clint knows what he means. "Trees are different in different places," the boy asserts. "Illinois trees look like Illinois trees. I drive six hours, and it's a huge difference."

Sitting on his mother's patio the day after Eid, I ask Clint if he has a favorite tree, and after chiding the line of inquiry as a "loaded question," he recalls seeing a twisted, gray shrub during a trip to Biscayne Bay in Florida. The ancient tree was short and wrinkly, measuring about six or seven feet in height, and it had been destroyed in its attempt to weather the passage of time. "The way the world looks must have been so different when that tree was there," Clint had thought to himself. "The park that I was in, the glaciers must have been just so much more dramatic. The animals that were around there, the native people, we'll never know what it exactly looked like."

Despite his participation in this book, Clint hasn't changed his mind regarding his relationship to transness, still believing that his independence means some necessary distancing from his identity. At a recent HRC dinner, Clint told Maha something he'd never let himself express— that he was grateful for everything she had done for him and for other kids like him—but as significant as that milestone was, he has remained unmoved. Preferring to walk alone, to find his own way through the wilderness, he still doesn't identify with her need to find a community who understands and shares her experiences. He doesn't need to be loud and proud when he already knows that Allah is so much bigger than all this: The Muslim divinity is not depicted as either male or female in the Quran, thought instead to have no gender at all. "When I think about God, it's just a blinding light," Clint says. "It's not a dude in the skies. God's not a man. We don't have depictions of gods or prophets, so every painting you see of Muhammad is just a cloud."

As my time with Clint draws to a close, I am left wondering why someone so resolute in his own solitude would agree to spend the end of his high school journey documenting his story with a journalist. Prom is in two weeks and graduation not long after, and I am occupying valuable real estate in his young life by keeping him from the classmates he may only see after this on social media, not to mention the best friend who he has yet to convince to attend his same chosen college. As a pair of birds squabble somewhere in the unseen distance, he says that it was important for him to tell other kids his age that being transgender doesn't have to define them or be the most important part of their life, that it can be just one small aspect of the messiness that makes them human. He says that, after today, he never plans to engage in any form of LGBTQIA+ advocacy ever again.

"Being trans is not a part of my identity," he says. "My Muslim friends, that's a group where I talk about things that culturally nobody else understands. I feel like that's a bigger part of my personality. Really, I'm just some boring dude with not a lot going on. I hope people think, 'I wasted my life reading this chapter.'"

AUGIE AND JACK

PENSACOLA, FLORIDA

MAY 2023

I. SOMETHING INHUMAN

Today is Jack and Augie Holliday's second day in their new apartment, and absent a couch, they squat together on a purple suitcase in the mostly empty living room, alternating turns resting their heads on each other's shoulders. Taking a hiatus from an afternoon's worth of heaving boxes up a perilously narrow flight of stairs, the two engage in a bit of good-natured sibling rivalry—their favorite pastime—by comparing their respective double-jointedness. Dressed in black military boots and a matching black t-shirt featuring a skeleton wearing a top hat, Jack shows off her ability to bend her pinky all the way back to her wrist. Augie, peering out from behind the split-level bangs of their sixties shag haircut, responds by twisting their foot all the way behind them; the move, though, is as much a testament to the ballet classes in which Augie was once enrolled as it is the uncanny mysteries of physiology.

Behind them during the demonstration is Van Helsing, a deceased betta fish named for the fictional monster hunter. Augie has been preserving the fish's remains in a mason jar filled with alcohol solution because they couldn't bear to bury him. "He's keeping his color well, but his eyes are gone," Jack says as she lifts the glass container, drolly remarking that Augie has been carrying the frilly little corpse around for weeks. "It's kind of creepy."

As their U-Haul's innards accumulate in the apartment, so do a series of random foodstuffs and objects indiscriminately scattered across the kitchen's faux-marble countertops—a miscellany of microwavable ramen, boxes of whole kernel corn, Gain detergent, and a skull ring gifted to Jack from a former coworker. Its previous owner claimed the heirloom was fused together from five hundred nickels, but the appraisal appears to be less than reliable: The same woman once boasted that she had shot her husband decades ago and that he had it coming. "She was a pathological liar, so . . ." Jack says, experiencing a delayed realization of the ring's sketchy provenance.

Jack's most prized possessions have yet to arrive: the tank holding her turtle, Franklin, and her twin buckets of DVDs, mainly consisting of entries from the Criterion Collection of art house movies. Her current favorite is 3 *Women*, an experimental film from the seventies that unfolds with the misty logic of a half-remembered dream. Jack likes the movie so much because she has no idea what it's about, so she comes away with a new theory each time.

The day's major focus is getting Jack and Augie's mattresses moved into their respective bedrooms, but their mutual laboring in the thick heat of Pensacola, Florida, is a reminder of all that has yet to be acquired. They still don't have towels, trash cans, shower curtains, ice trays, or even a bed for their mother, June, who slept the previous evening on a bed sheet spread across the carpeted floor. When June fires up a frozen veggie pizza for the hungry crew, she uses its flattened box as a tray and a bath towel as an oven mitt. Our feast is served on paper plates from the nearest Target store.

The family's lack is a byproduct of everything it took to get where they are now. They spent two months homeless and living in Airbnbs as June begged relatives, her college classmates, and even total strangers for enough money to house them. The displacement was extremely abrupt, following a blowout fight with her former boyfriend after June naïvely brought up the idea of buying Jack a car for her nineteenth birthday. The unexpectedly heated discussion ended in an argument over policies pushed by Florida governor Ron DeSantis (R) targeting transgender children, which was then followed by demands that June and her children vacate the premises. Overlooking the balance of negative six dollars in her checking account, June's ex offered to let her use his car—at the rate of seventy-five dollars a day—to find somewhere else to live.

June, a navy veteran, is finishing her master's degree in occupational therapy and couldn't afford the security deposit on a new place, so Jack paid it to ensure they weren't forced out onto the street. With the wages she had earned from working at the bargain retail stores Goodwill and Dollar General, Jack also rented their U-Haul and gave June money to buy groceries, but the still-escalating expenses have left Jack with little else to give. She has just three hundred dollars remaining in her savings, down from three thousand when they first became unhoused.

The financial and psychological stressors of homelessness have only added to Jack's ever-growing list of resentments, which are aimed at both her parents and the state where she has lived for most of her life. She is angry at June for poor decisions that she feels have contributed to their displacement and also feels increasingly trapped and alone in Florida, as lawmakers further intensify the Hollidays' already overwhelming problems. Just twenty-four hours after Jack is able to sleep in her own bed again, Governor DeSantis will sign a law that bans transgender minors from receiving treatments like hormone therapy and puberty suppressors from medical providers.[1] But the statute doesn't merely pertain to transgender youth, tacking on burdensome restrictions for adults seeking gender-affirming health care as well. It prohibits trans-affirming medications from being prescribed through telehealth appointments or by a nurse practitioner,[2] which is how the vast majority of transgender people in Florida get their prescriptions.[3]

The situation is sadly familiar for Jack, who already lost her health care once because of Florida's regulation. Although the state didn't revoke transition coverage through its Medicaid program until August 2022, a miscommunication with Jack's former medical provider—who no longer practices in Florida—led the Hollidays to believe that it had been banned well before that decision was officially made.[4] The last of Jack's estrogen ran out in November 2021, and she started seeing a gender-affirming medical provider again the following April, in time for her eighteenth birthday. Over those five months, she watched her femininity become something she no longer recognized, comparing the transformation in her flesh to the oeuvre of body-horror maestro David Cronenberg. "For me, it didn't feel like changing back into a man—it felt like turning into something inhuman," she tells me after learning the law is signed, upon getting an email from her telehealth provider explaining that they can no longer treat her.

During the time that she spent without estrogen, Jack barely left the dark of her room because she didn't want anyone to see her. The feeling was mutual: She didn't want to see herself, either. She says it took an intense willpower to wonder, "OK, what changed now?" when she woke up every morning and, in spite of her dark thoughts, still choose to get out of bed anyway. "You watch your body that you were so happy with deteriorate," she says, "and you don't know if it'll ever come back the same way." That period of her life has scarred her irreparably, and she worries for all the transgender kids who will suffer the same ordeal under Florida's new regulations.

Jack isn't out to anyone but close friends and family members she trusts, and when her medication was taken away from her, she began carrying around an electric razor for fear of her facial hair growing in; she, in particular, dreaded the sight of the frightful down sprouting from the edge of her chin. On HRT, Jack only had to shave once every three days to get by, but off it, she started timing when she would need to excuse herself to the bathroom. Terrified that a voice crack would unintentionally out her, she would take a drink before speaking to warm up her vocal cords. Jack was constantly second-guessing herself—afraid that she had missed something, that one slip-up could jeopardize the safe cocoon she had worked for years to build—and knowing that her own elected lawmakers were responsible for her torment only made it so much worse. "Like any teenager, you don't think people understand you," she says, "but it was taken to such an extreme, where the government doesn't understand you so much that they want you eradicated."

Jack knows that their new apartment should represent a fresh start, an opportunity to begin again in a place where she can finally decorate the walls the way she wants them—hanging posters of the cyberpunk anime *Ghost in the Shell* and *The Walking Dead* television series—but it's hard to feel much of anything. She spends most days on the dwelling's enclosed balcony dangling a cigarette as she stares vacantly into the expanse of the parking lot, wondering if the girl she was prior to her forced detransition will ever come back.

When she came out at fifteen, Jack took her first steps into womanhood by borrowing her mother's sale-rack bohemian threads—floral dresses, mesh crop tops, tattered jean shorts—before progressing to her now-trademark monochromatic wardrobe. Jack's only item of clothing that isn't solid black is a sweater covered in cartoon demons, which she finally surrendered to Augie because she had rarely ever worn it. While Jack saw a distinct utility in wearing one color all the time, the goth metamorphosis was also inspired by fictional characters she admired: the chain-smoking Marla Singer of the misunderstood fascism parody *Fight Club*, the hacking avenger Lisbeth Salander of Stieg Larsson's Millennium novels, and other feminine outsiders whom she felt simultaneously projected confidence and a defiant unknowability. But behind the pop culture homage of her dyed black hair, labret piercing, and shaved eyebrows, a part of Jack is struggling with her identity; she wonders who she is after so much has been taken from her and who she will become now that she survived it.

What concerns her family is that Jack no longer dreams of the future the way she used to. She's hesitant to discuss her goals and ambitions—both professionally and personally—and her loved ones worry that she's lost sight of her life beyond the horizon of now. June is the family's inveterate idealist, constantly repeating *everything is going to be OK* to herself until her hands physically shake. Jack, on the other hand, can't muster up the energy to do more than just last another day. "I feel like too much optimism has plagued so much of my life," she tells me as the balcony's dutiful ceiling fan soundlessly whirls, curling a gale of smoke around us. "I'd just rather not think about a future or a past."

Jack and her best friend used to fantasize about running away together to Portland, Maine, where they would live in a lighthouse on the cliffs and stroll along rock beaches together with their arms linked. But if the past has taught her anything, Jack believes, it's that she can't rely on anyone but herself. She has strongly considered the possibility of disappearing altogether: changing her name, getting new bank cards, and cutting off all ties with family and friends, even those she holds dearest. It's been so long since she was happy, she says, that she almost doesn't remember what it was like. "I'm not cripplingly depressed all the time," she clarifies. "I'm just so disconnected from everything that I don't really care about anything."

Jack will spend the duration of my time in Florida searching for reasons to resume her regularly scheduled life, signs that the gravitational pull of possibility is something she can still feel. As much as she thinks she doesn't need other people, Jack will find glimpses of the renewal she seeks in someone who also knows what it's like to feel so alone that it seems like nothing could ever be different: her younger sibling, Augie.

A sixteen-year-old high school sophomore, Augie picked a tremendously unlucky time to come out as nonbinary. In February of this year, they told their mother in a Walmart parking lot, "I'm not a chick, but I'm not a dude, either," choosing the big box chain to unburden themselves because they'd seen other kids come out in parking lots on social media. The very same month, Florida's Boards of Medicine and Osteopathic Medicine pushed ahead with banning transgender care to all minors who receive gender-affirming treatment in the state, not just Medicaid recipients.[5] That decision effectively made Governor DeSantis's transgender health care law a moot point before it was ever signed, but he continued to up the ante anyway, in hopes of fueling his political aspirations. Just days after approving legislation limiting the public restrooms that transgender people are permitted to use and making it a misdemeanor for drag artists to perform in view of minors,[6] he will officially declare his long-expected bid for president.[7]

Because they can't always rely on the adults around them—whether their state's political leadership or those entrusted with their care—Jack and Augie have learned to lean on each other for support. Before they even had the words to describe their relationship to gender, they were each other's best allies. Jack would swap her monster trucks for Augie's Barbie dolls the moment their biological father—with whom they no longer have a real relationship—left the room. When Jack found a pair of plastic cockroaches on the sidewalk last year, she made them into earrings to give to Augie as a present, and Augie now wears them all the time.

The siblings love, quarrel, and tease like family, never afraid to weaponize an embarrassing anecdote to get a rise out of the other, such as the time that Jack says Augie "ripped the fattest fart" after drinking too much kombucha before seeing *The LEGO Batman Movie* in theaters. "You had to pick the quietest moment," Jack recalls of watching the animated meta-superhero comedy together. "Everyone knew it was you." Legs akimbo on their newly situated mattress, Augie explains that they were attempting to time the fart's release to a dramatic moment in the film but woefully miscalculated the big drop: "I thought something big was going to happen and then nothing happened."

Jack and Augie have braved so much turmoil together, both the comical variety and the kind they struggle to extricate from their minds. In addition to surviving homelessness and Jack's medical trauma, they spent the early years of their respective adolescences watching their biological father routinely hit their mother, a years-long torrent of terrors from which June is still healing. They have endured because of the special relationship that guided them through the bleakest of hours—having someone in the next room to play video games with, to hate the world with, to know that one person understands what they are feeling. During the months that Jack spent without her medication, it was Augie who kept their big sister from succumbing to the gloom, knowing that the world would be sadder and lonelier if they didn't have each other. "I would probably be a shell of a person," Augie says of a hypothetical life without Jack. "We go to each other and complain about how stupid this situation is. We can just be mad about it together, be broody and angry."

Jack comes very close to giving into sincerity, to confessing just how much it has meant to her to have someone who sees her for exactly who she is, but at the last second, a glint flitters across her eyes; she has chosen violence instead. She says, with a rare smile: "You'd be so boring without me."

II. **VACATION FROM HELL**

When June first moved her family from Georgia to Florida many years ago, she had hoped that the calm of the ocean waves and the soothing coarseness of the shore would heal her family. "I expected everything to be fixed," she tells me as she drives toward her new home with the window open, unable to afford the extravagance of air conditioning. "I expected to walk every day at the beach. The sand is refining. It would buff it all out, like sand does."

Pensacola—a resort town of 54,000 positioned at the furthest edge of the Panhandle, right along the Alabama border—often bills itself as America's first city, owing to its sixteenth-century colonization by Spanish explorers. June fell in love with Pensacola's white beaches and forever summers during an idyllic trip in her youth when she traveled to the area with her preacher father for a Southern Baptist convention. She couldn't believe that people actually *lived* here, which seemed as unreal to her as renting a condo on the moon. "Of course people live here," her father assured her with a smile. "When you grow up and you're a big girl, you can live here, too." When her marriage to Jack and Augie's father fell apart in spectacular fashion, she still had that idea in the back of her mind: that somewhere out there lay paradise, still waiting for her after all this time.

But to get to know the Hollidays is to see how little the sand has cleansed them, to witness the layers of grime through which they are still shifting. June tends to have trouble finding her own apartment, driving the wrong direction several times before a gentle prodding reminds her to simply follow the directions clearly laid out by Google Maps. Often, the only way she can navigate the streets of her city is if the route is gently narrated aloud by another passenger. June's lack of direction is a combination of both trauma and predisposition: By her own admission, she walks faster than she runs, failing to keep up with the pace of her own thoughts. Except for her delicate frame, everything about June is big, from her winding hair and planetary eyes to the colossal laugh that feels as if it were compensating for years of its absence. Even her highlighter-yellow compact car, with its faulty transmission grinding like rusted teeth, is loud.

Even just a few days into the trip, this car ride has been one of many accidental tours of Pensacola—which June says, in a standard tangent, translates to "long-haired people" in the language of the Indigenous tribe who settled the area. She confesses that moving to the city has only added to their legion of woes. June suffered from acute PTSD following her marriage, sleeping with the lights on in fear that her former husband would break in, and her need to find another partner for security led her to make a series of regrettable choices. Her most recent boyfriend, the one who eventually forced her into homelessness, barely spoke to June's children over the course of their relationship—to the point where Jack and Augie still don't know basic information about him, such as his favorite food. If Augie wanted to meet up with friends to go roller skating, June's boyfriend would make them deep scrub the kitchen or spot clean the entire house first, with the goal being to dissuade Augie from wanting to leave; they eventually stopped asking to go out at all. "It was really hard to say, *Goddammit, I got with another asshole*," June admits.

June describes the time they spent unhoused, moving from one Airbnb to another, as the "vacation from hell." In any other circumstance, the two-bedroom condominium that kept them off the street would have been an absolute dream: The walls were covered in seashells, anchors, and pictures of boats, as well as fishing gear that travelers could bring to the beach with them. But June and Jack clashed constantly in a confined space where they got little distance from one another, their screaming fights bleeding together into a single run-on squabble. They were barely getting by, in any sense of the term. June was forced to pick change out of the couch to afford the toll to take Augie to school, and she got very little sleep at night, waking up to check the locks of her Airbnb every few hours; she slept by the door for added security.

The Hollidays were able to relocate to a more spacious Airbnb rental—with the help of a generous discount from its proprietor—while awaiting an official apartment, but the tensions of that transitional period have lingered into the present. Jack, who is as restrained as June is wild, sits silently in the back seat as her mother goes in circles, and when we arrive at the apartment at last, Jack immediately retreats to the balcony. As she stands next to a sun-faded lawn gnome that the Hollidays have named "David," I presume that Jack's gloomy reserve is an aftershock of intense grief, that she is just a deeply sad girl who has been asked to mourn far too much. But the situation reveals itself to be more complex than mere sorrow allows: She isn't speaking because she and June have barely said a word to each other in weeks, because she's so eye-poppingly furious at everything right now but doesn't know where to aim those frustrations.

Jack, igniting her lighter's flame, tells me that she knows that her anger is unfair to June, but it can be easy to hate someone when you're so close to them, when you've seen the worst of them and they've seen the worst of you. That painful intimacy terrifies her even more than it infuriates her—because what if that person who knows everything about you, even the parts you try to hide, betrays or suddenly abandons you? "You can love a person and still be scared of them or scared of things they'll say or do or scared they'll leave," she says. "I love my mom, and she scares me. I love Augie, and I'm still scared for them. I love my friends, and there's always that fear that they'll find someone better or less complicated or someone that makes them happier."

When it comes to June, Jack worries that too much has happened to ever repair what has been broken: too many hurtful words exchanged, too many doors slammed, too many days they'd both like to forget. "When you take a bite out of a sandwich, you can't really put it back together again," she says. "For the soul, anyway, there's no healing that. There's no reparations that can be made. It's just going to be there."

Jack says that her whole life, she has felt like she can't really trust others; the people who were supposed to protect her from evil would turn out to be the evil from which she needed protecting. One of Jack's earliest memories is hearing her mother and father arguing downstairs after their daughter had been tucked in for the night, followed by the stinging arrow of June's scream. Her father came upstairs and got in bed with Jack, and because she had already spied enough violent tussles through the crack in her bedroom door to know the truth, she asked him plainly: "What did you do to Mom?" He told Jack, cryptically, that he had put her mother on the stove. "That's the only time I've ever been able to ask my dad something like that and he answered honestly," Jack tells me. "And then we sat in silence."

As she's grown older, Jack hasn't been shown many reasons to put her faith in humanity. She was forced to finish high school at home when administrators wouldn't allow her to use the girls' bathroom on campus, instead making her use the restroom in the guidance counselor's office. She couldn't attend prom and didn't participate in graduation, and the diploma she received in the mail had her deadname on it. There is so much in Jack's universe that she cannot control: the politicians hell-bent on legislating her out of existence, the ex who wouldn't tell his family that she was transgender, the former boss who laid her off when she couldn't make her scheduled shift because her family was looking for somewhere to live.

But from the chaos of a life in transition, there springs order, first slowly and then all at once. While the majority of their first week is spent with Jack splayed across the floor as she fights the wireless company about the non-operational router, clicking a retractable knife to pass the time, by the sixth day the apartment begins to resemble a home. A path now winds through the mound of occupational therapy books that had previously taken over the dining area, and a fruit bowl filled with apples, tomatoes, and pears has appeared on the stove. Yard-sale art decorates the walls, including a faux-impressionist depiction of the drowning of Ophelia, the tragic paramour of Shakespeare's *Hamlet*. A portrait of an old man with a pipe comes with what is, by Jack's own admission, a thoroughly confusing backstory: They dubbed the bearded gentleman "Earl" after their former neighbor, but its would-be namesake was actually named Ernie and they didn't really know him at all. "We never met him and then he died," Jack says.

As the week carves out its natural trajectory, the apartment blooms with charming decay from the private collection of June, who never met trash that she couldn't repurpose as custom luxury. Below the newly hung wooden signs reading "Grow Through What You Go Through" and "Our Home" is a kitchen candle that was once a bottle of sake in its former life. On the balcony is a convocation of corroded effects: a peeling green bench, a rusted metal shelf that looks like it was left out in the rain, a black filing cabinet that screeches when anyone tries to pull open its laggard drawers. Secondhand tchotchkes far outnumber the apartment's human residents, such as a ceramic cat with a pincushion derriere and the genetically improbable combination of a rabbit father and pig wife holding a felt bunny infant.

June believes these earnest touches are a sign that after years of wrong turns, of feeling lost in her own life, she's headed in the right direction at last. Even if those predictions are a tad premature, she's determined to will them into coming true. "Mom's back," she announces to her children, who are so dazed from a week of reacclimating that they barely even register her presence in the room. "She's feeling better."

Jack tells me that she knows that she's reached a new chapter of her life when the air feels different and everything suddenly has a new smell, the kind that comes from opening the windows and allowing the breeze to cleanse a musty house. Their situation may be imperfect, but Jack takes comfort in having her own space, somewhere to analyze the work of ponderous existential philosophers in relative peace. She has been reading *Fear and Trembling,* a foundational study of moral philosophy authored by the nineteenth-century Danish theologian Søren Kierkegaard; some scholars now believe the text was an attempt to work through Kierkegaard's then-recent uncoupling from his muse and fiancée, Regine Olsen. In Genesis, the Bible tells of God's demand that Abraham sacrifice his son, Isaac, a commandment that is then abandoned at the actual moment of bloodshed. If an all-knowing, all-powerful God personally wills such beastly acts—or, in its metatextual reading, allows Kierkegaard to have his heart broken—*Fear and Trembling* posits that believing in the heavenly divine requires a temporary suspension of ethics. God, he argues, must operate on an entirely different moral plane than the rest of us, one that we simply cannot understand.

While Jack is not a Christian, reading the thin volume as she lies in bed allows her to ponder a related set of questions: *What world is this that operates along such blurry ethical lines? How can this be what life is?* Unfortunately, Jack knows that she will never know why things happen as they do, why these are the burdens she was asked to carry, or why some people have so much when others are given so little. As we go for a rare walk around the apartment complex, Jack tells me that it feels like she's been asleep for two years and that she's only now starting to wake up. Her eyes readjusting to the light of the day, she doesn't know what happens now or whether there's anything out there for her. "I don't think we arrive on Earth with a purpose," she says. "I think that's silly. God isn't sitting you down and saying, 'You're going to be a contractor.'"

But despite her lack of belief, whether in the hereafter or humanity itself, there's a part of her that wants the faith Kierkegaard ultimately chooses for himself, even though he has every reason to abandon a God who stood idle while his heart was shattered. "I do not want to exist in a reality where nothing means anything and when you die there's no more thinking," Jack says. "But it doesn't matter what I want because it's going to happen either way. I don't get to decide, so I'm going to either be at peace with that or let it eat at me for the rest of my life."

III. **BLACK HOLE**

A procession of ants parades across our picnic table to drink from an inlet of splattered butterscotch coffee, a man-made reservoir that has regrettably claimed several of their compatriots. Adding to the panorama is a mystery island within the lake's syrupy surface that Augie decides must be either squirrel or cat vomit, but Augie appears unbothered; they instead gaze out into the counterfeit green of the dyed lake just beyond the apartment complex's gazebo. They've always had an admiration for bugs, Augie says, because they feel these tiny creatures are misjudged and unfairly maligned. "I always try to save the bugs in our house," Augie tells me. "It makes me feel like I have a sense of humanity. They're important to how everything works." Ants, for instance, help to enrich the earth's soil by creating tunnels in the dirt, and they aid in decomposition by feasting on rotting carcasses. Spiders are a particular favorite of theirs, Augie declares: "They help with getting rid of the bugs that you hate."

Augie's admiration for insects is grounded in a mutual understanding of powerlessness, what it feels like to be beholden to the whims of giants with the will to crush. Augie's parents split up when they were ten, and the early years of their upbringing were characterized by the hollow slap of their father striking their mother, heard through the wall of an adjacent room. Police failed to stop the periodic abuse, even as Augie says their home became known as the house that "always had the cops called on them," including twice on Augie's birthday. "My birthday is cursed," they say with the dry laughter of someone used to using dark humor as a coping mechanism. "My dog died a couple of days just before my birthday last year."

Although the children were never physically harmed by their father, the violence against their mother only escalated, culminating in permanent brain damage following an incident in which he repeatedly slammed June's head into the dirt. By the time June's subsequent partner forced them out of their home eight years later, Augie had come to expect that grown-ups would make them feel small and helpless, close to invisible.

What got Augie through the two months they spent homeless, through the relentless nightmares of their teeth falling out that kept them awake in their temporary bed, was being able to escape into cinema. They particularly like horror movies, which share their affinity with the chronically downtrodden. A preteen screening of the gonzo Stephen King adaptation *The Shining* led Augie to films like the *Evil Dead* franchise and *Bride of Re-Animator*, the latter a cult horror-comedy paying homage to both James Whale's *Frankenstein* adaptations and the cosmic dread of author H. P. Lovecraft. What Augie loves about these movies is their use of practical effects, that the over-the-top gore is created not through CGI shortcuts but pure ingenuity. Augie was disappointed, however, by a climactic cheese-grater attack in the *Evil Dead Rise*—the latest entry in the long-running zombie series—for not going far enough. "I'm so mad about that part because it was just on the leg, and it barely did anything," Augie laments, wishing for a more substantial desecration. "That's so boring."

Their obsession with horror movies is yet another reminder for Augie that their destiny is to one day leave home to pursue a career in makeup or special effects, whether that's in Hollywood or elsewhere. Growing up in Florida's conservative panhandle—the reddest part of an increasingly cherry-colored state—has often made Augie feel as if they are the monstrosity, a hunted beast being chased with torches and pitchforks.

This will be Augie's final year attending in-person school after June chose to pull them out due to merciless bullying from their peers, who frequently threw French fries and basketballs at them. The assaults began during middle school when classmates would taunt them with the body-shaming nickname "Bowling Ball" and dare their friends to ask out Augie on a date as a cruel joke. "I stopped looking at pictures of myself," they say. "I didn't want to see how repulsive I was." After they came to the realization of their nonbinary identity during the pandemic, the mistreatment was compounded by constant misgendering and dead-naming at school. They compare going to class to wading in an endless pool of tar: "You're in it, but you don't know how you got there and now you're suffocating. You're moving your body, but you can't feel it."

Augie is still struggling to find their voice in a household where it doesn't always feel like they have one; it seems as if there's no space in others' bereavement for what they think and feel. June often relies on Augie to be an ear as she processes the pain still stored inside her body, recounting stories of violent suffering that her youngest doesn't want to hear. When Augie tries to return the gesture by talking about what's going on with them, June tends to accidentally steamroll the conversation, listening without listening at all.

Though Augie knows that Jack is a thin bedroom wall away, the two can't always relate to each other's journey as transgender people, even being as intimately close as they are. Even before Jack came out, others tended to assume this feminine imp was the girl she just so happened to be, but for Augie, there's no widely understood template to be recognized as nonbinary, no way to "pass" as anything. Strangers instead just shove them into the closest box they have available: Whenever Augie goes to the grocery store with Jack, the checkout cashier will inevitably bid the duo goodbye with a congenial "Good night, ladies!" Last year, Augie became so exhausted with others' assumptions that one day they started hacking off clumps of hair, resulting in a tortured bob they describe as reminiscent of Ramona Flowers, the unattainable dream girl of the *Scott Pilgrim* graphic novels, but if she got her head caught in a lawnmower. "I regretted it so much because I really love my hair," Augie sighs.

Although there are nonbinary people who describe themselves as synchronously balancing masculinity and femininity, Augie views their own identity as not *both* but *neither*, embracing not gender's multiplicity but rather its absence altogether. They compare their gender to a black hole—a hungry nothingness that swallows whatever is in its reach—but also to the horror films that have shaped how they view the world. "I feel very connected gender-wise to horror, the aesthetic of it," they say. "I consume it and then it becomes a part of my identity."

Augie believes there's something inherently genderless about cinema's archetypal monsters, pointing out that the earliest film adaptation of Mary Shelley's *Frankenstein* never specifies whether the gender of the brain given to the doctor's creation is male or female. Instead, the jar of floating human remains is simply labeled as "abnormal." "Frankenstein's monster could be a girl—or nothing at all," they say. "It's a corpse. It doesn't care." Augie has always felt an affinity with zombies because they walk the earth totally irrespective of gender, focused solely on the interminate task of acquiring more brains. If zombie movies envision a post-apocalyptic hellscape in which society has collapsed and the undead now dine upon the weary living, Augie wonders: *What good is the gender binary in such a world, anyway?*

Augie comes home from school every day exhausted—tired of malevolent smiles in the hallways, tired of gender boxes they didn't create—and lies in bed until the sunlight melts away, less to recharge than to hide for a while. There is one place, however, where Augie feels like they can be their whole self without effort or explanation: the local haunted maze where they volunteered last Halloween, painting the faces of demonic clowns and mad doctors.

Working every Friday to Sunday at the haunt, a place where others respected them for what they had to offer, gave Augie the energy to outlast their school week. As one of just two makeup artists in the crew, Augie was tasked every shift with painting dozens of sunken cheekbones and tumescent veins in less than four hours, before guests arrived to have the wits scared out of them. Augie nearly had a panic attack the first time they went through the maze, but it was worth it to see their creations in action, the monsters squirting syringes of fake blood as they chased June around. For as wearying as it can be to envision a future when the past has been so relentlessly dire, Augie found at the haunt what they had needed for longer than they can remember: a band of outsiders finding camaraderie in the parts of themselves society taught them to scorn.

Their job won't start up again until September, but while they wait, Augie is trying to make the rest of their life just as marvelously macabre. That work begins with some feverish interior decorating: Since their move-in last week, Augie has been toiling at dressing the naked walls of their bedroom in a wide array of cultural mementos, such as a wrinkled poster from the live-action *Scooby-Doo* film and an archipelago of magazine clippings from a standalone issue of *Entertainment Weekly* devoted to the *Scream* slasher franchise. A vintage movie poster from the verbose nineties original has not fared so well. Now that Florida's soggy late spring air has peeled every scrap of tape off the walls, it swings back and forth, a single thumbtack keeping the laminate from falling to the ground.

Spread across Augie's bed is an enviable collection of unopened action figures, including Pennywise, the phantasmagoric clown of the television miniseries adaptation of Stephen King's *It*, and the titular Egyptian menace from the inaugural Boris Karloff version of *The Mummy*. The mummy figurine helpfully comes with a set of spare hands and two backup heads, one of which trades the plastic corpse's placid countenance for a whimsical O-face.

Augie still has a great deal left to sort through before their room is neatly settled, including the contents of an entire chest of drawers that, for the time being, is weighed down by their childhood book collection. Key titles include *Basic Witches, Frankenfrog, Hooray for Pig, The Foot Book,* and a copy of the puzzle book *Where's Waldo?* in which Augie—never one to leave a job half-done—has circled every appearance of the striped fugitive, severely limiting repeat enjoyment. "I couldn't help myself," Augie explains, their mouth askew with moderate embarrassment.

As a neurodivergent person, Augie expresses a particular affinity for Amelia Bedelia, the title character of a series of illustrated books in which an obtuse housekeeper misinterprets common American idioms to teach young children about the idiosyncrasies of language. For instance, when one of the protagonist's employers requests that she "draw the curtains," Amelia Bedelia understands the command literally, quickly sketching an illustration of the living room drapes. Augie says the books always felt like an unintentional reflection of the way in which autistic people navigate existence: with a slight remove from the way others experience it, a single step out of sync from the chorus line.

For Augie, finding joy in the mundanity of everyday life isn't just about sorting their most exalted belongings but also asserting their right to take up space, which they would be the first to admit is not one of their strong suits. When their classmates started teasing them for the way they talk, Augie simply stopped speaking. *What's the point of talking if people can't understand me in the first place?* they wondered to themselves. Even today, Augie's voice rarely rises above a tense hush, constrained by the threat of saying the wrong thing, of sounding foolish, of unintentionally confirming that they are the loser everyone at school believes them to be.

That's why Augie takes such pride in their ability to communicate nonverbally through makeup. They often stay up past midnight to experiment with designs that are neither masculine nor feminine but distinctly them: not somewhere in between but entirely outside of the bounds of gender's matrix. Augie's usual 1:00 a.m. looks—black lipstick, squiggles around the eyes—are inspired by their nonbinary idol, the glam rock god David Bowie, who embodied an ever-expanding menagerie of personae like his own private zodiac. "He didn't look like anyone else," Augie says. "He could just transform into anything." Once they live in a place where they feel safe enough to dress the way they want in public, Augie hopes to exude Bowie's commitment to shape-shifting: serving glitz and glitter one day and then the next looking like nothing human-kind has ever seen. "I want to keep people on their toes."

Augie would like to assert themself more, but they admit that what's holding them back is the obligation to be the family's emotional care-taker: the one who listens, the one who puts others' wants and desires before their own. Their days begin with making Jack and June coffee—just in time for their mother's regularly scheduled trauma dumps—and end with fixing everyone salmon pasta, stir-fry, or whatever happens to be in the cupboard. "My purpose is to take care of the people around me," Augie says in resignation, slumping forward into themselves. "I try to see what they need and then I'll give them what I'm capable of doing."

Acting as their family's support system doesn't leave Augie much room for their own healing, and they are only now realizing how much they have yet to process, how badly they need to be the one who is consoled, and how fervently they wish to be the baby of the bunch, not its most mature adult. Sometimes June will tell Augie how wise and perceptive they are for their age, but the truth is that they don't want to be. They would rather not have had to mature this quickly. They don't want to be a grownup yet; they just want to be.

IV. GREASEBALL

June doesn't have many happy days, but today is one of them. After two weeks of finding ways to fall asleep on the pink rose bed sheets laid out across her floor, she has a real bed. It comes with a pleasingly spongy gray living room couch and a set of incongruously crunchy feather pillows donated by the local Veterans Affairs (VA) office. June was touched that the movers, many of whom are also former military, thanked her for her service as they dropped off her new furniture. "Because you were a homeless veteran, we wanted to do this for you and your kids," one of the movers told her. She had almost forgotten that's why the helpers were there: She gave to her country, and now it was giving back to her.

June is used to making the best out of unenviable circumstances, but there's comfort in knowing where she'll sleep tonight, that she will no longer have to worry. She can lie in her own bed working on her watercolors—a medium she likes because it is forgiving to the untrained hand—as she steals sporadic glances at her newly arrived piano, which sits by the window with a ukulele perched on top of it.

After the movers are gone, June and I walk past the apartment complex's pool, where a group of women defy the heat by soaking their feet in the community hot tub, before settling on a picnic bench underneath a willow tree. She breathes more deeply today, as if until now she'd forgotten how, because she finally feels at ease. June can tell that her children are also feeling that internal quiet: Their house is filled with the sounds of hesitant laughter, Jack and Augie trading cackles as they chase each other around. They have begun having friends over, something the kids would have never done in the past. "We are speaking to each other more—actually speaking, having banter," June tells me. "I used to walk on eggshells around Jack a lot. I think she felt that way about me, too. We're both not feeling that as much anymore."

June is grateful for these past few days—watching Jack put her feet in Augie's face, Augie giggling as June playfully showers them in bug spray—because she was once so scared that her family would never get here. The fact that they did make it June attributes to the kindness of others—her father bought her the car she now drives so she wouldn't have to rent her ex's—but their persistence is also the result of obduracy. June had to beg a housing coordinator to get them set up with an apartment viewing, all but demanding a new home for her family. "I've got babies," June told the staffer, shuddering as she acts out the dialogue now. "They're big babies, but they're still babies, and they've been through a lot. I've had it with people that said they would help me and they lied. I need this. The kids need this."

The very next day, the leasing agent at their then-soon-to-be apartment complex drove her in a golf cart to see the property, walked her up the stairs, and put the keys right in her hand. "Mrs. Holliday, this apartment is yours," the woman said. The agent had to repeat the offer several times when June didn't understand what she was saying, so predisposed to bad news that she couldn't fathom having something to celebrate, that she might finally get an overdue win after years upon years of unceasing loss.

No longer in fight-or-flight mode, June wants to focus on being the mother her children need her to be, but that's a tough assignment in a state where she can't provide for them the full range of resources to help them thrive, where her children can only grow so high. They have yet to find an in-person doctor for Jack now that telehealth is no longer an option, and someday, when they're ready, August plans to have top surgery, just one step toward becoming the otherworldly being to which they aspire.

June knows how important it is to be able to take those next steps because she saw in Jack the vicious strain of losing control over her body, of being forced to be someone she wasn't. During the lowest moments of Jack's detransition, she would beg June to let her die, and she got so skinny that June worried every night that Jack's heart would stop in her sleep. June sat by her daughter's bedside, pleading with Jack to stay with her. At the time, she didn't have the resources to move her children away from Florida, but after June takes her licensure exam for occupational therapy in July, she intends to save up to take them somewhere new, so they can feel the love they lacked for so long. "It's not safe here," she says, her words so painful that uttering them makes her flinch. "They can't become adults here. There's no future for them here."

Because tomorrow is our last day together, June brought with her a special surprise to share: *My Brave Little Chicken*, a children's book she started writing after leaving Jack and Augie's father. Writing the story—of a mother and her two baby birds sheltering together as a storm overtakes their nest—was an outlet for her trauma, a way to channel her innermost fear that a single gust of wind could demolish what little they had left. "It all changed in that instant, that dark and sleepless night," she wrote, in a scheme that rhymes except when June's flash of thoughts don't fit with the established pattern. "Blinded by the darkness with no peace in sight. All we had was each other. There was a night full of storming, holding each other tightly, hoping for the morning."

June only finished writing the book this very week because, until recently, she wasn't sure how it would end, either for her characters or the humans they represent. Once she had seen the sun begin to rise upon her own life, June felt ready to give their chicken avatars a happy ending; before now, she wasn't sure she could promise one. "And then finally it was morning," she wrote. "As the clouds broke for the sun, morning finally arrived. We hugged each other tightly, without a scratch. We had survived."

The fictional version of their lives obscures the fact that there still remain so many unresolved subplots, chief among them ongoing concerns regarding money. June is currently unemployed, and Jack is working to get her old job back at the Goodwill where she once found a deceased raccoon in the donation box. But what makes this time different is the brittle hope they share, the grace they are extending to each other as they clear the debris together. Jack is still holding on to so much resentment toward her mother, who she feels put her previous relationships before caring for her children, and she finds it hard to believe June when she says that all she really wanted was to give her kids a normal family, a stable living situation, a good father. It would be easier for Jack if June were to admit that she did it all for herself, that she got into one bad romance after another because she was lonely. "I know she loves me," Jack tells me later that day over the melodious gurgle of Franklin's tank filter. "I know a lot of people in my life do, but it's hard for me to accept love. Most of the love I've experienced has been conditional, so it's hard to really know what that word even means."

Jack is thinking about love a lot these days—how many different ways there are to love, how difficult it is to describe—and she keeps returning to a moment from her childhood in which she told June that she loved her more than she did her father. June, tucking Jack into bed, responded with all the diplomacy she could muster: "No, you just love him in a different way."

While Jack sometimes wonders if love's infinity-mirror multiplicity inevitably leads to dilution—that love refracted so many times is no longer truly love—she is coming to terms with the fact that she doesn't have the words to describe the way that she cares for June. She hates her mother sometimes, they quarrel, and they yell, but they always seem to find each other again after the squall. Watching the apartment come together has renewed Jack's once-anemic faith in June, sparking a realization that she needs to be kinder to this woman who has been through so much, even when Jack doesn't wish to be pleasant. "The fact that she was able to pull this out of her ass so quickly, that is really a marvel in and of its own," she says. "She's always done that her whole life." Jack pauses to consider that perhaps the reason she and her indomitable mother clash the way they do is precisely because they are like repellent magnets—so identical they push each other away. "I think that's where I get it from."

We spend our last night in familiar fashion: watching the movies and playing the video games that Jack and Augie use to mark time in an apartment still without clocks. The evening's feature presentation is *Angel's Egg*, a Japanese animated film about a mute young woman who guards a mysterious egg as she wanders a post-apocalyptic cityscape. Jack has chosen the film as a parting pop quiz before I go: She wants us to watch the movie and guess what its director, Mamoru Oshii, intended to say in making this nearly silent, virtually plotless film, which lifts its surreal imagery from a farrago of Christian symbolism.

As the credits roll over our shared befuddlement, Jack says that *Angel's Egg* was inspired by its filmmaker's loss of his Christian faith. The movie ends with the girl weeping in spiritual resignation after her egg is destroyed, but not before a deus ex machina wherein a profusion of embryos sprout from the trees. Hers is a satisfying explication of a noto-riously arcane work, but unfortunately, a Google search reveals Jack's analysis to be an urban legend among cinephiles: Oshii has admitted that he doesn't know what the film actually means, borrowing from various biblical passages because he thought they sounded cool. If Jack is disap-pointed by this reveal, she doesn't show it; we quickly pivot to *Lollipop Chainsaw*, a candy-colored hack-and-slash game following a pigtailed teenage girl as she vanquishes a horde of zombies. The action begins with protagonist Juliet, a sunny cheerleader in thigh-high schoolgirl stockings, decapitating her boyfriend after he's turned.

Sitting on Jack's bed next to a pillow of the actor Nicolas Cage regifted from June, I watch Jack and Augie fall back into tried-and-true rhythms, tossing out insults at one another with glee. Augie remarks during *Angel's Egg* that they wish their hair flowed with the gravity-defying ease of the film's nameless lead, whose pale locks appear to have their own personal airstream. "Too bad you're such a greaseball," Jack snips. As they trade barbs, Augie retorts that baby Jack looked like the snake-like infant from David Lynch's surrealist midnight movie *Eraserhead*, and Jack, ever at the ready with a sly riposte, says that Augie "smells like Play-Doh."

The two say that they've always wanted to see a sibling dynamic like theirs depicted in movies or television shows, and they've never witnessed that kind of relationship represented before: showing one's affection through fond mockery. While comparing one's family member to a slimy mutant baby may not be recognized as an official love language, their unique bond reminds them to laugh their way through whatever darkness fate has in store. If life is a sick joke, they may as well be in on it. "I'm glad I bullied you into being cool," Jack tells Augie with a laugh. "I got to be really cringey first and then you got to see what is cringey and what isn't."

In her black pencil skirt and fishnet stockings, Jack looks the most at ease that I've seen her since I arrived: laughing without reserve, allowing herself the vulnerability she often holds back. For a twitter of a moment, one could be forgiven for forgetting that we're still in Florida, still in this place that taught Jack and Augie that no good would come out of living. Slowly, the Hollidays are learning to trust not only each other again but also the society they had given up on. When the movers dropped off their couch earlier that day, Jack asked June how they could afford to pay the VA back, not understanding that it was a stringless gift; all that is expected of them is to enjoy their new furnishings.

Jack and Augie are in the process of learning how to accept hospitality, and they aren't yet convinced that they need the help, thinking that some other family out there must have it worse. As they ask each other a series of "Would You Rather?"-style questions—debating, for one, whether it would be preferable to live through a zombie apocalypse or a nuclear holocaust—I start to see that perhaps they're right about something. Maybe they don't have it so bad after all.

KYLIE

TORRANCE, CALIFORNIA

JUNE 2023

I. ALL-AMERICAN GIRL

Kylie Yamamoto smooths her orange bangs in the muted reflection of her iPhone screen as she prepares to look her very best for the commencement of the Los Angeles Pride Parade. Kylie is right at the front, just behind the parade's grand marshal, the comedian Margaret Cho, who sits atop a convertible painted in rainbow stripes that fan out like overlapping sunbeams. Cho, holding a chihuahua in her left hand and a parasol in her right, is the object of much attention among marchers with PFLAG, the national support group for LGBTQIA+ people and their families. The most excited member of the contingent is a peppy person in a rainbow NASA t-shirt loudly advertising the actress's resume like an overzealous talent agent. "There's Margaret Cho!" they say, approaching one bystander after another to bring them the good news. "I used to have the *All-American Girl* box set!"

Kylie is accompanied at the head of the parade by her equally lively mother, Janet, who pushes her to partake in the excitement by showing the guest of honor her sign: "I'm CuTie," with its conspicuously capitalized "T" decorated in the colors of the Transgender Pride Flag. Janet has her own corresponding posterboard reading "I Heart My CuTie," a message she felt was more subtle than the comparatively obvious alternative of "I Love My Transgender Daughter." "If you see it, you get it," Janet remarks, adding with a smirk: "And if you don't, I don't care." Margaret Cho does appear to get it, flashing a flit of a smile before resuming conversation with a bearded chaperone in Daisy Dukes and a dangly beaded top resembling a chandelier.

The signs are famed staples of Yamamoto prides, although they have evolved slightly over the years. When Kylie was much younger and her parents weren't sure whether she was a gay boy who liked to wear sparkly dresses or if there was something more to it, the "T" was designed in the colors of the standard Pride flag—that way, Kylie would be represented no matter where she ended up on the LGBTQIA+ spectrum.

Today, Janet has also brought everyone silken leis woven together from ribbon; hers is glossy rainbow, while Kylie sports a pink-and-blue necklace over her newly acquired PFLAG t-shirt. Although Janet chooses not to change into the tee, preferring instead to wear the flowing red velvet poncho she came in, Kylie almost didn't get a shirt at all. A volunteer organizer informed Janet shortly after we arrived that marchers had been expected to line up at 9:00 a.m.—almost two hours ago—if they hoped to secure one in their size. Luckily, a woman who sympathized with their plight gave Kylie a leftover large from her contraband stash, over which Kylie immediately draped an unzipped black hooded sweatshirt.

Janet is a longtime member of the San Gabriel Valley chapter of PFLAG, one of the only branches with its own space for Asian-American and Pacific Islander families. She is also a dedicated advocate for transgender rights: Janet has spoken at numerous conferences across the country, appeared in educational films with her daughter, and visited the White House last year to represent affirming families of transgender children.

But as Kylie will tell me later, she felt out of place among kids whose lives had been irrevocably altered by legislative attacks on their rights and health care, feeling as if she had nothing meaningful to contribute to the conversation. After all, she lives in one of America's most progressive and LGBTQIA+ friendly states: California, which last year became the first in the United States to declare itself a sanctuary for transgender people seeking gender-affirming medical treatments.[1] It felt so strange standing next to children who could feasibly be forced to travel to her state for their health care needs and realize that, aside from some minor quibbles, her life is actually pretty fantastic. "I'm always put in the situation where I'm the person from *Cali-forn-yuhh,*" she says, practically belching her home state's final syllable. "I'm listening to them talk about their issues and I'm like, 'Things are great. I'm in a supportive city. I have good friends. I don't have laws being made to limit my life.'"

Kylie almost didn't come today, attempting to back out just as her mother beckoned her to get in the van. She had preferred to stay in her room and play the first-person shooter game *Overwatch* with her circle of closest confidants, whose specific form of virtual bonding is dying together over and over again. Like many seventeen-year-old girls, Kylie just wants to be where her friends are, checking out creamy boys at the beach and gossiping about their school's continuous realignment of interpersonal constellations: which friends are fighting, who is cheating on whom. She had expressed her displeasure at being forced to attend Pride by giving Janet her famous silent treatment, barely speaking during their hour-long car trip from Torrance, the South Bay enclave their family calls home.

Kylie doesn't know where she fits in with her mother's crowd, always with their clipboards, visors, and travel-size sunscreen at the ready. Around Kylie is so much energy and excitement that she doesn't quite share: from the Disney Pride in Concert gays doing side-to-side stretches as the Psychedelic Furs' new romantic anthem "Love My Way" plays from distant speakers to the mob of brides flanking a wedding-cake car. In a scrumptious morsel of irony, our groups have been positioned crosswise from the Hollywood location of Chick-fil-A, which is surprisingly busy this morning.[2]

The parade itself goes by with a pop and flash, the bang of adrenaline compressing time with such force that the event feels over before it begins. Kylie, despite her earlier misgivings, warms up to the festivities as soon as she turns the corner of Hollywood and Highland, her face shining as she is greeted by a crush of body glitter and unconditional love from every direction. The sweet summer smell of bacon-wrapped bratwurst wafts from sidewalk grills as onlookers whoop and clap in their rainbow butterfly wings, sailor hats with matching white bibs, and scanty undergarments passed off as outerwear. Other spectators prefer message t-shirts, whether earnestly declaring that they are the "Proud Aunt of a Gay Nephew" or broadcasting their attraction to gentlemen of mature vintage: "I Heart Hot Dads."

After Kylie shares a sheepish wave with a queer woman wearing an "It Wasn't a Phase" tank top, an old friend spies her mother from the crowd and runs up to give them both a hug. "Hi, cuties! I love you!" she yells in reference to the sign that Kylie no longer knows what to do with, its novelty having worn off after the first few hoists. Janet doesn't make it through the entire route, her pulsing feet ready to burst, and she finds a nearby bench to rest, bequeathing to me her posterboard for the remainder of the march.

Kylie is so energized by the PFLAG group's reception that she wants to keep having fun even after the parade is over. As Janet enjoys a reprieve from her blisters, we walk past the muted counterprotest—a man in a red cap listlessly standing next to an "Ask Me Why You Deserve Hell" placard—to watch synchronized line dancers in chaps and fringe jackets hoedown to a medley of pop hits. First comes the cupid shuffle to Juice Newton's cover of the country-pop standard "Queen of Hearts," followed by an obligatory routine set to Kylie Minogue's "Padam Padam," already the gay anthem of the nascent summer, which the emcee explains the group threw together last night. The best performers are the ones who put extra flourish into it; a dancer with jean shorts ripped far up the sides is always adding an extra swish, kick, high knee, or clap to the choreography.

Seeing how much this day means to everyone and how much Kylie's group meant to the crowd—who kept cheering and shouting *thank you* to PFLAG parents for supporting their queer children—has been yet another reminder of how blessed Kylie is. "It made me really happy when

I saw how many people were supporting us and cheering for us," the girl tells me as the troupe dances to "Boys and Girls," the Britpop act Blur's paean to sexual fluidity. "I feel more conscious within my decisions and my life. I feel like I almost gained consciousness during COVID, not in the literal way. I became aware of my actions and how everything affects me. I think I woke up."

Kylie has led a rarefied existence, and if her mother sometimes accuses her of being coddled, too comfortable with the charms of her life, the allegation is something of a backhanded compliment to Janet's own parenting. Kylie has never wanted for anything, whether the latest iPhone model or the love of her parents, who were her most vocal supporters even before she had the words to express who she was. When Kylie was seven, Janet took her to the mall after her daughter told her that she no longer wanted to wear boys' clothes, and they spent three hours trying on anything Kylie wanted: flowy dresses, short skirts, dangly bracelets, and virtually everything else they saw. With the help of a sympathetic retail assistant at a tween clothing store, they left with fourteen outfits, treating Kylie's father, Dave, to a fashion show when they got home. Kylie began taking puberty suppressors at thirteen in consultation with doctors and psychologists and got her birth certificate corrected shortly after at a courthouse near their local mall.

The Yamamotos were the very last people in the courtroom to be called that day, and when the judge asked Kylie to state her deadname one final time for the court record, he added with a laugh, "Well, I bet you don't want to say that anymore. Why don't we make that happen then?" After she was legally recognized as the girl that she had always been, their family members each took turns taking photos with the judge, who gave them a tour of his office to celebrate the milestone. Further adding to the spirit of triumph, Kylie cartwheeled all the way to the exit elevator like an overeager pageant contestant, except she had already won the whole thing.

In my time spent with the Yamamotos, watching game show reruns and eating Dave's delicious fried fish, Kylie will tell me that she doesn't "have any problems," and that coy admission isn't entirely off base. On one of our daily walks to a playground in her neighborhood, she recalls that the only time she's ever been bullied for her gender was when another student shouted, "Kylie is a trans girl!" in the middle school locker room. Her peers responded with bored shrugs, not understanding what the fuss was about. Now in her senior year at Torrance High School, Kylie says that being transgender is a non-issue, joking that her classmates are too busy thinking about themselves to worry about her. "My whole friend group is gay," she says. "The majority is still straight and cis, but I feel like it's about fifty-fifty. Our school is really, really diverse."

Torrance High's Gender-Sexuality Alliance (GSA), she adds, is among the school's largest student groups, at around two hundred members. That's a tenth of the entire student population; the club is so big that it's forced to break into smaller groups to accommodate everyone who wants to attend its weekly meetings. When the full group gathers—which can only happen once a month for logistical reasons—they have to use the gymnasium. Kylie timidly admits, however, that she doesn't usually show up to GSA because the meetings have a habit of conflicting with her commitments for Botany Club, in which she serves as vice president, and Japanese Club. While she loves her queer friends, Kylie says they can't compete with Mother Nature: "A lot of people ask me, 'Why are you in that club?' and I'm like, 'Girl, I love plants. I love gardening!'"

But if Kylie is living a teenage dream of her parents' tenacious creation, the fortress built to keep her safe feels newly vulnerable, cracks splintering across its surface as June's infamous gloom settles over greater LA like drying concrete. Just five days before she marched at the front of the Pride parade, violence had erupted outside the school board of the Glendale Unified School District, which had voted that same day in favor of a resolution recognizing Pride month.[3]

Despite LA's reputation as a bulwark against intolerance, a liberal bubble within one of America's most progressive states, this wasn't even Southern California's first such incident within the past year. Just days before the beginning of June, a transgender teacher's Pride flag was burned outside of Saticoy Elementary School in North Hollywood after conservative parents protested *The Great Big Book of Families*—a book recognizing that some children are raised in same-sex households—being read aloud during a school assembly.[4] In April, the Chino Unified Valley School District (CVUSD) voted 4–1 to adopt a resolution requiring teachers to out transgender students to their parents if they begin using different names or pronouns at school.[5] CVUSD's policy mirrored a statewide bill proposed in the California State Legislature in 2023, which died after it failed to receive a hearing;[6] the legislation proved nonetheless influential, with conservative lobbyists pushing copycat proposals[7] at school boards throughout the state.[8]

As we sit on metal risers beside the park's baseball field, Kylie says she is exhausted at the mere thought of all this. She confesses that, if she's being completely honest, she has never been all that interested in political activism. When it comes to the anti-LGBTQIA+ policies being enacted in other states, she is only aware of Alabama's law limiting puberty suppressors and hormone replacement to minors because she has a friend there who is impacted by the legislation. "I can't even wrap my head around all that," she tells me.

As a toddler covers herself in sand from the baseball mound, Kylie explains that she feels enough pressure as it is without spending her time concerned that the realities kids in other states already face could soon disrupt her fantasy. While it might appear from the outside as if she's got everything a teenage girl could ever want, Kylie is still completely and utterly terrified about nearly every aspect of her future—terrified she'll be trapped in this moment forever, that she's going to screw it all up. She lies awake at night counting as high as she can until she falls asleep, sometimes getting all the way to seven hundred before she tires herself out. She can't be worried about being transgender, too, she asserts.

"I'm scared I'm not going to pass my classes," Kylie says. "I'm not going to get into college. I'm literally going to be a flop. That's what I worry about."

II. ANGEL NUMBERS

If Kylie has been pampered and cared for all her life, no one loves her more than she loves herself, even by her own admission. When I excuse myself during a tour of her bedroom to use the restroom, she takes the opportunity to grab my recorder and broadcast a message to what she assumes will be her scores of adoring fans. "You guys, I'm alone right now," she says, not sure what to say now that she can express whatever she wants. After a long pause, she offers a brief soliloquy: "How you been? I have a Tamagotchi, guys. It's pink, purple, and blue. It died at one year old. I let it stay alive for three days. It was embarrassing. I was trying these rollers out in my hair. They actually made my bangs look really cute. My bangs actually *ate down*."

Both brashly confident and totally guileless, Kylie approaches each of our interviews as if it were her personal podcast, a stream-of-consciousness guide to her likes, dislikes, and current roster of annoyances that tends to begin with a direct address to the intended public. "Hello, everybody," she will say, leaning directly into the microphone. Among her biggest gripes are the boys at school—whom she finds generally lacking in quality—and the friends that she thinks are ghosting her right now. It always feels as if everyone is hanging out without her, she says, which she deems to be as much an issue of bad taste as it is carelessness.

If one were curious about the loves in her life (aside from the solipsistic variety), all it takes is one glance at her room—a shrine to her myriad obsessions—to become apprised. The walls are shrink-wrapped with the posters of her favorite K-pop acts, including the girl groups Blackpink, NewJeans, and Twice, the latter of which she has seen in concert four times. Kylie first got into K-pop during the pandemic, when she was spending a great deal of time alone with her thoughts, and she grew attracted to the experimentation in the music, the way that Korean artists can make sounds and beats she has heard thousands of times in American pop songs feel brand new. She plays me Red Velvet's "Psycho," an ode to a codependent relationship that she praises for the tension between its polished concept and the incongruous sounds embedded within the verses. "It's supposed to sound elegant, but in the back, there's a game noise," she says, referring to the two-bit twinkle woven into the song's backing track. "Can you hear it? It's like a *duh-duh-duh-duh*. I really liked that."

Her bedroom is her refuge from the world, where she can go when everything becomes too much, where she can scream together with her friends over the phone to release personal demons, one of her favorite pastimes. There's a guarded girlishness to the space, as if the intent were to create a secret lair where the coming worries of adulthood wouldn't be able to find her, where she can hide for as long as she likes.

The most prominent feature of her private chamber is a mural of a princess and her castle, one depicting a kingdom of befuddling scale. Painted by a neighbor, the maiden is the same height as both her pet giraffe and a nearby tree, making the scenery either very tiny or her very tall. Questions of artistic verisimilitude do not concern Kylie as much as the fact that she wishes the blonde princess, with her bubblegum-pink dress covered in flowers, weren't a white girl. "I wish she was Asian or something, with brown hair," she bemoans, before moving on to a discussion of the stickers on the back of her door. Among them are decals reading "Sushi Rolls, Not Gender Roles," "Hot Queer Asian," "Maui Goat Yoga," and "Do Not Thaw, This Dinner Is Cooked From Frozen," the latter of which Kylie says was pulled off a microwavable meal and is now peeling off.

Kylie is torn between milking her adolescence and wanting to grow up all at once, and these days, she feels stuck somewhere in the middle, unable to move forward or step into the independence for which she thinks she might be ready. She has newly discovered her acute fear of failure after flunking her learner's permit test in November, which she has a year to retake. That existential panic deep in the sinkhole of her stomach revealed itself on question forty-four, when Kylie realized that she had already gotten six answers wrong and was only allowed to miss one more. She silently prayed that she would soon taste the flavors of liberty at long last, but alas, she flubbed the very next question.

The defeat came as a personal affront to Kylie, who has worked so hard to mask her insecurities and the uneasy parts of herself she is still learning to embrace: the shape of her cheeks and brows, the size of her feet. She began to wonder if all this confidence she had built had been for nothing, if her dreams of one day having an apartment with plants lining the staircases and a marshmallow-soft couch would never materialize. Kylie loves her life as it is, but she loves it far too much to let it stay like this forever.

Although she says that her long-term plan is to be a "sexy, young-looking" entrepreneur with "beautiful hair" to match her ten-digit net worth, Kylie's future brims with an uncertainty she had never before considered. She is presently weighing whether to enroll in a year-long cosmetology course after graduation—in hopes of becoming a beauty influencer—or going another route entirely, such as majoring in marine biology at a nearby state college. She gets such joy from doing her own makeup, which allows her to put on the face of anyone she wants, but she's been drawn to the water for as long as she can remember, as if she were accessing a memory from a previous life. And while the field of deep-sea research doesn't have, as of yet, many transgender women billionaires, there's no reason she can't be the first.

Kylie doesn't know who to be or how to decide which path to take, but she's doing everything possible to keep her terrible doubts from creeping in. "When I'm left to just my own thoughts, it'll get in there," she tells me, sitting cross-legged atop her bed. "That's why I'm always trying to do something, why I'm always playing music. When I forget my AirPods and I'm walking in the halls at school, all I'm doing is thinking—which is horrible."

On most evenings, Kylie and I take over her living room to watch *Buffy the Vampire Slayer*, the supernatural teen soap opera starring Sarah Michelle Gellar as a fifteen-year-old cheerleader who is likewise struggling with her destiny. This is Kylie's first time seeing the series, which was filmed at her high school, and every external shot of the sweeping Mediterranean revival campus—with its imposing entryway columns and porcelain courtyard fountain—triggers a burst of surprised ecstasy. "I was just sitting on that bench with my friend!" she shrieks. As a staunch fashion girl, Kylie loves the show's quintessentially late-nineties style, in particular the layered hair, leather jackets, and casual sundresses favored by its cosmically put-upon protagonist, Buffy Summers.

If she has an issue with *Buffy*'s early episodes, it's that the only cute boy at the fictional counterpart to Torrance High is the first to be turned: a geek portrayed by the inappropriately handsome Eric Balfour, who could only pass as a loser in an alternate universe. Kylie wishes the nerds at her school looked like him, she insists with a decisive nod. As we snack on the barbeque-flavored seaweed rolls her relatives shipped from Hawaii, Kylie wonders why the show couldn't have sacrificed someone else to the underworld instead; her personal suggestion is Xander, the toxically lovelorn sidekick played by Nicholas Brendon.

To watch a show about the emotional toil of battling inexhaustible evil is surreal in a year where a staggering five hundred anti-LGBTQIA+ bills have, thus far, been introduced in states across the country. And since April 2021, twenty states have passed laws limiting gender-affirming medical care for transgender youth, most recently Missouri.[9] But despite the seeming allegorical parallels afoot, Kylie says that Buffy's journey doesn't resonate with her own, and she likes it that way. While she can certainly relate to the struggles of trying to blissfully enjoy her youth even as dark forces encroach, the point is that she shouldn't have to make the same decision that the slayer does—of taking up the fight simply because others want her to. She should get to be a normal girl with normal friends and normal problems, rather than spending her free nights and weekends trying to prevent the end times. "I have enough to worry about," she says. "I'm rooting for y'all who have to worry about your lives, but I gotta do me."

During one of our regular park strolls, Kylie confesses that she initially didn't want to participate in this project, that she only agreed to be in this book because she knew it would make her mother happy. She is ultimately glad that she said yes because she's been having a much better time than she expected, as she'd initially figured she would be treated like a lab test subject rather than a person. Instead, we spend our days whiffing softballs at the batting cages, browsing her favorite stores at the mall in search of jeans, and seeing bawdy comedies at the fancier of the two AMC locations in town. Kylie especially liked *No Hard Feelings*, a raunchy-sweet Jennifer Lawrence vehicle about a slacker who answers a personal ad from parents offering a Buick Regal to any woman willing to date their socially awkward son.

The film, with its hard edges softened by neat third-act life lessons, reminded Kylie of the kinds of entertainment she had planned for her summer, a schedule of events that did not include baring her soul to a quasi-stranger she only just met. This is the last summer break she'll ever have before she graduates, and she's looking forward to it starting, to spending ten weeks free from others' expectations. But while we are still together, she is trying to decide what she wants from this experience, what she can derive from it. She would like to learn something about herself through the process, she thinks, to surprise herself with the emotions that rise from the depths.

The question of what Kylie is feeling these days is one she doesn't know how to answer, its very contemplation overwhelming her as we sit together at a table in the park. She has spent so long trying not to think about this, to hide her vulnerability and avoid looking too far within, afraid of what she will find. As a few tears tumble through our tabletop's black metal web, she buries her face in her arms, embarassed to be seen this way. She is quiet for a long time before composing herself. She is so done with it all, she says: with needing to explain herself, with worrying what the old white men who make decisions think about her existence, with constantly feeling as if everyone is enjoying themselves at her expense.

"I'm just tired of everything at this point," she says, more empty than sad. "I'm tired of not being invited out by my friends. I'm tired of being trans. I wish I felt like I didn't have anything to worry about. It's so minuscule, but I just feel like it adds up and I'm just tired."

Kylie asks if we can start walking back to her house, so I change the subject as she reapplies her lip pencil, asking her to expound upon the difference between "mid-ugly boys" and boys that are "ugly-ugly," a theory she had briefly elucidated earlier in the day. Initially, she puts forward the actor Michael Cera as an example of the former—his tenuous chin and bird-like features have a certain appeal from the right angle, perhaps—before moving him into the latter category. "You're not hideous," she says of what makes a man passably unattractive. "You're OK. You have maybe one person going for you."

The conversation shifts, as it often does while recording the Kylie podcast, to a range of other topics: her favorite episodes of the sci-fi series *Black Mirror*, why she never got into the unhinged *Archie* comic pastiche *Riverdale*, which of the neighbors have Trump signs in their yards. Sliding into her unmistakable *I've-got-juicy-gossip* voice, she says there's a house that has an "Impeach Biden" sign that the owners illuminate at night; another home had security cams all over the property to make sure no one stole their Trump gear. "I was just like, 'Take that down!' and everyone else who walked by was like, 'Take it down!' and then he did," she tells me.

While Kylie wants to get unstuck, she knows that there's no forcing it; maybe crying in front of a journalist today is a solid step. The universe appears to think so, as she takes advantage of the walk to add to her growing collection of angel numbers, repeating combinations of digits that she believes confer good luck. She spots a 444 combination on a license plate, which she says is her favorite because it's the one she sees the most often, and also a rarer 555 sequence.

Kylie is aware that the concept of enchanted integers sounds silly, but a fateful trip to her mother's psychic—who, with each reading, never fails to make Janet weep uncontrollably—taught her to be open to the unknowable. The medium wrote "Kylie" on a piece of paper with three stars, saying that she envisioned the celestial bodies floating above the girl's head; she then asked if the symbols meant anything. Kylie responded, through her own tears, that she sleeps under a trio of glow-in-the-dark stars affixed to her bedroom ceiling, which were hidden under a tapestry at the time. Seeing the serendipitous repetition of 111 or 777 similarly helps Kylie to remember that it's OK if she doesn't have it all figured out yet because some benevolent force out there does.

"This is actually crazy," she says, satisfied with her gospel of prosperity. "We're protected right now."

III. THE BUBBLE

The parking lot of Dodgers Stadium is eerily devoid of rainbows as Janet searches for a spot among the typical pre-game chaos—a silver Honda in front of us thumping the curb as its driver speeds away from the parking booth. This is Janet's first LA Dodgers game in at least ten years—it takes hours to get home to Torrance, she says, because of the traffic—and this is a decidedly strange time for her to become reacquainted with Major League Baseball.

For weeks, the Dodgers' annual Pride night has been the subject of controversy after conservatives, including Florida senator Marco Rubio,[10] criticized the team for giving its Community Hero Award to the Sisters of Perpetual Indulgence, a satirical drag troupe that dresses like harlequin nuns. The honor was rescinded following accusations from the right that the Sisters comprise an "anti-Catholic hate group," but the street performers were reinvited after LGBTQIA+ organizations like GLAAD and Equality California denounced the decision, calling attention to the group's decades of HIV/AIDS fundraising.[11] Although picketers had lined the boulevard outside the stadium earlier in the day with signs like "Satan Has No Rights" and "Dodgers Sold Their Soul," the ashes have cooled for the evening.[12] There are no protesters or even visible members of the LGBTQIA+ community as Janet's car circles the lot, and the jerseys we pass are bereft of bling. Pride night, at a glance, is reminiscent of the physicist Edwin Schrödinger's reality-bending cat: simultaneously queer and not queer.

Janet is directed to an open space as she searches through her emails for the free tickets she got through the Laurel Foundation, a Pasadena-based support group dedicated to both children living with HIV/AIDS and the families of transgender youth. For the first time since 2019, Kylie is preparing to attend the organization's summer retreat for transgender children—seven days of hiking, archery, ropes courses, gender euphoria workshops, and the occasional intra-camp rivalry. Back in her days as a tween troublemaker, Kylie was disciplined after a fellow girl tried to pour glue on her during the camp's fashion show. Kylie, never one to be made look like a fool, deflected the attempted incursion and wiped the colorless goo on the girl's jacket instead.

Although Kylie had been three years below the cutoff age of thirteen the first year she attended, Janet had begged the Laurel Foundation to let her enroll, crying over the phone that her daughter needed to be in a community of kids who share and understand her experiences, to know that she's not the only one. By the very next week, the organization had informed the Yamamotos they would make an exception, and now children as young as six are able to attend. "I'm just really happy she's going back this year," Janet tells me, collecting her purse. "I hope she finds friends because I always felt that it was important. She didn't want to go, but I always felt like you need to go to a place where you meet people who are like you."

The scene doesn't seem to be any gayer as we stroll past the line of transparent tote bags handed out by security and into the stadium, until a ponytailed woman in black aviator glasses clarifies that we have come to the wrong place. "If you are joining us for the ticket package this evening, you must enter through right center field to receive your Pride jersey," she announces through her bullhorn. Following her directions reveals a vista of blazing rainbow: visors, tube tops, sequin jackets, and cheap thick plastic sunglasses of gas station vintage. As an electronic sign inside announces "LGBTQ+ Pride Night," butches in crew cuts and femmes with asymmetrical bangs carry the tallest vodka lemonades I've ever seen, and a baby chews on a diminutive Pride flag as the child's parents await their hot dogs and fries. An adjacent gaggle dressed in bucket hats and Nikes passionately debates the back catalog of Taylor Swift; sides are taken as to the pop titan's best album—perhaps *Folklore*, what about *Red*—before *1989* emerges as a consensus answer. Selfie-takers block would-be passersby in pink anime cartoon pigtails and backward baseball caps as they document their ornamental corn dogs for posterity. "Sorry, we're just really excited about our Dodger Dogs," the wearer of a Bisexual Pride scrunchie shrugs apologetically.

The stands are sparse with occupants as we take our seats among the other Laurel Foundation parents, including a volunteer who hands out public transit passes to help members make the commute home. After the Dodgers' eventual 7–5 loss to the rival San Francisco Giants, Governor DeSantis will tweet photos of the empty stands, with the Florida politician intending to suggest that fans boycotted the game in objection to the Sisters.[13] But in reality, it just took a while for people to show up: The viral photos were captured earlier in the day as the group accepted its award, around an hour before the Olympic diver Tom Daley and his husband, screenwriter Dustin Lance Black, threw the first pitch. The stadium, adhering to stereotypes about gay tardiness, doesn't fill until around the fifth inning.

For all the contention surrounding it, the game is the selfsame blend of corporate sponsorship, jock jams, and stubbornly lengthy crowd waves that one would expect at any average baseball game. The hairbow-loving children's musician JoJo Siwa urges the crowd to "make some noise!" as another parent in our section asks Janet about her husband's upcoming fishing trip to the Channel Islands, an island chain twelve miles from the coast. Before Kylie was born, Dave was among the top tuna fishers in the world—one time catching two 300-pounders on the same trip, a feat considered a once-in-a-lifetime achievement for most. Instead of taking eighteen-day voyages to South America, he now enjoys short weekend getaways with friends, bringing home a surplus of fish that he gifts to neighbors and the first friends to respond to Janet's mass text: "Hey, everybody, the Yamamoto Fish Market is open!"

Janet decides to leave early—during the seventh-inning stretch—to avoid the post-game deluge, and we miss the advertised rainbow lights show following the final out. On our car ride back to the South Bay, she seems to know little about the Pride night backlash because, as she tells me, she doesn't watch the news. It's not willful ignorance, she explains, but an act of self-preservation: Janet needs to stay focused on raising her daughter—teaching her to be a good, thoughtful person who cares for others—rather than worrying about the people who wish them ill. "I never have it on because I don't want to know," she says. "As long as nobody's rocking my world, then I'm OK, then I've done OK, and she's going to be fine. She's going to be strong."

A major component of her reticence to engage with current events is that Janet has built a wonderful life for herself. She has a husband who cooks for her every night and a daughter she loves deeply when they aren't grating each other's nerves, but she hasn't always enjoyed such splendid serendipity. She hasn't seen her mother since the age of seven, when the woman who too briefly raised her moved back to Japan to get remarried, and her father is a recovering alcoholic. Dave was her third marriage, and when they first met on a group fishing trip with friends almost two decades ago, she almost didn't give him a chance because she thought he would be yet another regret. "I thought it was too good to be true, so I wanted to end it before he would leave me," she says. "I've been abandoned all my life."

The Yamamotos are, indeed, very fortunate, and Janet knows well enough not to undervalue her long-awaited rapture. So often in their lives, things could have gone wrong and didn't. When Kylie was young, an anonymous tipster called California Children's Services with a claim that her parents were forcing her to be transgender. A child welfare agent came to their house to investigate the allegation, and Janet was terrified that her daughter was going to be taken away from her, telling Kylie to go play in her room while the adults talked. The investigator spent almost two hours asking questions about their life and her daughter's gender journey, and every so often, Kylie would run out into the living room to sneak her mother a kiss or to pass her a note that read, "I love you, Mom."

Eventually, the agent concluded that she had all the information she needed, telling Janet that the Yamamotos would receive a letter in the mail the following month dismissing all charges against them. "People need to mind their own fucking business," the woman told her. The two ended the visit with a hug, and Janet fails to restrain her tears as she remembers how relieved she was to feel the woman's weight against her, to know everything was going to be all right.

Throughout Kylie's life, Janet has always focused on making sure her daughter had a healthy childhood, that there was no opportunity or wish denied to her simply because of who she is. They enrolled Kylie in everything from soccer to ice skating and pulled her out of her Catholic elementary school when administrators—citing the gendered rules on hair length—wouldn't let her grow out her wedge haircut, which made her look like the Olympian Dorothy Hamill. Janet and Kylie have been getting their nails done together at the same salon they have been going to since Kylie was just four years old; this month their nails have been painted chromatic pink like matching automobile wraps, in honor of Kylie's favorite color.

Janet knows that, much to her daughter's chagrin, she is constantly pushing Kylie to share her story and be a voice for transgender children who need advocates right now, but that's because Janet knows how felicitous their lives have been. She wants to share those blessings with others, to return what they have been given. "It's not a burden," Janet tells me as we pull into her driveway, well past her usual bedtime. "I'm not suffering. I'm not sad. I'm not, 'Why did God give this to me?' I look at it as a gift. She's changed my life. I would have never known how kind people are in this world if I didn't have her. I wouldn't be where I am today."

But as much as Janet attempts to keep the outside world from trespassing on their little heaven, she worries the day will come soon where they face the same hardships as other families. A few days after Pride night, Janet looks over my shoulder as we watch a school board meeting of the Glendale Unified School District (GUSD) from the glow of my laptop, during which speakers debate LGBTQIA+ inclusion as police gather in riot gear outside the building's doors.[14] For the second time in as many weeks, the crowd of hundreds breaks out in a chaotic brawl; at least one individual is injured.[15]

The meeting inside the school board chambers, although non-violent, is no less contentious. Speakers who oppose the board's previously announced decision to recognize Pride month claim that Glendale schools are promoting "sterilization, castration, and mutilation" and teaching children that they can "cut a body part off" just because they feel like it. A woman who says that she's been a children's pastor for the past twenty-nine years claims that LGBTQIA+ inclusion in schools is "equivalent to child abuse." "I beseech you to stop confusing loving kindness and acceptance with sexual confusion and pornographic images," she says through the glitchy live feed. "There is an agenda behind this, and it is not creating strong, independent, loving children. It is creating confusion, mental instability, and fear."

Although most of those who address the GUSD school board express support for the LGBTQIA+ community, the negative comments are shocking for Janet, who speaks back to the screen as if she were watching a torrid soap opera. "You have no idea!" she yells at the pastor. "I pray to God that you get a grandchild that is trans. I wish that upon you and then you'll see."

The pill is especially bitter because while Glendale is twenty-eight miles away—on the opposite side of the LA city limits—the threat feels nearer than ever. In a meeting held the very same night, the Torrance City Council votes unanimously to ban Pride flags from being flown on city light poles following a string of vandalism incidents targeting LGBTQIA+ affirming businesses.[16] In June 2022, after business owners began reporting that their flags were being desecrated or stolen, the city stopped allowing storefronts in the downtown entertainment district to hoist rainbow banners over public sidewalks. This year, Torrance's mayor, George Chen, doubled down on the city's decision to distance itself from the LGBTQIA+ community by discontinuing the tradition of issuing Pride proclamations. We open the Torrance council meeting's livestream just in time for Chen to refer to LGBTQIA+ identities as a "certain choice of lifestyle for some people."[17]

Janet wants to believe that she did everything right by raising Kylie in this community that has appeared to support their family for so many years, but she just doesn't know anymore. Los Angeles County voted overwhelmingly Democratic in the 2020 election—by a forty-five-point margin[18]—and Torrance has among the largest concentrations of Asian Americans in the entire country, but it seems as if the world is going backward, regressing so quickly that she can't process it.[19] "This is what scares me: that this becomes something that's going to start to creep into our world, into my bubble," Janet says. "If I ever have to deal with this, I don't know what I'll do. I'm grateful that she's gonna be a senior this year and be done with it. If this is the trend that's happening in California? Just get her through one more year and we're done."

The foibles of local government leaders and low-level religious authorities cannot change the overwhelming love that the Yamamotos feel for their daughter, which can be so smothering that it sometimes makes Kylie feel as if her parents are sitting on her. Kylie often complains that her mother's overly involved tendencies border on codependency, but everything one needs to know about their relationship is on display in their front room. The parlor is a tribute to just about every school art project Kylie has ever brought home; standouts include cardboard hands shaped like turkeys and zebras, a portrait of wrestler-turned-actor Dwayne Johnson on a paper grocery bag, and a picture of Kylie dressed in piñata paper that reads: "Love You Like Peaches and Strawberries." Janet says her wish is that Kylie, many years from now after her mother has passed, will look back on her childhood home so full of memories that they overflow into the kitchen and think: "My God, my mom did so much for me. She was always there for me, and she pushed me to do things to make me realize how great my life was."

Janet holds out a tentative hope that she might not have to wait quite that long, that her flowers may arrive sooner rather than later. "She might not understand that now," Janet says, "but I'm really hoping one day she will."

IV. BADDIE

The family dogs pace the living room as the annual Founder's Day fireworks crackle like confetti bombs in the night air, the detonations so close to the Yamamotos' home that the smell of gunpowder wafts through the front door. Janet gave the dogs anxiety pills to help them sleep through the concert of blasts, but Oreo stubbornly refuses to rest, meandering haltingly before flopping onto a shag throw rug in front of the television. Kylie, who put off packing until the very last night before camp, abandons her checklist to comfort Oreo; she sits on the floor next to the wheezing Australian shepherd mix, petting her until she passes out. Janet, demonstrating the same indecisiveness as the petrified animal, watches two minutes each of a series of Netflix movies before settling on a rerun of *America's Funniest Home Videos*. The long-running clip program's canned laugh track, set to a medley of comical sledding injuries and toddlers spraying themselves with fire hoses, is a dissonant companion to the bedlam unfolding around it.

Her mother puts aside any irritation with Kylie's lack of punctuality to lavish her with words of praise, lauding her every time another item is packed away: sleeping bag, *check;* pillowcase, *check.* "I'm so proud of you!" Janet says, adding that she hopes Kylie returns to camp as a counselor next year. "Do you know how many little girls are going to look up to you because you're so beautiful?"

Janet has spent the past several days waxing nostalgic about camp, blushing wistfully as she recalled how Kylie called home crying after her very first day, begging Janet to pick her up. Ultimately, Kylie had such a good time that she started hanging a Transgender Pride flag in her room for the first time ever. "She came home very proud of who she was," Janet had told me earlier in the week. "She made some friends." The counselors and other campers even gave Kylie an affectionate nickname: Walmart Moana, referencing the Disney animated film following the adventures of a Polynesian island chief's daughter. That kind of kneejerk association might have been considered offensive, Janet had noted, if Kylie didn't legitimately look like Moana when she was ten years old, the resemblance due to her father's Japanese-Hawaiian heritage.

But as the evening trudges forward, it becomes abundantly clear that Kylie doesn't really want to attend camp this year, joylessly dragging her bright pink suitcase to the car as if it were a lead pipe. As a car alarm echoes across the empty neighborhood streets, Kylie crouches on the sidewalk, repeating twice to herself, "I don't want to go." Janet initially ignores the signs, thinking that it's either teenage melodrama or yet another instance of a very stubborn girl letting her fear get the better of her, but eventually she collides headfirst into the granite wall of her daughter's resistance; their misalignment results in a confrontation outside Kylie's bedroom door. "I don't want to go!" Kylie insists. "I really don't want to go. I'm not going."

"You don't even know how privileged you are to go!" Janet shoots back, furious that the soon-to-be-wasted spot could have gone to another camper. Her mother attempts one last time to force the issue, telling Kylie to go to bed because they have to be up at 6:00 a.m., but Kylie is unflinching in her opposition. "I don't want to go because none of my friends are there," she says, noting that the campers she's gotten closest with over the years won't be present.

The fight, as is often the case between them, is about the fact that they each have trouble seeing the world through the other's eyes. Kylie has no interest in advocacy and just wants to have fun; she doesn't understand why her mother won't let her be her own person. *Why can't I decide for myself how I spend my summer?* the girl wonders. Janet, meanwhile, has clothed and fed Kylie for seventeen years and can't comprehend why her child doesn't recognize the sacrifices that she continues to make for her comfort.

Janet had had the entire day planned out, intending to stop by a PFLAG San Gabriel Valley Asian Pacific Islander meeting after camp drop-off to visit the fellow parents who have become like family in the seven years since she went to her first meeting. Before Kylie came into the world, Janet wasn't even aware someone could be transgender, and these people—the fellow PFLAG mothers, the camp directors who made sure there was a place for her daughter—were the ones who helped her along the way. She wants to give back so badly, knowing how much that support has meant to her family, how it got them to where they are today, and she doesn't understand why Kylie doesn't want the same thing. "It's hard to be a parent," she tells me, now that Kylie has firmly shut the door on her mother's intransigence. "You try to do everything the best you can. I probably made a lot of mistakes on this journey. She's a beautiful girl, thriving, but she's spoiled as shit."

Janet is obsessed with the idea of making the right choices for her daughter, but what she is failing to recognize in her frustration is that she already has. She has raised a strong, confident young woman—maybe a little *too* confident—who is able to ask for what she wants and won't stop until she gets it. Getting unstuck takes courage and determination, the ability to not only speak one's wishes but also act upon them, and what might appear to be a childish tantrum is actually Kylie's biggest break-through yet. She agreed to be in the LA Pride Parade, even though she really didn't want to go, and she agreed to be in this book, even though she really didn't want that either. Kylie made both impositions work for herself, but she is tired of holding her breath as she goes along with others' plans; she feels ready and able to start making her own instead. She is prepared to spend her summer exactly how she should have to begin with: being a teenage girl with a teenage social calendar.

Transgender kids want the same things that all other kids want, and that begins with the ability to make their own decisions and choices, to find their way through trial and error, to feel validated and seen for who they are and what they desire. They want to be loved with the same compassion and care that was so freely given to the children they recently were, but they also want to be respected as the adults they are very rapidly becoming. They want to know that they matter—that their thoughts matter, their voices matter—and that others will listen when they choose to speak. That doesn't mean their parents are required to give their kids everything they desire all the time, such as the pink convertible that Kylie fantasizes about owning one day; it means that parents simply demonstrate that they hear and are trying their best to understand.

When Janet knocks on Kylie's door to tell her that she doesn't have to go to camp, her daughter thanks her for validating her feelings, and even though the remark is intended to be half snide, they do share a brief moment of mutual recognition. As Janet wipes her tears away, Kylie promises to study for her permit test, telling Janet earnestly that she will go in her room and start now. Janet wants to respond by explaining to Kylie that she will always be her little girl, that Kylie could never do anything that would make Janet love her less, but they settle for a hug. "You better!" Janet says with a sniffle, glad for a small win.

The next day is our last together and my last of researching this book—marking nearly nine months since I first set off to spend time with transgender youth and their families, hoping not only to be a spectator in their lives but also to watch them heal and grow together. With Dave now back from his fishing trip, bearing enough raw cod to feed the entire block, we celebrate by releasing monarch butterflies that Janet raises from ova in a pair of netted enclosures in her living room. One might consider the timing to be rather on the nose if thematic literalism weren't such a major facet of the Yamamotos' existence. Earlier in the week, as we farmed oysters together at a shop on the pier, Kylie selected a shell with a black pearl inside, yet another testament to unexpected transformations.

The new batch of monarchs is ready to fly today, and Kylie and I delicately cup them in our hands to release them outside one by one. As I let them go, I think of all the young people I've met over the past year, the ones whose wings are drying for flight: Wyatt, who has since decided to leave South Dakota and attend ballet school in another state; Rhydian, who was able to get his top surgery in time to have his fantasy prom; Mykah, who graduated on time and is planning to attend Marshall University in the fall; Ruby, who has officially exchanged *I-love-you*s with the beau she now calls her boyfriend; Clint, who is preparing for his big move to the West Coast for college; Augie, who is hoping to work at the mall goth clothing store Hot Topic while they wait for the haunt to begin again; and Jack, who got her old job at Goodwill back, rotting animal carcasses and all.

Kylie, for her part, is looking forward to relaxing at home over the next few weeks as she prepares for her permit test; she made it all the way through the first of her three study packets last night. Sitting on her front steps wearing a turtle necklace Janet bought her in Hawaii, she tells me that she had initially hoped that participating in this project would make her want to start engaging in activism, to be the kind of person who marches proudly at the front of parades, but the opposite has been true. It's made her more resolute in being her own kind of role model; rather than being someone who is praised for bravely speaking their truth as a transgender woman, she wants to be the kind of person others look up to because she's—in her words—"a baddie just living my life."

If she attends Pride in the future, Kylie hopes to go with her friends, wearing a glanorous outfit inspired by Anna Nicole Smith. When she attended the West Hollywood parade in 2005, the late model and heir-ess donned a now-iconic silky white dress split up the sides, which she accessorized with Mardi Gras beads and a tiny Pride flag. Kylie loves being transgender—which she says is a great help in weeding out jerks from her friend circles—but she knows that there's so much more to her than just one thing, that she has so much more fabulousness to give. "Being trans is not my full story," she says.

As I think back on my time with Kylie in Torrance and with the other kids I've met throughout my travels, I think about something that Dave—the most elusive member of the Yamamoto household—told me during my stay. Outside of his home-cooked meals of spaghetti and unthawed fish, Dave and I rarely got to converse at length because he goes to bed at 5 p.m. for his job as the chief engineer of a local beer plant, where the top priority is to keep operations running. In one of our few conversations, Dave told me that he and Janet had Kylie late in life, and many of their friends and work colleagues had advised them against becoming parents. A coworker whose infant daughter had died after being born with too much fluid in her lungs said that the loss of a child ruined him, urging Dave not to take the risk that Kylie might not survive.

The Yamamotos decided to ignore those warnings and take a leap of faith, and when Janet asked Dave whether he wanted a boy or a girl, he simply responded, "I want a healthy baby." The only thing on his wish list was enough time with his child so they could enjoy being a family together, and when it turned out that the smiling baby he ini-tially assumed was his son was actually his daughter, the news changed nothing for him. "Have kids," Dave implored, looking me straight in the eye as he rocked back and forth in his living room recliner. "They make your life full. They do."

All of our lives are fuller when transgender kids have the freedom to grow up happy and healthy, to greet the universe on their own terms, to not only tell us who they are but also show us. Every Kylie, Mykah, and Wyatt documented in this book represents countless teenagers whose stories may never be told—because they aren't in a place safe enough to tell them or because they aren't that interested in visibility—but who are nonetheless moving through the world, finding their way. They are our neighbors, our classmates, our relatives, our friends, or the child walking past us off the bus as they hold tightly to both backpack straps, looking down at the ground as they try to make it home. They are everything that we can imagine, and they could be so much more if they were allowed to be, if only others would stop trying to make their decisions for them, thinking they know better than their parents, doctors, psychologists, or transgender kids themselves.

Kylie's wonderful, loving, overbearing mother was correct in wanting to share her daughter's lovely life with everyone, but the fact remains that the privileges Kylie has enjoyed should be the bare minimum. Every transgender child should get the chance to be spoiled rotten. America would be a better place if all its teenagers were so lucky.

ACKNOWLEDGMENTS

A project like this needed permission to exist, and I wouldn't have known it was possible to bring *American Teenager* into this world without Samantha Allen, whose encouragement of my literary aspirations was a seed planted. For years, I've wanted to write a book centering the experiences of transgender youth, but I was extremely skilled in talking myself out of it or creating excuses for why it wasn't the right time. In many ways, *American Teenager* is a call-and-response to Samantha's own *Real Queer America*, my *Exile in Guyville* to her *Exile on Main St.* Her extraordinary work helped me envision what I wanted to accomplish and to construct a template for how it might be done; it's not happenstance that our books are divided into the same number of chapters. I often preach that we, as queer journalists, must be the ones who believe in ourselves most; this industry is cruel, and it is not designed for our benefit. But after a string of professional disappointments, I had forgotten how to follow my own advice. Samantha reminded me at a time when I very much needed reminding.

Rick Richter and Caroline Marsiglia, my agents, saw the potential of *American Teenager* before I fully understood what it was, knowing only that our current political discourse required a moral intervention. It took flying to South Dakota and spending time with families on the ground to discover what this project needed to be: a cinéma vérité portrait of life as it is actually lived. I wanted the experience of reading *American Teenager* to feel like the great works of Steve James or Albert and David Maysles, documentarians who possess the radical empathy to create finely detailed portraits of people you come to feel that you know, as if they are your own family. Without Rick and Caroline's patience and their affirming notes on my early drafts, I never would have had the courage to go on that journey of discovery or to take the risk that writing the truth entails. From our very first meeting, I knew they were special because they really listened, rather than just waiting for their turn to talk. As someone who has spent so long fighting for my place in journalism, I am not always accustomed to being heard, and that phenomenon was intoxicating. With this book, I hope that I gave that feeling to others.

Zack Knoll, my editor at Abrams, opened so many doors for me that can never be closed. When my agents and I shopped our proposal around to publishers, many were confused about this idea or didn't understand it. Because there's never been a book quite like *American Teenager* before, we were told there must not be a market for it, as if the fact that it hadn't already been written was the gravest of condemnations. One editor felt the book "wasn't realistic" because none of the kids featured had been disowned by their parents. Zack, an angel of all angels, gave me the gift that I had needed for so long: He trusted me. He trusted that I knew how to handle these stories with thoughtfulness and care and that I could do the intensive work this level of ambition required. A book like this takes an extreme toll, and writing *American Teenager* has forever altered my body, not only its shape but also how it responds to the outside world. I am so thankful that he was willing to not only give me the time and the space I needed to process the collective trauma of seven families as they progress toward healing but also to sit with my own grief. So much of publishing is a game of access and gatekeeping, and he reminded me what matters most: our humanity.

American Teenager went through an extraordinarily rigorous reporting and editing process, much of which was a volunteer effort from the wonderful community that has supported my work for years. Brandon

Will, my ever-patient transcriber, made me feel like I wasn't doing this alone. Dozens of people read my rough manuscript and provided thoughtful feedback and suggested edits, including Aaron Lempert, Adi Barreto, Amanda Gammill, Angel Reneé Brondel, Anne Marie Dornoff, Bennett Kaspar-Williams, Brad Gorman, Brian Kennedy, Brody Levesque, Chelsa Morrison, Christina Liu, Danielle May, Devon Ojeda, Farah Sagin, Jane Anne Seagren, Khai Devon, Kristin Johnson, Lauren Rodriguez, Mackenzie Harte, Martha Madrigal, Natalie Daniels, Natalie Slack, Prerna Abbi, Sam Cocjin, Sheena Anne Kadi, Stefanie Nano, and Tiffiney McKee. They saw that this book was important before I was sure if it was even any good (I won't really be certain until the reviews come out and perhaps not even then). On the Abrams team, Melissa Wagner provided invaluable copy edits when my brain was all but inoperable, and Ruby Pucillo helped me see things that literally thirty other editors couldn't. I am impressed, amazed, and eternally grateful to you all.

Being part of this undertaking required immense sacrifice, and I am awed by how much the families featured in *American Teenager* gave of themselves to ensure its fruition, before we even knew it would ever see the light of day. You are my heroes and my teachers, and if I have little to say here, it's because I hope this book itself expresses my admiration. I am a different person—and more importantly, a better person—for knowing you all. You have enriched my life; taught me to be quieter, gentler, and more open; and expanded my world. As much as I remain a journalist doing my job, with the critical distance that requires, the bonds we forged remain unshakeable. I hope that I know all of you for the rest of my days and that we are still swapping GIFs and movie recommendations when we are ninety. (Ruby, if you haven't watched *Midnight* by the time this book goes to print, I am going to be severely disappointed. No one in history has ever looked better in a turtleneck than Don Ameche.)

Thank you to everyone who supported *American Teenager* on Patreon; to my Nana for demonstrating what it means to be truly selfless; to my Pops, for never holding it against me that we still haven't finished watching *The Wire* together; to my brother, Eric, for making me feel normal; to my chosen sister Jill, for helping me move so many times; to my late mother, for showing me how to live life on my own terms; to my best friend, Ryan, for putting up with me at my worst; and to my husband, my twin flame, for never making me explain myself. Thanks to the editors who have helped create opportunity for me during an era of journalism when that is increasingly scarce; organizations like GLAAD, the Association of LGBTQ+ Journalists, and Advocates for Trans Equality for tirelessly championing my work; and my group chat of fellow queer journos for reminding me that we're all in this together: Adam Rhodes, David Oliver, Jo Yurcaba, and Lauren McGaughy. And to my mentees, Oliver Haug and James Factora, thanks for letting me pay forward some of the love I have received. I know I probably owe you both a phone call, and for that I am deeply sorry.

And lastly, thanks to all the teachers who uplifted my writing long before *American Teenager* was even a twinkle in my eye. The first book I ever wrote was thinly veiled *Mulholland Drive* slash fiction during the height of my teenage David Lynch phase, and my only reader was my junior year English professor, Ms. Woods. In high school, I was very rarely the student who was told they could aspire to something bigger or be anything they dreamed. I listened to Peter Gabriel albums during lunch and spent my weekends rereading Gore Vidal essays, and adults generally didn't know what to do with me. I would find out that Ms. Woods read my book when I heard from a friend in her other period how much she liked it; usually, the stories that her students gave her to read were about werewolves, and she was relieved to read a bisexual noir melodrama for once. Her praise meant a great deal, and it's telling that I don't remember my first boyfriend's last name but I *do* remember what Ms. Woods wrote in my college recommendation letter: "Nico Lang has range." When we look up to someone, even the faintest hint of positive attention from them can change the very course of our lives. All of us should remember that we have that power.

NOTES

Foreword

1   Erin Reed, "US Internal Refugee Crisis: 130–260k Trans People Have Already Fled," *Erin in the Morning,* June 14, 2023. www.erininthe morning.com/p/us-internal-refugee-crisis-130-260k.

Introduction

1   Megan Munce, "Gender-affirming medical treatment for transgender kids would be considered child abuse under Texas Senate bill," *Texas Tribune,* April 27, 2021. www.texastribune.org/2021/04/27/texas-senate -transgender-child-abuse.

2   "Senate Bill 1646," Legiscan, 2021. capitol.texas.gov/tlodocs/872/billtext /html/HB00038I.htm.

3   "What Are the Penalties for Child Abuse?" Law Offices of Randall B. Eisenberg. www.rbisenberg.com/faqs/what-are-the-penalties-for-child -abuse/.

4   Nico Lang, "A Former Evangelical Minister Testified for the Equality Act Alongside Her Trans Daughter," LOGO News, April 15, 2019. www.logotv .com/news/u1zfd3/evangelical-equality-act-transgender-daughter.

5   Movement Advancement Project, "Assessing the damage: Reviewing changed state LGBTQ policies," *Los Angeles Blade,* July 30, 2023. www .losangelesblade.com/2023/07/30/assessing-the-damage-reviewing -changed-state-lgbtq-policies/.

6   Data provided directly by Advocates for Trans Equality.

7   Erin Reed, "Bill gives Florida 'emergency jurisdiction' over trans kids on custody disputes, targets adult care," *Erin in the Morning,* April 3, 2023, www.erininthemorning.com/p/bill-gives-florida -emergency-jurisdiction.

8   Jo Yurcaba, "From drag bans to sports restrictions, 75 anti-LGBTQ bills have become law in 2023," NBC News, December 17, 2023. www .nbcnews.com/nbc-out/out-politics-and-policy/75-anti-lgbtq-bills -become-law-2023-rcna124250.

9   Brandon Girod, "Florida's transgender affirming care ban is now law. Here's what SB 254 does," *Pensacola News Journal*, May 17, 2023. www.pnj.com/story/news/politics/2023/05/17/florida-sb-254-florida -abduction-transgender-bill-now-law-what-it-does/70206291007/.

10   Samantha Riedel, "Advocates say a controversial report on healthcare for trans kids is 'fundamentally flawed,'" *Them*, April 12, 2024. www .them.us/story/cass-review-nhs-trans-youth-healthcare-report.

11   "Research finds significant reduction in depression, suicidality in youth receiving gender-affirming care or puberty blockers," American Academy of Pediatrics, October 7, 2021. www.aap.org/en/news-room /news-releases-from-aap-conferences/research-finds-significant -reduction-in-depression-suicidality-in-youth-receiving-gender -affirming-care-or-puberty-blockers/.

12   Theresa Gaffney, "Mental health benefits of gender-affirming hormones for teens persist for two years in new study," *Stat*, January 18, 2023. www.statnews.com/2023/01/18/mental-health-benefits-of-gender -affirming-hormones-for-teens-persist-two-years/.

13   Heather Boerner, "What the science on gender-affirming care for transgender kids really shows," *Scientific American*, May 12, 2022. www.scientificamerican.com/article/what-the-science-on-gender -affirming-care-for-transgender-kids-really-shows/.

14   Dr. Jack Turban, "The evidence for trans youth gender-affirming medical care," *Psychology Today*, January 24, 2022. www.psychologytoday .com/us/blog/political-minds/202201/the-evidence-trans-youth-gender -affirming-medical-care.

15   James Factora, "Amid attacks on care for trans youth, new study confirms why it's life or death," *Them*, February 28, 2022. www.them.us /story/trans-youth-healthcare-study-puberty-blockers-hormones -depression-suicide.

16   "Medical organization statements," Trans Health Project. transhealth project.org/resources/medical-organization-statements/.

17   Jonathan Allen, "New study estimates 1.6 million in U.S. identify as transgender," Reuters, June 10, 2022. www.reuters.com/world /us/new-study-estimates-16-million-us-identify-transgender -2022-06-10/.

18   Kate Sosin, "More Americans now know transgender people, but most still don't seem to understand them," *The 19th*, July 27, 2021. 19thnews.org/2021/07/more-americans-know-transgender-people -gender-assignment/.

19 Rob Todaro, "Personally knowing a transgender person correlates with increased sympathy for transgender people and support for LGBTQ+ issues," Data for Progress, October 11, 2023. www.dataforprogress.org /blog/2023/10/11/personally-knowing-a-transgender-person-correlates -with-increased-sympathy-for-transgender-people-and-support-for -lgbtq-issues.

20 Paul J. Weber, "Texas governor order treats gender-confirming care as abuse," *Associated Press*, February 23, 2022. apnews.com/article /texas-child-abuse-child-welfare-greg-abbott-ken-paxton-65c054b6 ccd9040e81ad1a4be11403b9.

21 Jack Forrest, "Texas governor signs ban on gender-affirming care for minors," CNN, June 2, 2023. www.cnn.com/2023/06/02/politics/texas -gender-affirming-care-ban-minors/index.html.

Wyatt

1 Nico Lang, "Transgender restroom use: America's next battle for equality and recognition," *The Guardian*, February 19, 2016. www .theguardian.com/commentisfree/2016/feb/19/transgender -restroom-use-americas-next-battle-for-equality-and-recognition/.

2 Laura Wagner and Bill Chappell, "South Dakota governor vetoes bill stipulating transgender students' bathroom use," NPR, March 1, 2016. www .npr.org/sections/thetwo-way/2016/03/01/468732723/south-dakota -s-transgender-bathroom-bill-hits-deadline-for-governor.

3 Kiara Alfonseca, "South Dakota signs 1st anti-transgender sports law of 2022," ABC News, February 4, 2022. abcnews.go.com/US/south-dakota -signs-1st-anti-transgender-sports-law/story?id=82672739.

4 Morgan Matzen and Joe Sneve, "Gov. Kristi Noem won't sign transgender sports bill," *Argus Leader*, March 19, 2021. www.argusleader.com/story /news/education/2021/03/19/gov-kristi-noem-wont-sign-transgender -sports-bill-south-dakota/4671608001/.

5 "Judge's ruling allows South Dakota school for deaf to close," *Rapid City Journal*, October 5, 2010. rapidcityjournal.com/news/judges -ruling-allows-south-dakota-school-for-deaf-to-close/article_39ed 54e4-d0bb-11df-8921-001cc4c03286.html.

6 Shelly Conlon, "South Dakota deaf education: Students share struggles," *Argus Leader*, December 4, 2019. www.argusleader.com/in-depth /news/education/2019/12/04/hard-of-hearing-deaf-students-struggle -south-dakota-education-asl/4177702002/.

7   Nico Lang, "South Dakota anti-trans bill's defeat is part of larger pattern, advocates say," NBC News, February 12, 2020. www.nbcnews.com/feature/nbc-out/south-dakota-anti-trans-bill-s-defeat-part-larger-pattern-n1135741.

8   "South Dakota's Equality Profile," Movement Advancement Project. www.lgbtmap.org/equality-maps/profile_state/SD.

9   HRC staff, "How one small South Dakota town became a champion for LGBTQ equality," Human Rights Campaign, January 18, 2019. www.hrc.org/news/how-one-small-south-dakota-town-became-a-champion-for-lgbtq-equality.

Rhydian

1   Mike Cason, "Alabama lawmakers pass ban on transgender medical treatments for minors," AL.com, April 7, 2022. www.al.com/news/2022/04/ban-on-transgender-medical-treatments-for-minors-at-top-of-alabama-house-agenda.html.

2   Brian Lyman, "Gov. Kay Ivey signs bills targeting transgender youth in Alabama," *Montgomery Advertiser*, April 8, 2022. www.montgomeryadvertiser.com/story/news/2022/04/08/gov-kay-ivey-signs-bills-targeting-alabama-transgender-youth/9516134002/.

3   J. D. Crowe. "Trans youth medical ban: Did the Good Lord make Kay Ivey a bully?" AL.com, May 10, 2022. www.montgomeryadvertiser.com/story/news/2022/04/08/gov-kay-ivey-signs-bills-targeting-alabama-transgender-youth/9516134002/.

4   Kiara Alfonseca, "Judge partially blocks transgender youth care ban that makes treatment a felony," ABC News, May 14, 2022. abcnews.go.com/US/judge-partially-blocks-transgender-youth-care-ban-makes/story?id=84704580.

5   A January 2024 ruling from the U.S. 11th Circuit Court of Appeals would ultimately overturn the injunction, allowing Alabama to enforce SB 184. Jenna Stephenson, "Federal court ruling leaves families of Alabama transgender youth angry, uncertain," *Alabama Reflector*, January 16, 2024. alabamareflector.com/2024/01/16/federal-court-leaves-families-of-alabama-transgender-youth-angry-uncertain-about-future/.

6   Ivana Hrynkiw, "Neil Rafferty, Alabama's only openly gay legislator: 'Why can't we just let people live their lives in this state?'" AL.com, April 12, 2022. www.al.com/educationlab/2022/04/neil-rafferty-alabamas-only-openly-gay-legislator-why-cant-we-just-let-people-live-their-lives-in-this-state.html.

7   Jonece Starr Dunigan, "Birmingham board denies state's first LGBTQ charter school application," AL.com, January 29, 2020. www.al.com /news/2020/01/birmingham-board-denies-states-first-lgbtq-charter -school-application.html.

8   Trisha Powell Crain, "Alabama's LGBTQ charter school denied again by state commission," AL.com, September 10, 2020. www.al.com /news/2020/09/alabamas-lgbtq-charter-school-denied-again-by-state -commission.html.

9   Trisha Powell Crain, "Birmingham LGBTQ safe space charter school approved for 2021 opening," AL.com, November 2, 2020. www.al.com /news/2020/11/magic-city-acceptance-academy-gains-approval-to -open-charter-school-in-2021.html.

10 Kim Chandler, "Trans kids in Alabama are officially banned from playing sports that don't correspond to the gender they were assigned at birth," *Business Insider*, April 24, 2021. www.businessinsider.com /alabama-anti-trans-bill-sports-teams-2021-4.

11 Jo Yurcaba, "Alabama passes bills to target trans minors and LGBTQ classroom discussion," NBC News, April 7, 2022. www.nbcnews.com /nbc-out/out-politics-and-policy/alabama-passes-bills-targeting-trans -minors-lgbtq-classroom-discussion-rcna23444.

12 In the 2023 legislative session, Florida would go onto one-up Alabama by extending its "Don't Say Gay" law through the end of high school. But after LGBTQ+ advocates sued over the Florida statute, portions of the Florida legislation were rescinded in a settlement. Mike Schneider, "Florida teachers can discuss sexual orientation and gender ID under 'Don't Say Gay' bill settlement," AP News, March 11, 2024. apnews .com/article/florida-dont-say-gay-bill-settlement-987904b3e19122d 719cf468034746b6e.

13 Aggregation based upon data from the Human Rights Campaign's hate crime reporting ("Fatal Violence Against the Transgender Community in 2016," "Fatal Violence Against the Transgender Community in 2017," et al.).

14 Mathew Rodriguez, "Black transgender woman Jazz Alford shot and killed in Birmingham, Alabama, hotel room," *Mic*, October 7, 2016. www.mic.com/articles/156135/black-transgender-woman-jazz-alford -shot-and-killed-in-birmingham-alabama-hotel-room.

15 Christina Caron, "Alabama woman becomes first known transgen- der person killed this year in U.S.," *New York Times*, January 11, 2019. www.nytimes.com/2019/01/11/us/transgender-black-woman-killed .html.

16 Jeffery Martin, "Murder of nonbinary teen killed at Christmas party broadcast on Facebook," *Newsweek*, December 23, 2020. www .newsweek.com/murder-non-binary-teen-killed-christmas-party -broadcast-facebook-1557089.

17 Nico Lang, "Alabama GOP prepares war on transgender teens," *Rolling Stone*, March 12, 2022. www.rollingstone.com/culture/culture -features/trans-teen-healthcare-alabama-law-1320337.

18 Much to Mima's chagrin, Jennings will later win the job full-time.

19 For more examples of the confusion caused by Alabama's trans medical care ban: Nico Lang, "Despite legal gender-affirming care, Alabama pharmacies are denying trans kids refills," *Reckon*, October 30, 2023. www.reckon.news/lgbtq/2023/10/despite-legal-gender-affirming -care-alabama-pharmacies-are-denying-trans-kids-refills.html.

20 Steve Almasy and Amanda Musa, "Alabama governor signs into law two bills limiting transgender youth protections," CNN, April 8, 2022. www.cnn.com/2022/04/08/us/alabama-transgender-bills/index.html.

21 Rhydian will be nineteen when the courts permit Alabama to enforce its trans medical care ban, meaning that he is not affected. However, countless minor children in Alabama are.

Mykah

1 Curtis Tate, "HB 2007: What gender-affirming health care means for minors," West Virginia Public Broadcasting, February 7, 2023. wvpublic.org/hb-2007-what-gender-affirming-health-care-means-for -minors/.

2 Corrine Hackathorn, "Wheeling becomes third West Virginia city to ban conversion therapy," WTRF.com, May 3, 2022. www.wtrf.com/wheeling /wheeling-becomes-3rd-west-virginia-city-to-ban-conversion-therapy/.

3 "The lies and dangers of efforts to change sexual orientation or gender identity," Human Rights Campaign. www.hrc.org/resources/the-lies -and-dangers-of-reparative-therapy.

4 "Report on conversion therapy," United Nations Office of Human Rights, May 1, 2020. www.ohchr.org/en/calls-for-input/report -conversion-therapy.

5 "Conversion 'Therapy' Laws," Movement Advancement Project. www .lgbtmap.org/equality-maps/conversion_therapy.

6 Donna Fuscaldo, "Ten states with the lowest life expectancies," *AARP*, February 17, 2022. www.aarp.org/health/conditions-treatments /info-2022/life-expectancy.html.

7   Steven Ross Johnson, "The ten states with the highest infant mortality rates," *U.S. News and World Report*, November 1, 2023. www.usnews.com/news/health-news/slideshows/infant-mortality-rate-by-state.

8   Julianna Furfari, "West Virginia schools ranked near worst in country, teachers respond," WTOV, July 31, 2019. wtov9.com/news/local/west-virginia-schools-ranked-near-worst-in-country-teachers-respond.

9   "Best States: Health Care," *U.S. News and World Report*. www.usnews.com/news/best-states/rankings/health-care.

10 Jeff Morris, "West Virginia trails neighboring states, finishes near bottom of Best States ranking," WCHS, May 14, 2019. wchstv.com/news/local/west-virginia-trails-neighboring-states-finishes-near-bottom-of-best-states-ranking.

11 "Drug overdose mortality by state," Centers for Disease Control. www.cdc.gov/nchs/pressroom/sosmap/drug_poisoning_mortality/drug_poisoning.htm.

12 "Foster care in West Virginia," Legal Aid of West Virginia, August 23, 2021. legalaidwv.org/legal-information/foster-care-in-west-virginia/.

13 Staff reports, "WV one of two states with population decline over past decade," *Charleston Gazette-Mail*, July 8, 2018. www.wvgazettemail.com/news/wv-one-of-two-states-with-population-decline-over-past/article_a34ce34b-3bd6-5a68-9838-d399c4cb7247.html.

14 Rodney Lamp, "West Virginia has third-oldest population in the United States," WBOY, April 8, 2020. www.wboy.com/news/west-virginia/west-virginia-has-third-oldest-population-in-the-united-states/.

15 Nico Lang, "The life-changing power of West Virginia's only queer youth summer camp," *Xtra*, September 7, 2022. xtramagazine.com/power/activism/west-virginia-aclu-queer-youth-summer-camp-235382.

16 Curtis Tate, "House passes bill limiting medical care for transgender youth," West Virginia Public Broadcasting, February 3, 2023. wvpublic.org/house-passes-bill-limiting-medical-care-for-transgender-youth/.

17 John Raby, "GOP increases supermajorities in West Virginia House, Senate," AP News, November 9, 2022. apnews.com/article/general-elections-west-virginia-wheeling-government-and-politics-20003d4aece817fe37cdea0b5d341635.

18 Karla Hubbard, "The ten states with the least racial diversity," *U.S. News and World Report*, August 23, 2021. www.usnews.com/news/best-states/slideshows/the-10-least-racially-diverse-states-in-the-us.

19 WGN Weather Team, "What is the flattest state in the United States? And the most mountainous?" WGN-TV, August 1, 2017. wgntv.com

/weather/what-is-the-flattest-state-in-the-united-states-and-the
-most-mountainous/.

Ruby

1   Sneha Dey and Karen Brooks Harper, "Transgender Texas kids are terrified after governor orders that parents be investigated for child abuse," *Texas Tribune*, February 22, 2022. www.texastribune.org/2022/02/28 /texas-transgender-child-abuse/.

2   Eleanor Klibanoff, "Texas resumes investigations into parents of trans children, families' lawyers confirm," *Texas Tribune*, May 20, 2022. www .texastribune.org/2022/05/20/trans-texas-child-abuse-investigations/.

3   Jo Yurcaba, "'Our state is terrorizing us': Texas families of transgender kids fight investigations," NBC News, March 9, 2022. www .nbcnews.com/nbc-out/out-news/-state-terrorizing-us-texas-families -transgender-kids-fight-investigat-rcna19282.

4   Sergio Martinez Beltrán, "Texas Republican Gov. Greg Abbott beats Beto O'Rourke, securing a third term," NPR, November 8, 2022. www.npr.org/2022/11/08/1134832026/texas-governor-election -results-greg-abbott-beto-orourke.

5   Gaby Del Valle, "Chick-fil-A's many controversies, explained," Vox, November 19, 2019. www.vox.com/the-goods/2019/5/29/18644354 /chick-fil-a-anti-gay-donations-homophobia-dan-cathy.

6   Manny Fernandez and Dave Montgomery, "Texas moves to limit transgender bathroom access," *New York Times*, January 5, 2017. www .nytimes.com/2017/01/05/us/texas-transgender-bathroom-access .html.

7   Alexa Ura and Ryan Murphy, "Here's what the Texas bathroom bill means in plain English," *Texas Tribune*, June 9, 2017. apps.texas tribune.org/texas-bathroom-bill-annotated/.

8   Julie Moreau, "No link between trans-inclusive policies and bathroom safety, study finds," NBC News, September 19, 2018. www .nbcnews.com/feature/nbc-out/no-link-between-trans-inclusive -policies-bathroom-safety-study-finds-n911106.

9   Eric Levenson, "Texas panel advances 'bathroom bill' after testy, lengthy debate," CNN, March 8, 2017. www.cnn.com/2017/03/08 /politics/texas-bathroom-bill/index.html.

10 Allison Scott, "The last piece of North Carolina's 'bathroom bill' is dead. It's time to move forward," *Them*, December 15, 2020. www.them .us/story/north-carolinas-bathroom-bill-transgender-rights-op-ed.

11   Yezmin Villareal, "Here's all the business N.C. has lost because of anti-LGBT bill," *The Advocate*, April 13, 2016. www.advocate.com/politics /2016/4/13/heres-all-business-nc-has-lost-because-of-anti-lgbt-bill.

12   "Anti-transgender sports ban, HB 25, goes into effect today," Equality Texas, January 18, 2022. www.equalitytexas.org/anti-transgender -sports-ban-hb-25-goes-into-effect-today/.

13   Megan Munce, "Texas Senate resumes push to ban transition-related medical care for transgender children, days after bill failed in House," *Texas Tribune*, May 17, 2021. www.texastribune.org/2021/05/17/texas -transgender-children-medical-care/.

14   Orion Rummler. "Gov. Greg Abbott signs Texas' first statewide anti-trans bill. What may come next?" *The 19th*, October 25, 2021. 19thnews .org/2021/10/gov-greg-abbott-signs-texas-first-statewide-anti-trans -bill-what-may-come-next/.

15   "Special session legislative bill tracker," Equality Texas. www.equality texas.org/special-session-legislative-bill-tracker/.

16   Peter Holley, "Fearing that state leaders want them 'eradicated,' some transgender Texans embrace firearms," *Texas Monthly*, May 17, 2021. www .texastribune.org/2021/05/17/texas-transgender-children-medical-care/.

17   C Mandler, "Texas Gov. Abbott signs bill banning transgender athletes from participating on college sports teams aligned with their gender identities," CBS News, June 15, 2023. www.cbsnews.com/news /texas-transgender-college-athletes-bill-greg-abbott-sb-15/.

18   Naheed Rajwani-Dharsi, "The cost of Texas' special legislative sessions," *Axios*, December 6, 2023. www.axios.com/local/dallas /2023/12/06/cost-of-texas-special-legislative-sessions.

19   "Cost of living comparison," Numbeo. www.numbeo.com/cost-of -living/comparison.jsp.

Clint

1   "Get the facts on gender-affirming care," Human Rights Campaign. www.hrc.org/resources/get-the-facts-on-gender-affirming-care.

2   "A binding guide for all genders and gender expressions," Trans Lifeline. translifeline.org/binding-guide/.

3   "Binding safely for your body: tips for all body types and sizes," Point of Pride. www.pointofpride.org/blog/binding-safely-for-your-body-tips -for-all-body-types-and-sizes.

4   "Nondiscrimination laws," Movement Advancement Project. www .lgbtmap.org/equality-maps/non_discrimination_laws.

5   "Gov. Pritzker signs sweeping reproductive rights protections into law," Illinois.gov, January 13, 2023. www.illinois.gov/news/press-release.25906.html.

6   Ariel Edwards-Levy, "Mitt Romney repeatedly references height of trees in Michigan," *HuffPost*, February 24, 2012. huffpost.com/entry/mitt-romney-michigan-trees_n_1299937.

Augie and Jack

1   Daniel Trotta, "DeSantis signs Florida ban on transgender treatment for minors," Reuters, May 18, 2023. www.reuters.com/world/us/desantis-signs-florida-ban-gender-affirming-treatment-transgender-minors-2023-05-17/.

2   Thalia Beaty, Brendan Farrington and Hannah Schoenbaum, "Transgender adults in Florida are blindsided that a new law also limits their access to health care," AP News, June 4, 2023. apnews.com/article/florida-transgender-health-care-adults-e7ae55eec634923e6593a4c0685969b2.

3   Nico Lang, "What happens when you're out of testosterone—and you live in Florida," *Slate*, September 6, 2023. slate.com/technology/2023/09/trans-health-care-florida-prescription-telehealth-testosterone.html.

4   Arek Sarkissian, "Florida bans Medicaid from covering gender-affirming treatments," *Politico*, August 11, 2022. www.politico.com/news/2022/08/11/florida-finalizes-ban-medicaid-transgender-treatments-00051259.

5   Natasha Lennard, "DeSantis-stacked medical boards ramp up bans on care for trans youth," *The Intercept*, February 14, 2023. theintercept.com/2023/02/14/florida-trans-health-care/.

6   Brooke Migdon, "DeSantis signs transgender bathroom bill, bans gender-affirming care, expands 'Don't Say Gay' law," *The Hill*, May 17, 2023. thehill.com/homenews/state-watch/4008737-desantis-signs-transgender-bathroom-bill-bans-gender-affirming-care-expands-dont-say-gay-law/.

7   Kevin Breuninger, "Florida Gov. Ron DeSantis joins presidential race, taking on Trump for GOP nomination," CNBC, May 24, 2023. www.cnbc.com/2023/05/24/ron-desantis-launches-white-house-bid.html.

Kylie

1   Samantha Riedel, "California is officially the first sanctuary state for trans youth," *Them*, September 30, 2022. www.them.us/story/california-sanctuary-state-trans-youth-gavin-newsom.

2   Beth Greenfield, "Why are people mad at Chick-fil-A? A rundown of the chain's past and present anti-LGBTQ controversies," Yahoo! Life, July 15, 2021. www.yahoo.com/lifestyle/why-are-people-mad-chick-fil-a-anti-lgbtq-controversies-205302238.html.

3   Samantha Riedel, "Violence broke out during a California school board meeting about Pride month," *Them*, June 7, 2023. www.them.us/story/glendale-school-board-meeting-proud-boys-violence.

4   Steve Scauzillo, "Rainbow flag burned at North Hollywood school where some parents oppose Pride event," *Los Angeles Daily News*, May 30, 2023. www.dailynews.com/2023/05/30/flag-burned-at-san-fernando-valley-school-where-some-parents-oppose-pride-event/.

5   Marc Cota-Robles, "Chino Valley Unified votes in support of proposed controversial gender reporting bill," KABC, April 7, 2023. abc7.com/chino-valley-unified-school-district-gender-reporting-bill-support-students/13098388/.

6   Salvador Hernandez, "California bill requiring schools to out transgender students to parents dies," *Los Angeles Times*, April 11, 2023. www.latimes.com/california/story/2023-04-11/outing-transgender-students-california-bill-dead.

7   Andrew Sheeler, "California attorney general warns school districts not to adopt forced outing policies," *Sacramento Bee*, January 20, 2024. www.sacbee.com/news/politics-government/capitol-alert/article284131728.html.

8   Months after the visit, the CVUSD policy will be temporarily enjoined by a court ruling. Jordan B. Darling, "Judge bars Chino Valley Unified from outing transgender students to parents," *Orange County Register*, October 19, 2023. www.ocregister.com/2023/10/19/judge-bars-chino-valley-unified-from-outing-transgender-students-to-parents/.

9   Kacen Bayless, "Missouri Gov. Parson signs bill banning gender-affirming care for minors during Pride month," *Kansas City Star*, June 7, 2023. www.kansascity.com/news/politics-government/article275761396.html.

10 Brody Levesque, "Rubio bashes LA Dodgers over honoring drag group, Dodgers fold," *Los Angeles Blade*, May 17, 2023. www.losangelesblade.com/2023/05/17/senator-rubio-bashes-la-dodgers-over-honoring-drag-group/.

11 Tomás Mier, "Dodgers apologize and reinvite sisters of perpetual indulgence to Pride night," *Rolling Stone*, May 23, 2023. www.rollingstone.com/culture/culture-sports/dodgers-apologize-reinvite-sisters-of-perpetual-indulgence-pride-night-1234740139/.

12 Andrew J. Campa, Saumya Gupta, Sarah Valenzuela, and Ruben Vives, "Religious groups protest Sisters of Perpetual Indulgence before Dodgers' Pride Night," *Los Angeles Times*, June 16, 2023. www.latimes.com/california/story/2023-06-16/protest-dodger-stadium-sisters-of-perpetual-indulgence-dodgers-pride-night.

13 Katie Balevic, "DeSantis claimed Dodgers stadium was 'virtually empty' after Pride backlash. The game actually sold more tickets than normal," *Business Insider*, June 22, 2023. www.businessinsider.com/desantis-falsely-claims-dodgers-stadium-empty-after-pride-backlash-2023-6.

14 Jeremy Childs and Christian Martinez, "At dueling LGBTQ+ protests outside Glendale school board meeting, violence erupts—again," *Los Angeles Times*, June 20, 2023. www.latimes.com/california/story/2023-06-20/glendale-school-board-meeting-once-again-ground-zero-for-dueling-lgbtq-protests.

15 Timothy Bella, "Protesters brawl over LGBTQ curriculum outside Calif. school board meeting," *Washington Post*, June 7, 2023. www.washingtonpost.com/nation/2023/06/07/california-glendale-school-board-brawl-lgbtq-pride/.

16 Teresa Liu, "Torrance moves to tighten policy on light-pole banners amid Pride controversy," *Daily Breeze*, June 22, 2023. www.dailybreeze.com/2023/06/22/torrance-moves-to-tighten-policy-on-light-pole-banners-amid-pride-controversy/.

17 Nico Lang, "A California mayor calls LGBTQ+ identities a 'choice of lifestyle,'" *Los Angeles Blade*, July 6, 2023. www.losangelesblade.com/2023/07/06/a-california-mayor-calls-lgbtq-identities-a-choice-of-lifestyle/.

18 "LA county election results," Los Angeles County Registrar-Recorder/County Clerk. results.lavote.gov/text-results/4193.

19 Ashar Jawad, "10 cities with highest percentage of Asian American population," Yahoo Finance, November 29, 2023. finance.yahoo.com/news/25-cities-highest-percentage-asian-002917750.html.

RESOURCES

Additional Reading

Aizumi, Marsha, and Aiden Aizumi. *Two Spirits, One Heart: A Mother, Her Transgender Son, and Their Journey to Love and Acceptance.* Minneapolis: Magnus Books, 2013.

Amer, Lindz. *Rainbow Parenting: Your Guide to Raising Queer Kids and Their Allies.* New York City: St. Martin's Griffin, 2023.

Bailar, Schuyler. *He/She/They: How We Talk About Gender and Why It Matters.* New York City: Hachette Go, 2023.

Boylan, Jennifer Finney. *Stuck in the Middle with You: A Memoir of Parenting in Three Genders.* New York City: Crown Publishing Group, 2014.

Brill, Stephanie A., and Rachel Pepper. *The Transgender Child: A Handbook for Families and Professionals.* Minneapolis: Cleis Press, 2008.

Brown, Christia Spears. *Parenting Beyond Pink & Blue: How to Raise Your Kids Free of Gender Stereotypes.* Berkeley: Ten Speed Press, 2014.

Bruesehoff, Jamie. *Raising Kids Beyond the Binary.* Minneapolis: Broadleaf Books, 2023.

Dawson, Juno. *What's the T?: The No-Nonsense Guide to All Things Trans And/Or Non-Binary for Teens.* London: Wren & Rook, 2021.

Ehrensaft, Diane, PhD. *Gender Born, Gender Made: Raising Healthy Gender-Nonconforming Children.* New York City: The Experiment, 2011.

Erickson-Schroth, Laura. *Trans Bodies, Trans Selves: A Resource by and for Transgender Communities.* London: Oxford University Press, 2022.

Feinberg, Leslie. *Transgender Warriors: The Making of History from Joan of Arc to Dennis Rodman.* Boston: Beacon Press, 1997.

Fisher, Owl, and Fox Fisher. *Trans Teen Survival Guide.* Philadelphia: Jessica Kingsley Publishers, 2018.

Ford, Vanessa, and Rebecca Kling. *The Advocate Educator's Handbook: Creating Schools Where Transgender and Non-Binary Students Thrive.* San Francisco: Jossey-Bass, 2024.

Gill-Peterson, Jules. *Histories of the Transgender Child.* Minneapolis: University of Minnesota Press, 2018.

Gillespie, Peggy. *Authentic Selves: Celebrating Trans and Nonbinary People and Their Families.* Boston: Skinner House Books, 2023.

Ivester, Jo. *Never a Girl, Always a Boy*. Phoenix: She Writes Press, 2020.

Jennings, Jazz. *Being Jazz: My Life as a Transgender Teen*. New York City: Ember, 2017.

Key, Aidan. *Trans Children in Today's Schools*. London: Oxford University Press, 2023.

Kokabe, Maia. *Gender Queer: A Memoir*. Portland: Oni Press, 2019.

Meadow, Tea. *Trans Kids: Being Gendered in the Twenty-First Century*. Oakland: University of California Press, 2019.

Mock, Janet. *Redefining Realness: My Path to Womanhood, Identity, Love, and So Much More*. New York City: Atria Books, 2014.

Nealy, Elijah C. *Trans Kids and Teens: Pride, Joy, and Families in Transition*. New York City: W. W. Norton & Company, 2019.

Nutt, Amy Ellis. *Becoming Nicole: The Transformation of an American Family*. New York City: Random House, 2016.

Serano, Julia. *Whipping Girl: A Transsexual Woman on Sexism and the Scapegoating of Femininity*. New York City: Seal Press, 2016.

Stryker, Susan. *Transgender History: The Roots of Today's Revolution*, Revised Edition. New York City: Seal Studies, 2017.

Tannehill, Brynn. *Everything You Ever Wanted to Know About Trans (But Were Afraid to Ask)*. Philadelphia: Jessica Kingsley Publishers, 2018.

——. *My Child Told Me They're Trans . . . What Do I Do?* Philadelphia: Jessica Kingsley Publishers, 2023.

Tobia, Jacob. *Sissy: A Coming-of-Gender Memoir*. New York City: G.P. Putnam's Sons, 2019.

Turban, Jack, PhD. *Free to Be: Understanding Kids and Gender Identity*. New York City: Atria Books, 2024.

Vaid-Menon, Alok. *Beyond the Gender Binary*. New York City: Penguin Workshop, 2020.

Whittlesey, Christy. *The Beginner's Guide to Being a Trans Ally*. Philadelphia: Jessica Kingsley Publishers, 2021.

Willis, Raquel. *The Risk It Takes to Bloom: On Life and Liberation*. New York City: St. Martin's Press, 2023.

Additional Viewing

Alencastre, Dante, director. *Raising Zoey*. Trans Media, 2017.

Barnett, Michael, director. *Changing the Game*. Hulu, 2019

Feder, Sam, director. *Disclosure*. Netflix, 2020.

Fisher, Luchina, director. *The Dads*. Netflix, 2023.

French, Pamela, director. *Becoming More Visible*. Alexander Street, 2016.

Haas, Shaleece, director. *Real Boy*. Independent Television Service, 2016.
Hyde, Jonathan C., director. *Always Jane*. Amazon Prime Video, 2021.
Juhola, Eric, director. *Growing Up Coy*. Still Point Pictures, 2016.
Knowlton, Vlada, director. *The Most Dangerous Year*. Passion River Films, Collective Eye Films, Academic Entertainment, 2018.
Kyi, Daresha, director. *Mama Bears*. The Film Collaborative, 2022.
Liese, Sharon, director. Transhood. HBO, 2020.
Navasky, Miri, director. *Growing Up Trans*. PBS, 2020.

Organizations to Contact for Support

Advocates for Trans Equality
a4te.org

GLSEN
glsen.org

PFLAG
pflag.org

Stand With Trans
standwithtrans.org

Sylvia Rivera Law Project
slrp.org

TransFamily Support Services
transfamilysos.org

TransFamilies
transfamilies.org

Transgender Law Center
transgenderlawcenter.org

TransLifeline
translifeline.org

The Trevor Project
thetrevorproject.org

ABOUT THE AUTHOR

NICO LANG (they/them) is an award-winning journalist with more than a decade of experience covering the transgender community's fight for equality. Their work has appeared in major publications, including *Rolling Stone, Esquire,* the *New York Times,* the *LA Times, Vox, Salon, Time, Harper's Bazaar,* the *Washington Post,* and the *Wall Street Journal.* Before becoming a freelance journalist, Nico served as the deputy editor for *Out* magazine, the news editor for *Them*, the LGBTQ+ correspondent for *VICE*, and the editor and cofounder of the literary journal *In Our Words*. Their industry-leading contributions to queer media have resulted in four GLAAD Media Award nominations and seven awards from the Association of LGBTQ+ Journalists (NLGJA), the most of any journalist. Lang is also the first-ever recipient of the Visibility Award from the Transgender Legal Defense & Education Fund (TLDEF), an honor created to recognize their impactful contributions to reporting on the lives of LGBTQIA+ people.